DIGITALLY MONITORED

This book explores the rights of individuals subjected to digital surveillance and monitoring through a range of legal and theoretical perspectives.

As digitisation transforms how states, private entities and individuals use surveillance – across criminal justice systems, workplaces, and in our personal lives – it enables increasingly pervasive forms of monitoring and blurs the boundaries between public and private spaces. This shift raises complex questions about privacy, discrimination and accountability.

While these issues have often been examined in isolated contexts, *Digitally Monitored* takes a broader view, establishing digital monitoring as a distinct field of enquiry. Together, the chapters address a set of overarching themes that emerge when digital monitoring is viewed more holistically. These include the justifications for monitoring (such as public safety and employee productivity) versus the protection of individual rights, potential infringements on individual liberty, evolving notions of privacy, heightened risks to vulnerable groups posed by biased technologies, and the role of Big Tech in the collection and use of data.

The chapters offer a range of perspectives on digital monitoring from various legal angles, including public, private and international law. By establishing digital monitoring as a distinct area of study, the book deepens our understanding of the values embedded in monitoring practices and advances the articulation and protection of the rights of those under surveillance.

Digitally Monitored

Freedom, Surveillance, and the Law

Edited by Hadassa Noorda and Jeevan Hariharan

•HART•
OXFORD • LONDON • NEW YORK • NEW DELHI • SYDNEY

HART PUBLISHING
Bloomsbury Publishing Plc
Kemp House, Chawley Park, Cumnor Hill, Oxford, OX2 9PH, UK
1385 Broadway, New York, NY 10018, USA
Bloomsbury Publishing Ireland Limited, 29 Earlsfort Terrace, Dublin 2, D02 AY28, Ireland

HART PUBLISHING, the Hart/Stag logo, BLOOMSBURY and the Diana logo are trademarks of Bloomsbury Publishing Plc
First published in Great Britain 2026

1

A catalogue record for this book is available from the British Library.

A catalogue record for this book is available from the Library of Congress.
Library of Congress Control Number: 2026030549

ISBN: HB: 978-1-5099-9189-1
ePDF: 978-1-5099-9187-7
ePub: 978-1-5099-9188-4

Typeset by Lumina Datamatics Ltd

For product safety related questions contact productsafety@bloomsbury.com

To find out more about our authors and books visit www.hartpublishing.co.uk. Here you will find extracts, author information, details of forthcoming events and the option to sign up for our newsletters.

ACKNOWLEDGEMENTS

This volume is the result of a two-day workshop held at the Netherlands Institute for Advanced Study (NIAS) in Amsterdam on 16–17 September 2024. The purpose of the workshop was to examine the rights of those under digital monitoring across several legal systems and areas of law, and to ensure these rights are safeguarded in the digital age. Accordingly, we invited scholars from a wide range of areas of law to reflect on the concept of digital monitoring and to explore its impacts and legal protection within their respective areas of expertise.

We are delighted that this exchange resulted in a collection of papers that each make a unique contribution and, taken together, establish a distinct field of inquiry. We therefore felt that these papers should be brought together in an edited volume, and this book is the result.

The workshop was generously supported by NIAS and through Digital Transformation of Decision-Making seed-funding from the University of Amsterdam. We would like to express our sincere gratitude to both institutions. Our thanks also go to our research assistants: Jessie Levano, for her invaluable help in organising the workshop, and Dana Seggev, for her careful work in editing the chapters. Many thanks are also due to Roberta Bassi and Sasha Jawed, of Hart Publishing, and two anonymous reviewers for their encouragement and engagement with the project.

We are very grateful to all the authors for their hard work and enthusiasm contributing to this project, to Silvia De Conca, Göran Sluiter and Marc Tiernan who also presented papers at the workshop, and to Agnes Akkerman, Wike Been, Marta Campos Pinto da Cruz, Michèle Lamont, and Bengi Zeybek for chairing workshop sessions.

We, as editors, have learnt an incredible amount from each of the chapters that follow; we are sure that you will too.

CONTENTS

PART III
PRIVACY, INITIMACY AND THE DIGITALLY MONITORED SELF

CONTRIBUTORS

Joe Atkinson is an Associate Professor of Employment Law at the University of Southampton, UK.

Eleni Frantziou is an Associate Professor in Public Law and Human Rights at Durham University, UK.

Marthe Goudsmit Samaritter is a Senior Researcher at the Max Planck Institute for the Study of Crime, Security and Law, Germany.

Jeevan Hariharan is a Lecturer in Law at University College London, UK.

Mireille Hildebrandt is an Emeritus Professor at the Faculty of Law and Criminology, Vrije Universiteit Brussel in Belgium and at the Faculty of Science, Radboud University in the Netherlands.

Tsachi Keren-Paz is Professor of Private Law at the University of Sheffield, UK.

Virginia Mantouvalou is Professor of Human Rights and Labour Law at University College London, UK.

Michele Molè is a Researcher in the Security Technology and e-Privacy Research Group, University of Groningen, the Netherlands.

Hadassa Noorda is an Associate Professor of Law at the University of Amsterdam, the Netherlands.

Nuna Zekić is an Associate Professor of Labour Law at the University of Amsterdam, the Netherlands.

1

Introduction

The Nature, Scope and Legal Complexity of Digital Monitoring

HADASSA NOORDA AND JEEVAN HARIHARAN

1 From Monitoring to Digital Monitoring

It is well documented that, in the early twentieth century, some American industrialists went to great lengths to watch over their workers. Perhaps most famously, Henry Ford created a team of investigators, known as the Ford Sociological Department, which would monitor employees on the job and make unannounced visits at their family homes, checking for cleanliness and noting any renters a worker might have living with them.[1] Employees had to abstain from alcohol and their bank records were accessed to ensure they were contributing to a savings account. As explained by website of 'The Henry Ford' (a museum established by Ford himself), the rules laid down by the Sociological Department had to be complied with for workers to be eligible for the highly lucrative $5 a day pay rate which had been advertised to attract and retain staff.[2] This was a scheme that Ford had implemented because of high turnover rate at his Detroit factory, where workers were severely dissatisfied with the difficult and tedious conditions that had to be endured.

As the Ford example reveals, monitoring is by no means a new phenomenon.[3] Workers have been tracked throughout history, sometimes in the most brutal

[1] See M Ballaban, 'When Henry Ford's Benevolent Secret Police Ruled His Workers' (*Jalopnik*, 23 March 2014). Available at: https://jalopnik.com/when-henry-fords-benevolent-secret-police-ruled-his-wo-1549625731; 'Ford Motor Company Sociological Department and English School' (*The Henry Ford*). Available at: www.thehenryford.org/collections-and-research/digital-resources/popular-topics/sociological-department.

[2] 'Ford's Five Dollar Day' (*The Henry Ford*). Available at: www.thehenryford.org/collections/explore/articles/fords-five-dollar-day.

[3] See GM Rejouis, 'Why Is It OK for Employers to Constantly Surveil Workers?' (*Slate*, 2 September 2019). Available at: https://slate.com/technology/2019/09/labor-day-worker-surveillance-privacy-rights.html.

circumstances imaginable, such as slaves in the United States being carefully observed when picking cotton.[4] Keeping people under watch has undoubtedly been part of the human experience throughout time in other contexts as well, including in law enforcement, educational settings, espionage, media reporting, and acts of stalking and voyeurism. In some of these situations, monitoring is (and always has been) clearly justified. For example, if a young schoolchild is on play equipment or a worker is operating heavy machinery, monitoring by a supervisor of some kind is necessary for the subject's health and safety. However, there are also a host of instances where the activity is completely unacceptable, and is used rather as a tool of oppression, discrimination and control.

In recent decades, with the rapid rise of digital technologies, the core motivations behind monitoring have not necessarily changed. What has changed, however, is the *way* in which monitoring occurs. In times gone by, monitoring has been highly time and resource intensive, requiring the person monitoring to be physically proximate to their subject. Discussing the monitoring activities of Henry Ford, scholars Ifeoma Ajunwa, Kate Crawford and Jason Schultz point to the invasive conduct of the Ford Sociological Department as an early example of modern workplace surveillance.[5] In the end, though, as they explain, the investigators could not be in two places at once, so their surveillance was thus limited by what they could see and record.[6]

Digitisation has profoundly changed how monitoring happens, and with it, the extent to which it occurs.[7] In the modern workplace, as we have highlighted in previous work, there are now a wide range of tools available to monitor employees, boasting features like keystroke logging, locational tracking, facial recognition, and video surveillance.[8] Today, a superior does not need to be proximate to a worker to see what they are doing, and they certainly do not need to be always watching over them. Digital technologies can be used to keep track of and record workers entirely remotely and with high levels of precision. As a result, workplace monitoring has become more granular. It also now occurs at a significantly larger

[4] See eg M Desmond, 'In Order to Understand the Brutality of American Capitalism, You Have to Start on the Plantation' (*The New York Times*, 14 August 2019). Available at: www.nytimes.com/interactive/2019/08/14/magazine/slavery-capitalism.html. Desmond traces the ways in which productivity was carefully measured on cotton plantations in the eighteenth century, and links this with the ubiquitous workplace surveillance practices employed by large companies today. As slave labour camps spread and the production of cotton increased, Desmond highlights that the owners of plantations, known as 'planters', implemented precise record-keeping systems and used 'overseers' to record the yield of each enslaved worker.

[5] I Ajunwa, K Crawford and J Schultz, 'Limitless Worker Surveillance' (2017) 105 *California Law Review* 735, 741–42.

[6] ibid 742.

[7] Rejouis (n 3).

[8] J Hariharan and H Noorda, 'Imprisoned at Work: The Impact of Employee Monitoring on Physical Privacy and Individual Liberty' (2025) 88 *MLR* 333. See also B Cyphers and K Gullo, 'Inside the Invasive, Secretive "Bossware" Tracking Workers' (*Electronic Frontier Foundation*, 30 June 2020). Available at: www.eff.org/deeplinks/2020/06/inside-invasive-secretive-bossware-tracking-workers; M Scherer, 'Warning: Bossware May Be Hazardous to Your Health' (*Center for Democracy & Technology*, 2021). Available at: https://cdt.org/wp-content/uploads/2021/07/2021-07-29-Warning-Bossware-May-Be-Hazardous-To-Your-Health-Final.pdf.

scale, impacting workers in a vast range of industries across the full spectrum of the economy. The deployment of monitoring technologies has exploded as a result of the sudden shift to remote working during the COVID-19 pandemic and the development of the modern gig economy.[9]

Work, of course, is far from the only context in which monitoring occurs in our modern lives and where digitisation has had a profound impact. In the context of criminal law, for example, modern technology generates both new forms of criminality as well as new tools to control and punish people. New technologies facilitate violence, for example, deepfake pornography and online gender-based violence, causing new legal and ethical challenges.[10] Law enforcement authorities are equipped with digital tools for gathering and sharing information; these are used to keep track of vulnerable groups including migrants and people on welfare benefits.[11] In many legal systems, electronic monitoring is used as a punishment. Instead of going to prison or paying a fine, the offender is placed under home surveillance using technologies that remotely check their location and constrain their liberty.[12]

The digital monitoring practices of the kind just sketched raise several legal and ethical issues, particularly regarding privacy, stigma and public shaming, the potential for net-widening, negative impacts on employment conditions, and collateral consequences for legally innocent parties.[13] Digital monitoring can perpetuate discrimination; studies show that surveillance can reproduce and entrench gender, race, class and immigration status inequalities.[14]

2 The Collection, Its Core Contributions and Common Themes

The purpose of this collection is to examine the rights of those subject to digital monitoring; it aims to ensure these rights are properly safeguarded in the digital age. This is an increasingly important but under-researched area in

[9] See K Ball, *Electronic Monitoring and Surveillance Workplace: Literature Review and Policy Recommendations* (Luxembourg, Publications Office of the European Union, 2021) 12.

[10] See eg M Goudsmit, 'The Wrongness of Image-Based Sexual Abuse' (DPhil Thesis, University of Oxford 2022); C McGlynn and E Rackley, 'Image-Based Sexual Abuse' (2017) 37 OJLS 534.

[11] See eg V Mantouvalou, *Structural Injustice and Workers' Rights* (Oxford, Oxford University Press 2023) 157.

[12] See eg H Noorda, 'Exprisonment: Deprivation of Liberty on the Street and at Home' (2023) 42 Criminal Justice Ethics 1; H Noorda, 'Imprisonment' (2023) 17 *Criminal Law and Philosophy* 691.

[13] See eg V Mantouvalou and H Noorda, 'Non-Custodial Sentences and Human Rights' (2024) 24(3) *European Human Rights Law Review* 228; W Bülow, 'Electronic Monitoring' in J Ryberg (ed), *Oxford Handbook on Punishment Theory and Philosophy* (Oxford, Oxford University Press, 2025).

[14] Studies demonstrate that automated facial analysis algorithms and datasets can discriminate based on classes like race and gender, see J Buolamwini and T Gebru, 'Gender Shades: Intersectional Accuracy Disparities in Commercial Gender Classification' (2018) 81 *Proceedings of Machine Learning Research* 77; Ball (n 9); On racially disparate impact of race neutral monitoring in the context of fines, see also E Hopkins and M Sanchez, 'Chicago's "Race-Neutral" Traffic Cameras Ticket Black and Latino Drivers the Most' (*ProPublica*, 11 January 2022). Available at: www.propublica.org/article/chicagos-race-neutral-traffic-cameras-ticket-black-and-latino-drivers-the-most.

legal scholarship. The collection's focus is on legal and theoretical perspectives, exploring digital monitoring practices in several legal systems and across different areas of law.

Sitting underneath the collection as a whole is the core idea that digital monitoring is a worthy of attention as a distinct field of enquiry. This is not to say that digital monitoring takes the same form or raises the same issues in all the settings in which it occurs. In our view, however, by recognising digital monitoring as such, we can come to a deeper understanding of the values implicated by such monitoring, better explicate the rights of those under surveillance, and ensure that those rights are properly safeguarded in the digital age. The contributions in the collection speak directly to these issues. Individually and taken together, the chapters build a complex picture of the nature and extent of monitoring, and the different parts of the law which need to be called upon to address digital surveillance adequately.

All the chapters are the product of a two-day workshop that took place at the Netherlands Institute for Advanced Study (NIAS) in Amsterdam on 16–17 September 2024. Contributors to the project were asked at the outset to reflect on the concept of digital monitoring, and to explore its impacts and legal protection within a particular field of their choosing. For many authors, what emerged was an investigation of digital monitoring within a particular context, such as the monitoring of migrants, of workers or of women (as in the case of FemTech). For others, the focus was broader or more conceptual, looking at the different regional human rights frameworks that regulate digital monitoring, or the interface between monitoring and privacy in a digital age. From the outset, the goal here was never to present an exhaustive picture of digital monitoring. Instead, consistent with the above, the core idea driving the collection is that by starting to think about digital monitoring as a distinct field of enquiry, we can deepen our understanding of the values embedded in such practices, more effectively articulate the rights of those subject to surveillance, and work to ensure these rights are adequately protected in the twenty-first century.

Given the significant licence that was initially given to individual authors to take the topic in different directions, there was a risk that the contributions in the collection might not speak to similar ideas. As it happened, however, conversations over two days in Amsterdam repeatedly highlighted various common themes and questions at the heart of the papers. To be sure, each of the papers takes a very different approach and offers a unique contribution. At the same time, we as editors would argue that there are five core themes that emerge from the project as a whole; these are worth identifying before we turn to provide a brief synopsis of each of the chapters in turn.

The first common theme that emerges is that the justifications for monitoring are often framed around public safety, national security and company productivity; however, the legitimacy of monitoring typically depends on balancing these objectives against the protection of individual rights, as highlighted in frameworks like Article 8 of the European Convention on Human

Rights (ECHR). From a legal perspective, Article 8 guarantees the right to respect for private and family life, home and correspondence. But the extent to which this provision covers digital monitoring and deals with it satisfactorily is a matter of debate. In this context, a core question is the extent to which additional values should guide the benchmarks for determining when monitoring is acceptable or unacceptable. And a key consideration in assessing the legality and ethics of monitoring is whether the starting point should be no monitoring at all, or whether monitoring is justified in certain contexts as a lesser evil than a more invasive practice-like incarceration. This debate touches on broader issues of authority, accountability and the justifications for state or corporate entities to monitor individuals.

Second, there are complex questions about the 'private' and 'public' that come to the fore when considering the nature and extent of digital monitoring. The modern landscape of digital tools that blend public and private realms often operate in the space between these categories, creating new challenges for domains that are traditionally considered as private, such as homes and workplaces. Personal devices, online activities, and health data are routinely collected and analysed, often without explicit consent. Moreover, in the digital world, there are also spaces that may not fit neatly into either the public or private category, such as 'non-public' or 'non-private' data, which still has significant implications for individual rights.

Appreciating the complex way in which the 'public' and 'private' interact opens the way to deeper thinking about the values implicated by digital monitoring practices. Whether or not monitoring occurs in a strictly 'private' space, privacy is usually seen as a core interest implicated by these activities. However, we should be alive to the fact that there are different dimensions of privacy at play in these situations beyond 'data privacy' or 'informational privacy', such as 'physical privacy'. And, in some cases, there are other values at stake as well, including freedom and individual liberty. There are difficult questions here about the boundaries of individual liberty and how legal freedom is understood. In a digital era, legal freedom arguably goes beyond mere non-interference to include the right not to be fully captured or defined by computational systems. Protecting this requires legal frameworks that allow individuals to contest how they are represented or processed. Legal freedom, in this sense, depends on enabling people to challenge algorithmic framings, shifting the burden of proof onto powerful actors, and ensuring rights are practical and effective. Law can help safeguard freedom by protecting both the ability to act and the right to be shielded from being fully codified or controlled.

Third, while digital monitoring practices generate issues across the full spectrum of society, vulnerable groups face heightened risks as biased technologies exacerbate harms such as stigmatisation and exclusion. For example, facial recognition systems have been shown to perform less accurately for people of colour, leading to discriminatory outcomes. Beyond bias in technology, the very act of monitoring can become a tool for reinforcing discrimination. For marginalised groups, including women and racial minorities, monitoring can have a particularly harmful impact, as it can result in stigmatisation, exclusion, and unjust treatment.

Fourth, digital monitoring highlights concerns about the operation of Big Tech companies. These platforms collect vast amounts of personal data, raising ethical and legal questions about data handling and potential abuse. While individuals are directly affected by monitoring, the role of these platforms in the collection and dissemination of information is central to the issue. Addressing these challenges effectively requires a nuanced understanding of the dynamics between those being monitored and those conducting the monitoring, including questions of agency and subjectivity.

Fifth, examples such as the operations of Big Tech companies, as well as the monitoring of migrants, workers, women and students, demonstrate that concerns about digital monitoring go further than the 'individual'. In certain chapters, there is explicit acknowledgement of the difficulties which are faced when, for example, privacy issues are understood merely through an individualistic, atomistic lens. More broadly, though, many of the contributions in the collection speak to the idea that privacy not only affects individuals but also operates at a collective level. It impacts groups, communities and societies as a whole, creating challenges that require collective responses, such as collective bargaining and consultation frameworks.

3 The Chapters

The individual contributions in the collection are divided into three parts. Part I contains two chapters by Eleni Frantziou and Virginia Mantouvalou which, in different ways, speak to the crucial role of human rights law in addressing digital monitoring concerns.

Chapter 2, by Eleni Frantziou, helps frame the book's overall focus by offering a comparative analysis of how major regional human rights frameworks address privacy issues in the digital age. As Frantziou explains, in the absence of a globally applicable human rights framework, examining regional human rights regimes and their jurisprudence provides a mechanism for assessing the resilience and drawbacks of existing human rights structures to deal with privacy violations in the digital age. Examining the jurisprudence of (i) the European Court of Human Rights (ECtHR), (ii) the Inter-American Court of Human Rights (IACtHR), and (iii) the African Court of Human and People's Rights (ACtHPR), Frantziou sketches (for the first time in the academic literature in this field) an emerging practice on digital monitoring which cuts across different regional human rights systems.

Analysing the case law through the lens of four principal issues (mass surveillance and monitoring; access to data; publication of information obtained through monitoring; and targeted surveillance/monitoring by public or private actors), Frantziou argues that the jurisprudence of the three regional systems is defined by a number of core themes. First, all three systems show significant concern for state abuses of power in the field of mass or generalised surveillance, and the various instruments enumerate safeguards to ensure such monitoring is lawful and non-arbitrary. Second, however, there is much greater disparity between the systems and a lower standard of protection when it comes to digital monitoring conducted by private, not state, actors. A third point, which emerges particularly from the more developed ECtHR jurisprudence, is that an open-ended approach is taken to the justifications for monitoring (including, for example, economic considerations in in cases involving employee monitoring). As Frantziou points out, this suggests that the ECtHR is adopting the same stance in digital monitoring as it has traditionally held in other areas in terms of non-intervention in private matters. This reluctance to see control over one's data as a core element of Article 8 is arguably mirrored by the hesitancy of the ACtHPR to accept data violations as a harm in itself, with the added feature that the African system has an absence of directly relevant case law on point. By contrast, the emerging jurisprudence of the IACtHR is framed more expansively and clearly, reflecting a more active development of privacy law in the digital sphere.

The overall message that emerges from Frantziou's analysis is that regional human rights regimes are crucial for regulating digital monitoring. Such systems have a wide jurisdictional reach, a strong normative force, and have been able to bring about real and rapid changes. At the same time, the jurisprudence of such courts has arguably remained rather limited, and there remain key challenges in capturing the precise specificities of the digital age, particularly in terms of the conduct of private actors and the nature of the countervailing factors used to justify monitoring. In highlighting these points, Frantziou's chapter speaks directly to many of the core themes identified above, especially in terms of the open-ended nature of the balancing exercise in this field and the interface between 'public' and 'private' realms. More generally, the chapter aptly demonstrates the legal complexity of regulating monitoring in a digital age, which in different ways features in all the other contributions as well.

Chapter 3, by Virginia Mantouvalou examines the electronic monitoring of migrants, emphasising the significance of human rights law in challenging current practices. To date, much of the important literature examining digital monitoring by the state has concerned the use of digital tools such as electronic tagging as an alternative to traditional forms of criminal punishment which typically involves confining offenders to a cell, under lock and key. In writings elsewhere, for example, Noorda has developed the concept of 'exprisonment' to describe and capture the significant impacts such measures have on a subject's freedom and liberty despite the absence of physical incarceration.[15] Mantouvalou's chapter extends the relevance of the concept of 'exprisonment' to the electronic monitoring of migrants.

[15] On exprisonment, see H Noorda, 'Preventive Deprivations of Liberty: Asset Freezes and Travel Bans' (2015) 9 *Criminal Law and Philosophy* 521; H Noorda, 'Exprisonment: Deprivations of Liberty on the Street and at Home' (2023) 42 *Criminal Justice Ethics* 1.

As Mantouvalou points out, in political discourse, such monitoring is often presented as an acceptable and effective measure pursuing the legitimate aim of immigration control. Moreover, immigration monitoring is often seen as a less problematic mechanism for such control compared to more restrictive measures such as immigration detention and collective expulsions. In this way, we can observe the justifications for the digital monitoring of migrants mirroring the rhetoric around non-custodial surveillance in the criminal justice context. Yet, as Mantouvalou argues, the digital monitoring of migrants should be recognised to be *more* problematic than it is as a non-custodial sentence for a crime. Such monitoring is typically imposed not by a court order but by an administrative decision, without close scrutiny of the necessity of the measure and the implications on the lives of those monitored. Crucially, it extends criminal justice measures to the immigration context where no crime has been committed – in doing so, it can be understood within a broader practice of 'crimmigration' whereby immigration is increasingly being considered as tantamount to criminality.

At the heart of Mantouvalou's chapter is a careful analysis of the monitoring technology used and its effects. Often, when digital monitoring is being discussed, it can be difficult to grasp fully the negative impacts of such technology. However, Mantouvalou's use of examples throughout the chapter paint a stark and troubling picture of what such monitoring actually entails. Drawing in particular on interviews conducted in the *Every Move You Make* and *Constantly on Edge* projects, the chapter highlights the way that the tagging restricts freedom, causes social isolation and has grave physical and psychological effects.[16] The result, as Mantouvalou explains, is that while monitoring may at first seem less intrusive than immigration detention, its effects are deep and significant, with an added impact that such technologies ultimately lead to 'net-widening', increasing the number of people under state control.

From a legal perspective, Mantouvalou argues that the human rights implications of such technology are wide-ranging and serious, extending not just to an individual's private life but also, for example, to the right to work, freedom of association and freedom of religion. Looking at the United Kingdom (UK) context in particular, Mantouvalou shows that such practices have already been the subject of complaints and enforcement action by the Information Commissioner's Office (ICO). There is also an emerging body of case law from UK courts and scrutiny from Parliamentary Committees which have found problems with the monitoring regime. Looking forward, Mantouvalou urges that an even broader consideration of human rights principles is important for such practices to be challenged, including through Article 3 (inhuman and degrading treatment) and Article 14

[16] J Hynes and M Leslie, '"Constantly on Edge": The Expansion of GPS Tagging and the Roll-Out of Non-Fitted Devices' (Medical Justice, Bail for Immigration Detainees and Public Law Project, 2023); 'Every Move you Make: The Human Cost of GPS Tagging in the Immigration System' (Bail for Immigration Detainees, Medical Justice and Public Law Project, 2022).

(discrimination) of the ECHR. Here, again, therefore we see the panoply of issues raised by digital monitoring and the legal complexities involved.

Part II shifts to consider the specific context of digital monitoring in the modern workplace. To date, workplace surveillance has probably been one of the most widely documented and discussed areas of digital monitoring. Each of the three chapters in this part of the book adopts a novel line of enquiry in relation to this important and difficult topic. Consistent with the core premise of this whole collection, the main thread running through these chapters is that while monitoring has always been a part of workplace environments, digitalisation has fundamentally shifted the *way* in which it occurs. In properly analysing monitoring practices we need to pay attention to the granular way employers now watch over their employees, using sophisticated 'bossware' which can log keystrokes, take photographs and closely track the location and activity rate of workers in real time.

Chapter 4, by Joe Atkinson, examines how employment law should respond to these new electronic capabilities, adopting a unique line of argument that this question can only be addressed by examining the normative foundations and extent of employers' legitimate authority to monitor their workers. As Atkinson highlights, despite labour law being centrally concerned with defining and limiting managerial authority, the theoretical foundation of such power is under-explored in the specific context of workplace monitoring. As a default, an employer's power to monitor workers in whatever way they want is generally seen as an aspect of their broad authority to organise their business as they see fit. Such authority, where it is not expressly conferred, will generally form part of the implied terms of obedience and co-operation read into an employment contract by courts. There is, moreover, a residual liberty for employers as private entities to act freely at common law, provided that their activity is not prohibited by some area specific area of law (such as anti-discrimination or data protection law).

As Atkinson forcefully highlights, contemporary digital monitoring practices force us to confront the appropriateness and extent of this broad default authority. Digital tools, in Atkinson's words, 'create *qualitative* and *quantitative* changes to previously analogue oversight', and such monitoring is in a symbiotic relationship with 'algorithmic management'. The impact of monitoring is stark, implicating physical and informational dimensions of privacy, workers' rights to liberty as well as other rights such as free expression or the ability to engage in political association. For Atkinson, the intensity of monitoring necessitates an examination of the normative foundations of managerial authority, and in particular, the leading theories of such authority which have found favour in labour law scholarship. In this vein, the chapter undertakes a close interrogation of justificatory theories of managerial authority grounded in property rights, worker consent, and the fulfilment instrumental goals such as economic efficiency. The conclusion is that none of these approaches legitimises the current legal default, and at most there is justification for a qualified power to monitor. This means that law reform is required to better track employers' legitimate authority to monitor, which includes enshrining a right to justification for monitoring and the facilitation of strong collective voice on the issue.

Whereas Atkinson is primarily focused on the scope of managerial authority, Chapter 5, by Nuna Zekić, explores the relationship between digital monitoring in contemporary workplaces and the concept of a 'right to disconnect'. By linking the nature of the right to disconnect to the technological processes that are used to keep workers tethered to their jobs – often beyond designated workplaces and working hours – Zekić brings into focus the core questions and tensions that arise when thinking about disconnection from the digital sphere of work.

The chapter begins by examining how digital tools and devices have enabled a state of constant connectivity, rendering employees reachable – whether voluntarily or at an employer's request – outside regular working hours. As the boundaries between working and non-working time blur, the growing need to disconnect from work becomes increasingly apparent. Against this backdrop, the European Parliament has called on the European Commission to introduce legislation securing a right to disconnect, and several Member States have already taken steps in this direction. At the same time, in some jurisdictions, the added value of such new legislation is still questioned. One of the main arguments is that the EU already has strong working time legislation, which offers sufficient protection of workers' free time. Moreover, the EU has a strong legal protection of privacy to ensure that employee monitoring does not go too far. Taken together with general labour law protections, these frameworks are, according to some, adequate to safeguard workers in an increasingly digital work environment.

Zekić challenges this assumption. The core question she poses is whether workers can, in practice, choose to disconnect – or whether existing legal frameworks fall short, particularly for non-standard workers who may be implicitly expected to remain available. She argues that neither working time rules nor privacy laws sufficiently empower workers who seek to withdraw from their 'digital workspace'. The chapter therefore calls for a broader reflection on whether a newly articulated right to disconnect can meaningfully address the challenges of the 'digital workspace', especially when workers are only implicitly obliged to remain connected.

Chapter 6, by Michele Molè, adds a further layer to the concerns raised by Zekić and Atkinson by shifting attention from employer expectations and the exercise of managerial authority to the market for technology that structures and intensifies the monitoring practices that employers adopt. Molè questions the idea that regulating workplace monitoring should focus primarily on limiting excessive employer power. Instead, he highlights that employees' rights and well-being are shaped not only by employers but also by the monitoring tools they purchase. While recognising that these tools amplify employer authority, Molè argues that the form and scope of this authority are increasingly shaped by the design and operational choices of third-party providers, with significant implications for workplace hierarchies and dynamics of subordination. There are clear connections to be drawn here with Atkinson and Zekić's chapters, especially Atkinson's discussion on the symbiotic relationship between monitoring and algorithmic management, given that the monitoring systems under consideration are often designed by precisely the third-party providers which are the focus of Molè's chapter.

Molè introduces the novel framework of 'authority-commodity', drawing on Bernard Stiegler's critique of consumer society, to illustrate how employers function simultaneously as holders of authority over employees and consumers of monitoring services.[17] This perspective calls for a rethinking of regulation: rather than focusing solely on employer behaviour, legal frameworks should address which monitoring technologies can be developed and marketed, taking into account the hidden asymmetries of information and power between providers and their clients.

Part III, the final part of the collection, contains three chapters on privacy, intimacy and the digitally monitored self. Compared to many of the previous chapters which are primarily directed at monitoring within a single context or setting, each of these chapters draws in a range of examples to make a broader normative point about the impact of digital surveillance on individuals and society.

Chapter 7, by Tsachi Keren-Paz, explores the interface between digital monitoring and intimate privacy through the lens of two case studies: FemTech products and non-consensual intimate images (NCII). FemTech, as Keren-Paz explains, is a broad umbrella term capturing 'the wide range of digital products designed with women's health in mind',[18] including 'menstrual, sexual and procreative health as well as nursing [breastfeeding] care'.[19] By contrast, NCII, also referred to as intimate image abuse or image-based sexual abuse, is the taking, making (as in deep fakes) and sharing of intimate images without consent.[20] While NCII has received significant attention in recent years, including in a detailed report by the England and Wales Law Commission which led to legislative amendments, FemTech has been under-explored from a legal perspective.[21] One of the important contributions of Keren-Paz's chapter is to draw attention to the proliferation of FemTech products and the range of issues they raise, including in relation to sexual privacy, product functionality, unequal access for different groups, the facilitation of domestic violence and the reinforcement of existing gender inequalities.

Having set out the two case studies, Keren-Paz makes three primary claims in his chapter. The first is that the FemTech and NCII case studies can be mapped respectively onto narrow and broad understandings of surveillance. This distinction in some ways tracks the distinction between physical and informational

[17] B Stiegler, *Symbolic Misery, Volume 1: The Hyper-Industrial Epoch*, English edn (Cambridge, Polity Press, 2014); B Stiegler, *Automatic Society* (Cambridge, Polity Press, 2016).

[18] LA Balfour, *The Digital Future of Hospitality* (London, Palgrave Macmillan, 2023) 105.

[19] Tereza Hendl and Bianca Jansky, 'Tales of Self-Empowerment through Digital Health Technologies: A Closer Look at "Femtech"' (2022) 80 *Review of Social Economy* 29, 29.

[20] N Henry et al, *Image-based Sexual Abuse: A Study on the Causes and Consequences of Non-consensual Nude or Sexual Imagery* (Abingdon, Routledge, 2020).

[21] Law Commission, *Intimate Image Abuse: A Final Report* (Law Com No 407, 2022). Following the report, the Online Safety Act 2023 (OSA) partially implemented its recommendations, adding offences to the Sexual Offences Act 2003 (SOA) for *sharing* and *threatening to share* intimate images. See OSA, s 188, which inserts ss 66B–66D into the SOA. Further offences have now also recently been added into the SOA (ss 66E–66H) by the Data (Use and Access) Act 2025 in respect of deepfakes (going beyond the Law Commission's report which had not recommended deepfake offences).

privacy flagged above and in that way gives us a better understanding of the different types of harms that are perpetuated by these activities. The second claim is that NCII raises specific issues about monitoring viewers of intimate images, which Keren-Paz argues can be justified based on principles of reciprocity and 'poetic justice'. That is to say, a viewer's privacy interest 'should be discounted due to the serious invasion of privacy they inflict on NCII victims'. Third, and perhaps most significantly, the chapter argues that both FemTech and NCII can be understood within a normative framework which: (a) underscores the gendered power dynamics at play in both phenomena; (b) emphasises the role of private law in allowing marginalised people to keep excessive and illegitimate monitoring in check; and (c) acknowledges that such monitoring is usually conducted by private actors not the state. In doing so, the chapter lies directly at the intersection of many of the core themes already identified, particularly in the way that Keren-Paz emphasises the impact of monitoring on marginalised groups, the role played by Big Tech companies and, in the case of viewers of NCII, that monitoring can be justified by placing appropriate (ie minimal) weight on the user's own privacy interests.

As already noted, NCII is often also referred to as image-based sexual abuse (IBSA). The latter is the term preferred by Marthe Goudsmit Samaritter who, in Chapter 8, also uses it as a core case study of digital monitoring, alongside public surveillance and digital proctoring. As with Keren-Paz's discussion on FemTech and Mantouvalou's chapter on the monitoring of migrants, Goudsmit Samaritter's analysis of digital proctoring makes a novel contribution to the literature in the way that it calls attention to an under-explored phenomenon. The use of proctoring technology, which is used to track students taking exams, is increasingly widespread but it has had surprisingly little attention in the academic literature so far.

For Goudsmit Samaritter, the purpose of the three digital monitoring case studies (IBSA, public surveillance and digital proctoring) is to make a significant theoretical claim that many contemporary privacy infringements are best understood through a relational, not atomistic, framework. The point here is that privacy must be understood as more than just a 'defensive shield around the individually conceived person', which is what typically lies behind traditional theories of privacy (eg the influential idea that privacy involves a spatial 'right to be let alone' or even a right to 'informational privacy'). Instead, on the relational account of privacy for which Goudsmit Samaritter advocates, privacy involves the 'the protection of a shared space in which persons can appear to one another in ways that affirm their subjectivity'.

The picture which Goudsmit Samaritter presents shows the way in which digital monitoring forces us to confront fundamental ideas about concepts such as privacy. The key point that emerges from her analysis is that being visible or 'seen' is not inherently a *threat* to privacy; in fact, in many circumstances, 'being seen' can be privacy *enhancing*. The wrongfulness of activity in the three case studies lies therefore not merely in being seen, but rather in the fact that a subject's 'normative authority' to determine how and the terms on which they are seen is compromised.

One reason why this is important is that it helps explain why practices can be privacy infringing even when they occur in public spaces. The relational account also allows us to observe an additional dimension of privacy harm; namely, the 'objectification' that occurs when a person's subjectivity is denied.

Chapter 9, by Mireille Hildebrandt, the last chapter of this volume, addresses the impact of a specific type of digital monitoring, called profiling or computational targeting, which comes up in a variety of different fields and contexts. Building on her earlier work on 'privacy as the protection of the incomputable self' and her call for 'a philosophy of technology for law', Hildebrandt brings the assumptions of computer science into conversation with those of law and the Rule of Law.[22] Understanding privacy as the protection of the incomputable self allows for a conception of privacy that combines negative and positive freedom, based on the fact that the self cannot be reduced to numbers, however complex the calculation.

In this chapter, Hildebrandt moves beyond a narrow focus on privacy protection to make a broader argument: that law must respect the underdetermined nature of human agency and offer ways to resist and contest being defined in computational terms. Achieving this, she argues, requires that lawyers deepen their understanding of the conceptual assumptions underlying computational systems, equipping them to avoid both naïve incorporation and naïve rejection of what are now called AI systems.

Hildebrandt then briefly argues how the EU legal framework, more specifically the GDPR and the AI Act, already offers some of the legal instruments to protect against such monitoring. Finally, she introduces a critique of unrestrained global capitalism that aligns with the computability that is core to behavioural profiling. For legal frameworks to truly protect the incomputable self, Hildebrandt argues, we must reshape the economic incentives driving public and private surveillance. Key to this critique is that legal frameworks constitute economic markets, thereby rejecting economic determinism.

4 Conclusion

From this collection of chapters, it is clear that digitisation is fundamentally reshaping how states, private entities and individuals engage in monitoring activities. Across criminal justice systems, workplaces, and in our personal lives, we can observe that such practices enable increasingly pervasive forms of oversight, blur the boundaries between public and private spaces and often have particularly stark impacts on vulnerable members of society.

[22] M Hildebrandt, 'A Philosophy of Technology for Computational "Law"' in D Mangan, A Daly and G van Dijck (eds), *Philosophical Foundations of IT Law* (Oxford, Oxford University Press, 2025).

While the individual chapters raise a broad panoply of issues, taken together, we hope that they underscore the urgency of recognising digital monitoring as a distinct field of enquiry. Our goal in putting together this collection has been to begin, rather than conclude, a dialogue about digital monitoring across the different domains in which it occurs. As such, there are necessarily many dimensions of digital monitoring which this book does not fully explore. At the same time, by bringing the diverse perspectives within this field into conversation, we hope that this volume deepens our understanding of the values that underpin monitoring practices and to support more robust articulation and protection of the rights of those subjected to them in an increasingly digital world.

PART I

Digital Monitoring and the Role of Human Rights Law

2

Privacy and Digital Monitoring in Regional Human Rights Law

Moving Forward, One Step at a Time

ELENI FRANTZIOU*

1 Introduction

More than fifty years since the advent of closed-circuit surveillance technology and thirty-five years since the creation of the World-Wide-Web, human rights law continues to struggle to accommodate the challenges of the digital age. This can be attributed to two structural issues: first, the right to privacy is traditionally viewed as an individual right, developed at a time when the possibilities of generalised and indiscriminate forms of surveillance were limited in terms of means and methods. Second, human rights law is typically considered 'vertical by default', since it was designed to be used primarily in the state–individual relationship.[1] Even if a vertical understanding of privacy had been capable of capturing communications monitoring in the early human rights era, it presents considerable deficiencies today.[2] Digital infrastructure has always been privately owned and there is considerable legal debate about the functioning of cyberspace not only in terms of international human rights law, but also in terms of jurisdiction

* I am very grateful to two anonymous reviewers and the participants of the Workshop on Digital Monitoring held at NIAS, Amsterdam, 16–17 September 2024, for their thoughtful comments and suggestions on an earlier draft of this chapter. I am especially indebted to the editors, Dr Hadassa Noorda and Dr Jeevan Hariharan, for their comments, edits, and impeccable coordination of this project.

[1] G Bhatia, *Horizontal Rights: An Institutional Approach* (London, Bloomsbury Publishing, 2023) 20.

[2] Arguably, a vertical understanding of privacy is more broadly deficient, given that it does not capture workplace monitoring, which was not only physical, but also records-based.

and governance, more broadly.[3] While there have been attempts to address these issues at the international level through a Global Digital Compact, there is currently no binding instrument that governs digital monitoring on a global scale.[4]

In the absence of a globally applicable human rights framework for privacy in the digital age, the advances made through regional human rights law and case law can be used to assess the resilience and drawbacks of existing human rights structures, and to support a more incremental development of human rights to address privacy violations in the digital environment. While several regional and sub-regional systems have emerged over the last few years, little attention has so far been paid to how their specialised human rights courts interpret digital forms of surveillance and communications monitoring within the framework of their existing jurisprudence and, especially, how the jurisprudence of each system resonates with that of the others. This chapter takes up this task. It aims to sketch, for the first time within the academic literature in this field, the contours of an emerging practice on digital communications monitoring which cuts across different regional human rights systems. To do so, the chapter focuses on the approach taken in the adjudication of the three main regional human rights treaties with dedicated courts: the African Charter of Human and Peoples' Rights (ACHPR), the American Convention on Human Rights (ACHR), and the European Convention for the Protection of Human Rights and Fundamental Freedoms (ECHR). The chapter analyses the extent to which the case law of the European Court of Human Rights (ECtHR), the Inter-American Court of Human Rights (IACtHR), and the African Court on Human and Peoples' Rights (ACtHPR) tackle digital monitoring or can be interpreted or applied to digital monitoring cases, highlighting both common patterns and gaps in existing case law.[5] A clearer understanding of this framework is necessary to assess how regional human rights law can develop to better protect the rights of the victims of digital monitoring across the globe.

More specifically, even though these three human rights protection systems are not applicable on a global scale, they have near-universal application in their

[3] 'Submarine Cables, the True Communication Highway' (*Mapfre Global Risk*, 22 July 2019) www.mapfreglobalrisks.com/en/risks-insurance-management/article/submarine-cables-the-true-communication-highway/; see, eg, D Guilfoyle, T Philippa Paige and R McLaughlin, 'The Final Frontier of Cyberspace: The Seabed Beyond National Jurisdiction and the Protection of Submarine Cables' (2022) 71 *ICLQ* 657.

[4] 'Global Digital Compact Must be Guided by Human Rights, Says Türk' (*Office of the United Nations High Commissioner for Human Rights*, 8 May 2023). Available at: www.ohchr.org/en/statements/2023/05/global-digital-compact-must-be-guided-human-rights-says-turk; 'UN High Commissioner Urges Human Rights-Centric Approach to Mitigate Risks in AI Development' (*Digital Watch*, 14 February 2024). Available at: dig.watch/updates/un-high-commissioner-urges-human-rights-centric-approach-to-mitigate-risks-in-ai-development; 'Principes directeurs relatifs aux entreprises et aux droits de l'homme' (*Nations Unies*, 2011). Available at: www.ohchr.org/sites/default/files/documents/publications/guidingprinciplesbusinesshr_fr.pdf.

[5] As the case law of the IACHR and ACtHPR is more limited than that of the ECtHR, I include in this analysis some of the key decisions of the respective quasi-judicial commissions (the Inter-American Commission of Human Rights and African Commission on Human and People's Rights).

respective regions and are binding on 104 of the 193 member states of the United Nations, with 46 states having signed and ratified the ECHR, 34 the ACHPR and 24 the ACHR.[6] On a political level, all three systems have established guidelines and strategies that recognise the challenges of the digital age for equality, freedom of expression and privacy.[7] As such, the present analysis offers scope for both inter-systemic comparison and for broader, cross-cutting patterns that are endemic to digital monitoring. Based on the comparative analysis that follows, the chapter argues that the practice of all three systems is characterised by a focus on mass, rather than individualised, forms of surveillance and monitoring; a lower standard of protection from monitoring by private actors, as opposed to state actors; and an open-ended approach to the justifications of monitoring, which requires refinement in the digital age. Despite differences in the structure and development of the case law of the three systems, the above patterns present ongoing common challenges for affirming a human right to privacy as a self-standing feature of regional human rights law. At the same time, regional particularities, such as the application to the digital context of a 'balancing' technique by the ECtHR and the absence of a dedicated protection of privacy in the ACHPR, reveal important deficiencies within some of these systems, exposing potentially deep-seated disagreements about how privacy ought to be defined in the digital age, especially with regard to questions of access to data and control over an individual's digital footprint.

The chapter is structured as follows: Part 2 defines the main terms of reference for the comparison and briefly presents the basic features and differences of the systems examined, to the extent that these are relevant to digital monitoring. Part 3 sets out the analysis of the case law, based on four principal themes: mass surveillance and monitoring (section 3.1); access to data (section 3.2); publication of information obtained through surveillance/monitoring (section 3.3); and targeted surveillance and monitoring by public or private actors (section 3.4). Part 4 provides comparative reflections. Part 5 concludes.

[6] In this analysis I include states that have ratified the American Convention of Human Rights (currently 24, following Venezuela's re-admission).

[7] E Lanza, 'Standards for a Free, Open and Inclusive Internet' (*Inter-American Commission on Human Rights*, 15 March 2017). Available at: www.oas.org/en/iachr/expression/docs/publications/internet_2016_eng.pdf; CB Marino, 'Freedom of Expression and the Internet' (*Inter-American Commission on HumanRights*, 31 December 2013). Available at: www.oas.org/en/iachr/expression/docs/reports/2014_04_08_Internet_ENG%20_WEB.pdf; 'Resolution on the Right to Freedom of Information and Expression on the Internet in Africa - ACHPR/Res. 362(LIX) 2016' (*African Commission on Human and Peoples' Rights*, 4 November 2016). Available at: www.oas.org/en/sla/dil/docs/acceso_informacion_desarrollos_UA_ACHPR-Res_362_LIX_2016.pdf; 'Déclaration de principes sur la liberté d'expression et l'accès à l'information en Afrique 2019' (*African Commission on Human and Peoples' Rights*, 10 November 2019). Available at: achpr.au.int/fr/node/902; Council of Europe, 'Council of Europe Strategic Framework 2022-2025 in the Digital Environment'. Available at: www.coe.int/en/web/freedom-expression/internet-governance.

2 Principles for the Regional Comparison

2.1 Data Collection

To identify case law related to digital monitoring, I conducted a keyword search of the term 'surveillance' on the following official databases: AfricanLII, for the ACtHPR; Corteidh, for the IACtHR; and HUDOC, for the ECtHR.[8] I limited my search to judgments in English and French, which are the principal working languages of both the ECtHR and the ACtHPR.[9] For the IACtHR, where the working languages are English and Spanish, I employed the embedded automatic translation function (Spanish to English) on the Corteidh database. I supplemented this search with further thematic searches of judgments relating to online expression and privacy.[10] The following analysis highlights the decisions and principles that I considered most relevant and representative of the jurisprudence of the three courts for the purposes of cross-regional comparison. It is not suggested, however, that these are the only relevant decisions or cases. The case law analysis was last updated on 6 September 2024.

2.2 Overarching Differences between the Three Systems

In light of their jurisdictional and remedial similarities, the three regional human rights systems examined in this chapter lend themselves naturally to an analytical comparison of their approach towards surveillance/monitoring – a broad human rights issue that touches on rights cognisable to a degree in all of the examined systems.[11] There are, however, three key differences between these systems, which are worth mentioning at the outset: first, unlike the ECtHR and ACtHPR, the IACtHR does not accept direct complaints by individuals and, even within the ACHPR system, individual complaints are uncommon.[12] While this

[8] 'African Court on Human and Peoples Rights'. Available at: africanlii.org/judgments/AfCHPR/; 'Base de Datos de Jurisprudencia' (*Corte IDH*). jurisprudencia.corteidh.or.cr/search/jurisdiction:EA/Internet; (*HUDOC European Court of Human Rights*). Available at: hudoc.echr.coe.int/eng#{%22documentcollectionid2%22.

[9] NB: the African Court also uses Portuguese and Arabic as working languages, but these were not included in my search.

[10] I am grateful to Anna Thoomkuzhy for her assistance with the ECHR part of the project.

[11] B Çali, MR Madsen and F Viljoen, 'Comparative Regional Human Rights Regimes: Defining a Research Agenda' (2018) 16 *International Journal of Constitutional Law* 128, 133–35. See also, more generally, L Burgorgue-Larsen, *The 3 Regional Human Rights Courts in Context: Justice That Cannot Be Taken for Granted* (Oxford, Oxford University Press, 2024).

[12] See 'Declarations' (*African Court on Human and Peoples' Rights*). Available at: www.african-court.org/wpafc/declarations. More specifically, 54 of the 55 Member States of the African Union (AU), with the exception of Morocco, have ratified the African Charter, but only 34 Member States have ratified the Protocol relating to the establishment of the African Court. Amongst these 34 states, only seven have a valid Special Declaration permitting individual complaints by citizens and NGOs at the time of writing (this follows several withdrawals of such declarations, the last of which was by Tunisia in March 2025).

procedural difference does not necessarily suggest a different interpretation of rights, it often means that fewer cases reach the IACtHR and ACtHPR than the ECtHR, as complaints are addressed in the first instance by the Inter-American and African Commissions on Human Rights, respectively. This is compounded by the significant age gap between the three systems, the larger number of ECHR contracting states (and corresponding 46 dedicated judges), and comparative wealth of resources of the ECHR system, which permit the ECtHR to handle a much greater number of cases than the other two courts.[13] In turn, while an effort has been made in the following analysis to limit the dominance of ECHR case law within the comparison, this has not always been feasible, as the overall volume of ACtHPR and IACtHR case law remains limited compared to that of the ECtHR.

Second, although none of the three systems allows individuals to bring claims directly against other private actors, such as internet service providers or employers, all three recognise that contracting states must not only refrain from violating rights but also protect them in the context of private relationships. There are, however, differences in the ways and extent to which these systems include the conduct of private actors. Whereas the IACHR and ACHPR explicitly recognise the duty of states to legislate to 'guarantee' rights in domestic law and treat that obligation strictly, the ECHR does not contain this level of detail.[14] The ECtHR has, of course, also interpreted rights as entailing positive obligations for contracting states in its case law on the basis of Article 1 ECHR, which states that every contracting party must 'secure to everyone within [its] jurisdiction the rights and freedoms defined ... in [the] Convention'.[15] But while it has occasionally treated positive obligations as including duties for private actors (also in the digital monitoring context), the ECtHR has typically taken a narrow approach in economic and social rights cases, understood as cases with resource reallocation implications, while it also, in principle, resists jurisdiction in cases that concern the interaction of private individuals.[16] By contrast, the IACtHR and ACtHPR have generally taken a broader stance vis-à-vis the human rights obligations of private actors, with their findings often applying to actions of the state and to the actions third parties without distinction.[17] Thus, despite not yet having developed their jurisprudence on digital monitoring to the same degree as the ECtHR, the African and Inter-American systems of rights protection display, to a more limited degree,

[13] By contrast, the ACtHPR and IACtHR are composed of eleven and seven judges, respectively.

[14] ACHR, arts 1 and 2; ACHPR, art 1.

[15] *Plattform "Ärzte für das Leben" v Austria* Series A no 139 (1988) 14 EHRR 204; *Marckx v Belgium*, Series A no 31 (1979) 2 EHRR 330. For an in-depth analysis of the development of positive obligations under the ECHR, see A Mowbray, *The Development of Positive Obligations under the European Convention on Human Rights by the European Court of Human Rights* (Oxford, Hart Publishing, 2004).

[16] See, eg, *Bărbulescu v Romania* (2017) ECHR 742; A Nolan, 'Addressing Economic and Social Rights Violations by Non-state Actors through the Role of the State: A Comparison of Regional Approaches to the "Obligation to Protect"' (2009) 9 *Human Rights Law Review* 225, 251–52; *Pla v Andorra* (2006) 42 EHRR 25, para 59.

[17] Nolan (n 16).

some of the challenges that the following analysis identifies in the ECHR context, such as an inconsistent approach between states' obligation to protect privacy and violations of privacy that result from the conduct of third parties.

Finally, and perhaps most importantly, the three instruments adopt different approaches to the right to privacy, as well as to other rights associated with surveillance and monitoring, such as equality and the freedom of expression. It is worth briefly considering these differences in turn.

2.3 Privacy

The digital environment has radically altered the contours of the contemporary right to privacy in ways that could hardly have been envisaged by the drafters of the treaties under examination. Even beyond the specificities of the digital context, however, the substantive protection of privacy in the three systems differs in important ways, which condition the comparative assessment that follows. Crucially, while the European and American Conventions explicitly recognise the right to privacy in Articles 8 and 11 thereof, the African Charter does not.

Article 8 of the ECHR is the most detailed provision across the three instruments. It provides that:

1. Everyone has the right to respect for his private and family life, his home and his correspondence.
2. There shall be no interference by a public authority with the exercise of this right except such as is in accordance with the law and is necessary in a democratic society in the interests of national security or public safety, for the economic well-being of the country, for the prevention of disorder or crime, for the protection of health or morals, or for the protection of the rights and freedoms of others.

It follows from the text of Article 8 of the ECHR that this provision can be restricted by lawful and proportionate measures, based on one of the grounds enumerated in subparagraph 2. As has already been highlighted above, the ECtHR has developed positive obligations under Article 8, and has acknowledged that the provision encompasses individual notions of privacy including data privacy, noting that 'private life is a broad term not susceptible to exhaustive definition'.[18] What is somewhat problematic about the text of Article 8, from the perspective of capturing violations of privacy in the digital age, is that it only envisages interference by public authorities. The textual limitations on Article 8 could be understood as rendering more difficult its invocation in cases involving purely private action, thus presenting a challenge for regulating the application of human rights on the internet as a space of primarily private initiative.

[18] *Breyer v Germany* (2020) 71 EHRR 17, para 73.

Article 11 of the ACHR protects the right to privacy in broader terms. It states that:

1. Everyone has the right to respect for his honor and to recognition of his dignity.
2. No one shall be subjected to arbitrary or abusive interference with his privacy, family life, home or correspondence, nor to unlawful attacks on his honor and reputation.
3. Everyone has the right to the protection of the law against such interference or attacks.

By referencing the 'protection of the law' to guard against violations of privacy, the text of Article 11 of the ACHR lends itself more naturally to positive obligations on the part of the contracting parties to regulate the conduct of private actors, including in the digital environment – an understanding of the text that has been affirmed by the IACtHR.[19]

Unlike the ECHR and ACHR, the African Charter makes no reference to the right to privacy in its text. This is unusual, particularly because the African Charter is the youngest of the three instruments, but can be explained by reference to the Charter's drafting context. As Jimoh notes, during the drafting process privacy was viewed as an individual right that was unsuited to the Charter's broader philosophy, which was the creation of an instrument enshrining a more collective/communal conception of human rights than other international standards.[20] However, it has been suggested both in African Union declarations and in academic commentary that the right to privacy is already comprised in the protection of dignity, which is enshrined in Article 5 of the ACHPR.[21] Still, the absence of an explicit protection of privacy in the Charter's text complicates the regional comparison, and renders the contribution of the ACHPR to the development of privacy-protective jurisprudence more peripheral than that of the other two systems.

2.4 Other Relevant Provisions

Beyond the right to privacy per se, aspects of the right of access to information and the right to impart information can be relevant to digital monitoring case law, as monitoring often results in sanctions against the speaker as well as in information shutdowns. The right to receive and impart information is protected across all three systems.

[19] *Escher et al v Brazil* IACHR Series C no 200 (2009), para 115.

[20] M Jimoh, 'The Place of Digital Surveillance under the African Charter on Human and People's Rights and the African Human Rights System in the Era of Technology' (2023) 1 *African Journal of Legal Issues in Technology and Innovation* 113, 117.

[21] 'Déclaration de principes sur la liberté d'expression et l'accès à l'information en Afrique 2019', above n 7; see also A Singh and M Power, 'The Privacy Awakening: The Urgent Need to Harmonise the Right to Privacy in Africa' (2019) 3 *African Human Rights Yearbook* 202.

Article 10(1) of the ECHR states that 'everyone has the right to freedom of expression. This right includes the freedom to hold opinions and to receive and impart information and ideas without interference by public authority and regardless of frontiers.' Similarly, Article 13(1) of the American Convention provides that:

> everyone has the right to freedom of thought and expression; this right includes freedom to seek, receive, and impart information and ideas of all kinds, regardless of frontiers, either orally or in writing, in print or in the form of art, or through any other media of his choice.

Article 9 of the African Charter states that 'everyone has the right to information'. While the right to receive information has not been fully developed under ECtHR jurisprudence, it has played a greater role within IACHR case law. As the following analysis will demonstrate, all three systems place heightened significance on free speech issues resulting from monitoring.

Further, invasions of privacy through digital monitoring are often closely linked with protected characteristics, such as religious or political beliefs, as well as with membership of organisations, such as advocacy groups and trade unions. A range of provisions protect these rights within the three systems under examination. Articles 1.1 and 24 of the American Convention establish the rights to equality and non-discrimination. Article 1.1 of the Convention requires contracting states to respect and ensure the free and full exercise of the human rights contained in the Convention 'without distinction of any kind as to race, color, sex, language, religion, political or other opinion, national or social origin, economic status, birth, or other social condition'. Article 24 states that 'all persons are equal before the law. Consequently, they are all entitled to equal protection of the law, without discrimination of any kind'. Equality before the law is protected in similar terms in Article 3 of the African Charter. But the latter is unique in that it also contains a series of broader provisions on equality and non-discrimination for both individuals and groups, and protects them both as rights vis-à-vis the state and as 'duties' of each person under Article 2. It also stipulates in Article 27:

1. Each individual has duties towards the family and society, towards the State and other legally recognized communities, and towards the International Community.
2. The rights and freedoms of each person shall be exercised with respect for the rights of others, collective security, morality and the common interest.

In the same vein, Article 28 of the African Charter provides that 'everyone has the duty to respect and to regard his fellow men without discrimination of any kind, and to maintain relations which make it possible to promote, safeguard and strengthen mutual respect and tolerance'. The African Charter is unique in its inclusion of these obligations and, even though it is not always clear how they can be judicially enforced in their own right, they often supplement and strengthen the reasoning of the African Commission and Court.[22] By contrast, the main protection against discrimination in the ECHR system is Article 14, which prohibits any distinction 'based on sex, race, color, language, religion, political or other opinion, national or social origin, association with a national minority, property, birth or other status', but only as regards the 'enjoyment' of other rights protected in the ECHR. In other words, Article 14 is not a positive right aimed at guaranteeing equality in the Contracting States, but has a clearly auxiliary character that depends on the existence of another relevant provision.[23] As a result, questions of equality and targeting have been less prominent before the ECtHR than in the case law of the other two courts.

3 Thematic Comparison

Having broadly sketched the main terms of reference of the three regional systems with regard to digital monitoring, this section goes on to organise and juxtapose their practice in this context under the four themes outlined earlier: mass surveillance and monitoring; access to data; publication of information obtained through surveillance and monitoring; and targeted surveillance and monitoring by public or private actors. This comparative analysis shows that there is a focus, across all three systems, on mass forms of monitoring and surveillance; a lower standard of protection from monitoring by private, as opposed to state, actors; and an open-ended approach to the justifications of monitoring – findings which will be further detailed and nuanced in section 4 below.

3.1 Mass Surveillance and Monitoring

In its 1978 ruling in *Klass and Others v Germany*, the ECtHR held that the secret surveillance of correspondence was necessary in a democratic society in the interests of national security and for the prevention of disorder or crime.[24] Thus, even though its operation needs to meet conditions of legality and proportionality as set out in Article 8 of the ECHR, mass surveillance and monitoring are not deemed *ipso facto* incompatible with it. By the early 2000s, the ECtHR had started to develop this case law further as a result of new technologies, applying stricter criteria regarding the clarity and arbitrariness of the applicable legal framework. For example, in *Liberty and others v United Kingdom*, the Court found that the

[22] M Mutua, 'The Banjul Charter and the African Cultural Fingerprint: An Evaluation of the Language of Duties' (1995) 35 *Virginia Journal of International Law* 339.
[23] 'Guide on Article 14 of the European Convention on Human Rights and on Article 1 of Protocol No. 12 to the Convention' (*European Court of Human Rights*, 28 February 2025). Available at: https://ks.echr.coe.int/documents/d/echr-ks/guide_art_14_art_1_protocol_12_eng, 6.
[24] *Klass and others v Germany* Series A no 28 (1978) 2 EHRR 214, paras 51–58.

UK's interception of the communications of civil liberties organisations was not clear enough to be considered 'in accordance with the law' and therefore violated Article 8 of the ECHR.[25] Since 2015, the ECtHR has also started setting out a more principled approach towards large-scale targeted and mass surveillance practices, showing concern for the existence of legal safeguards for privacy in order for surveillance to be considered permissible. In its ruling in *Zakharov v Russia*, the Court found that Russian legislation governing the interception of communications did not provide for adequate and effective guarantees against arbitrariness and the risk of abuse, which is 'inherent in any system of secret surveillance, and which is particularly high in a system where the secret services and the police have direct access, by technical means, to all mobile-telephone communications'.[26] As such, the 'quality of law' requirement for an interference with Article 8 of the Convention to be considered justified was not met.

In *Szabó and Vissy v Hungary*, which concerned Hungarian legislation on secret anti-terrorist surveillance, the Court found that such legislation was incompatible with Article 8, both because it was too broad and lacked judicial scrutiny.[27] In a similar vein, in its ruling in *Big Brother Watch and Others v United Kingdom*, the ECtHR found that the UK's bulk interception of communications data, which was uncovered as part of Edward Snowden's revelations in 2013, violated Article 8 of the ECHR (as well as, in other respects, Article 10). The case clarified that to be considered compatible with Article 8, mass surveillance regimes must include 'end-to-end safeguards', meaning that an assessment of the necessity and proportionality of the measures should be made at the domestic level; that bulk interception should be subject to independent authorisation at the outset, when the object and scope of the operation were being defined; and that the operation should be subject to supervision and independent *ex post facto* review.[28] Applying this approach, the Court concluded that the UK's interception regime suffered from three key defects: the absence of independent authorisation for bulk interception warrants; the failure to include the categories of search terms ('selectors') in the application for a warrant; and the failure to ensure that search of an identifiable individual was subject to prior authorisation. However, in this case law, the ECtHR also confirmed that mass surveillance and the sharing of private information arising therefrom are not necessarily incompatible with the Convention. Moreover, the case does not go as far as to set out a requirement of *prior judicial authorisation* ahead of each instance of interception.

While sharing the main features of the ECtHR's approach, the IACtHR has been more specific about the need for prior judicial authorisation of all instances of interception of identifiable data (including some aspects of sensitive metadata,

[25] *Liberty and others v United Kingdom* (2008) 48 EHRR 1, para 69.
[26] *Zakharov v Russia* (2015) 63 EHRR 17, para 302.
[27] *Szabó and Vissy v Hungary* (2016) 63 EHRR 3, paras 81–86.
[28] *Big Brother Watch and Others v United Kingdom* (2021) 74 EHRR 17, para 350.

such as geolocation). From early on in its privacy case law, the IACtHR has held that the concept of private life within the Inter-American system comprises the monitoring of conversations and other communications, and that this may include not only listening to the content of communications but also the mere act of recording or storing technical aspects of their operation.[29] In *Escher v Brazil*, the Court also recognised that communications on the internet are protected by Article 11 of the ACHR, and noted that 'the State must make a greater commitment to adapting traditional forms of protection of the right to privacy to the present day'.[30] The IACtHR's most important contribution to this field is arguably its October 2023 judgment in the *CAJAR* case, in which it found that Colombia had violated the ACHR by using several invasive surveillance techniques against the members of CAJAR, a non-governmental human rights litigation organisation.[31] In this case, the Court found that Colombia had violated the rights to life, personal integrity, privacy, freedom of thought and expression, informational self-determination, truth, honour, judicial guarantees, judicial protection, freedom of association, movement and residence, protection of the family, rights of children, and the right to defend the human rights, of certain members of CAJAR as well as their families. In respect of the need for prior judicial control, the Court stated that

> the effective protection of the rights to privacy and freedom of thought and expression, combined with the extreme risk of arbitrariness posed by the use of surveillance techniques … of communications, especially in light of existing new technologies, *leads this Court to conclude that any measure in this regard* (including interception, surveillance, and monitoring of all types of communication …) *requires a judicial authority to decide on its merits*, while also defining its limits, including the manner, duration, and scope of the authorised measure.[32] (emphasis added)

Crucially, in the Inter-American system, judicial authorisation is also needed when state intelligence agencies request personal information from private companies that manage this data, as well as for 'surveillance and tracking techniques concerning specific individuals that entail access to non-public databases and information systems that store and process personal data, the tracking of users on the computer network, or the location of electronic devices'.[33] While the IACtHR broadly follows the same approach as the ECtHR in the sense that it highlights the need for safeguards without labelling the practice of mass surveillance as incompatible with the American Convention per se, it has gone further than the ECtHR in terms of its insistence on prior judicial control of state surveillance activities, as well as by including in more explicit terms in its jurisprudence the conduct of private internet actors.

[29] *Tristán Donoso v Panama* IACHR Series C no 193 (2009), paras 55 and 76.
[30] *Escher v Brazil* (n 19) para 115.
[31] *Miembros de la Corporación Colectivo de Abogados "José Alvear Restrepo" ('CAJAR') v Colombia* IACHR Series C no 506 (2023).
[32] ibid paras 132–35.
[33] ibid para 553.

Whereas the African Court has not directly considered issues of state surveillance at the time of writing, some indications of the overall approach taken under the African Charter can be seen in cases concerning the targeting of political dissidents. On the one hand, in *Media Rights Agenda v Nigeria,* the African Commission highlighted that enacting laws to protect communal interests protected by Article 27(2) of the Charter, such as national security, is a permissible limit to other Charter provisions, such as freedom of the press. On the other hand, the quality of the law that details the limitation is paramount in ensuring that the exercise of Charter rights is not rendered illusory.[34] As a result, safeguards are essential against any arbitrary or retroactive measures, such as the retroactive banning of publications.[35] Going further, in *Media Rights Agenda (Malaolu) v Nigeria*, Nigeria had tried for treason and imprisoned the applicant, who was the editor of an independent newspaper, under the provisions of an emergency law passed during a military coup, without any clear evidence or indication as to the basis of his trial and conviction. The African Commission found that the applicant had been targeted because of his political opposition to the regime, and that the state could not merely point to the existence of validly enacted law to eschew its obligations under the Charter.[36] It consequently found various violations of the Charter, including Articles 3(2) on the equal protection of the law, Article 9 on the freedom of expression, and Article 5 on human dignity. Similarly, *Article 19 v Eritrea* concerned the detention and ill-treatment on grounds of treason of eighteen journalists suspected of being members of the G15, an organisation which had authored a public letter criticising the government. Similar to the approach of the ECtHR, the African Commission found violations of several Charter rights and highlighted the significance of the quality of the law setting out restrictive measures within the African Charter system:

> [If] 'law' is interpreted to mean any domestic law regardless of its effect, States Parties to the Charter would be able to negate the rights conferred upon individuals by the Charter. However, the Commission's jurisprudence has interpreted the so-called claw-back clauses as constituting a reference to international law, meaning that only restrictions on rights which are consistent with the Charter and with States Parties' international obligations should be enacted by the relevant national authorities. The lawfulness of Eritrea's actions must therefore be considered against the Charter and other norms of international law, rather than by reference to its own domestic laws alone.[37]

As Mujib Jimoh notes, the principles of necessity of the measures, as well as of equal treatment and dignity that stem from this case law could be used to challenge

[34] *Media Rights Agenda v Nigeria* African Commission on Human and Peoples' Rights Communication nos 105/93, 128/94, 130/94 and 152/96 (1998), para 70.

[35] ibid paras 58–29.

[36] *Media Rights Agenda v Nigeria* African Commission on Human and Peoples' Rights Communication no 224/1998 (2000), para 75.

[37] *Article 19 v Eritrea* African Commission on Human and Peoples' Rights Communication no 275/03 (2007), paras 91–92.

general surveillance measures under the African system in the future.[38] Given its scrutiny of the laws authorising restrictions on rights by reference to international standards, the African system could develop strong protection of the individual against arbitrariness that resembles the approach of the other two systems. Its emphasis on *equality* before the law is also a noteworthy element of its jurisprudence, which is not yet present in that of the other courts.

3.2 Access to Data

The question of whether human rights law empowers data subjects to access the data that the state has collected about them is a necessary follow-up to the question of whether the interception or storing of that data was permissible in the first place. In its early jurisprudence, most notably in *Leander v Sweden*, the ECtHR developed a narrow concept of access to information, holding that this right 'basically prohibits a government from preventing someone from receiving information that others wish or may be willing to provide'.[39] More recently, however, the Court has begun to broaden its approach concerning information of a public nature, including information held on private internet repositories, citing the relevant case law of the Inter-American Court on this issue.[40] Further, although the ECtHR has consistently held states responsible for tracking and preventing access to specific websites, such as Google Sites and YouTube, it has not yet entrusted them with the positive obligation of guaranteeing individuals' access to their personal data against private companies refusing to share such information of their own accord.[41] While the ECtHR has occasionally endorsed 'the right to a form of informational self-determination' in the context of state disclosure of private information, it has been reticent to accept important aspects of that right in data privacy cases concerning private actors.[42] For example, it has resisted bringing automatically within the protective scope of Article 8 requirements for erasure or rectification, and has insisted on proof of the severity of the harm suffered being adduced by the applicant in seeking to ensure a fair balance between privacy and the exercise of free speech, as further discussed in the following section.[43]

By contrast, the rights of access to information and of control over personal data are more directly protected by the IACtHR. In *Claude Reyes v Chile*, the Court

[38] Jimoh (n 20) at 122. See also 'Principles and Guidelines on Human and Peoples' Rights while Countering Terrorism in Africa' (*ACHPR*, 3 August 2016). Available at: achpr.au.int/index.php/en/node/850 Part 11.

[39] *Leander v Sweden* Series A no 116 (1987) 9 EHRR 433, para 74.

[40] *Magyar Helsinki Bizottsag v Hungary* (2016) 71 EHRR 2, para 61, citing the judgment of the IACHR in *Claude Reyes et al v Chile* Series C no 151 (2006).

[41] *Yildirim v Turkey* (2012) App no 3111/10; *Cengiz v Turkey* (2015) App no 48226/10 and 14027/11.

[42] ECtHR 27 June 2017, *Satakunnan Markkinapörssi Oy and Satamedia Oy v Finland* (2018) 66 EHRR 8, para 137; *LB v Hungary* (2023) 77 EHRR 1, para 103.

[43] *Hurbain v Belgium* (2023) 77 EHRR 34, paras 199 and 210.

confirmed that it expects contracting states to actively facilitate access to information based on the principle of 'maximum disclosure', even though it must be noted that, in this context too, the case law has concerned state conduct.[44] More recently, in its decision in *CAJAR*, the IACtHR went beyond its own earlier jurisprudence, as well as that of its European counterpart, in finding that the 'right to informational self-determination' as it stems from various legal systems of the region and the protections set forth in both Articles 11 and 13 ACHR, is an autonomous human right recognised by the Inter-American system.[45] The existence of this right means, in the IACtHR's assessment, that it is essential that individuals have the right to know what data about them are contained in state records, where the data came from, the purposes for which the data is being kept, how long it has been stored for, whether and (if so) why it is being shared with outside parties and, more generally, how it is being processed. Alongside this protection, there is a right to rectify, modify or update their data if it is inaccurate, incomplete or outdated; a right to delete or suppress the data in justified circumstances; and the right to oppose the processing of the data in justified circumstances, as well as a right to data portability.[46] While the facts of this case concerned state data repositories, as highlighted earlier, the Court also recognises and includes in its judgment private actors who manage personal data.[47]

The ACtHPR has affirmed that the right to information is protected by Article 9 of the African Charter.[48] The Commission has also found that failure to explain the arrest and intimidation of journalists violates individuals' right to receive information.[49] However, the ACHPR system has not developed an active jurisprudence on access to personal data held in state or private repositories under this provision.

3.3 Balancing Freedom of Expression and the Right to Privacy in Cases Involving Monitoring and Surveillance

While a wealth of ECtHR case law is based on the principle of striking a 'fair balance' between competing rights – typically Articles 8 (privacy) and 10 (freedom of expression) – the nuances of the digital age have yet to be fully fleshed out, particularly in the context of the publication of information discovered as a result of surveillance. More specifically, the ECtHR traditionally recognises a high level of protection of freedom of expression for the media, which can, in some respects, extend to the publication of information obtained through covert surveillance of the data subject, as illustrated in cases such as *Mosley v United Kingdom* and

[44] *Claude Reyes* (n 40), para 92.
[45] *CAJAR* (n 31), para 586.
[46] ibid paras 582–600.
[47] ibid para 571.
[48] *Lohé Issa Konaté v Burkina Faso*, ACtHPR Application no 004/2013 (2005).
[49] *Dawda K Jawara v Gambia*, African Commission of Human and Peoples' Rights Communication nos 147/95 and 149/96 (2000).

Médiapart v France.[50] To determine whether a publication infringes privacy, the Court uses a five-step test, developed in *Von Hannover v Germany*, which examines: whether the expression in question contributes to a debate of public interest; whether the person concerned by the expression is a public figure; the previous conduct of the person concerned (ie whether they have already been the subject of publicity concerning their private life); the content, form and consequences of the publication; and the duties and responsibilities of journalists in collecting the data (eg, whether private information has been obtained clandestinely).[51] However, the Court's application of these criteria in cases of covert surveillance is fraught with contradictions.

For example, in the *Mosley* case, which concerned the online publication of an unlawfully obtained video with sexual content (thus going to the heart of the applicant's private life), the Court accepted that, given that the video had already been widely circulated, the national authorities' refusal to order its removal did not amount to a violation of Article 8. Since thousands of internet users had already accessed the video, the invasion of privacy had already been committed, and the removal of the video link would have had no real remedial effect. The ECtHR therefore approved the solution proposed by the national court, namely financial compensation. By contrast, in the more recent *Médiapart* case, the Court also accepted the Cour de Cassation's order to withdraw from online circulation a series of secretly obtained recordings of private discussions between Mrs Bettencourt (the owner, at the time, of the L'Oréal group) and her financial adviser, on the grounds that the wide online dissemination of the recordings had constituted a significant and long-standing violation of her privacy. These contradictory messages are not necessarily surprising in the context of the ECHR, where the operation of the margin of appreciation means that, insofar as national authorities assess the balance between the relevant rights in line with the *Von Hannover* criteria, the ECtHR will not normally replace their assessment with its own. They do, however, prevent the emergence of a coherent approach towards the publication of information as a result of surveillance in the ECHR system: they indicate an absence of red lines regarding violations of privacy that cannot be accepted under the ECHR system and a high degree of remedial deference to domestic courts. This can be questioned in the digital context in particular, which poses greater risks to privacy due to its amplifying effects and the fact that, as the Court has itself acknowledged, the internet extends the 'public watchdog' role of the press to a wider range of actors, such as bloggers and social media users.[52]

The IACtHR had traditionally taken a clearer approach in favour of the freedom of expression in cases concerning the press, in line with the prohibition of

[50] *Mosley v United Kingdom* (2011) 53 EHRR 30; *Société Editrice de Mediapart and others v France*, (2021) App nos 281/15 and 34445/15.

[51] *Von Hannover v Germany* (2012) 55 EHRR 15, paras 109–13; see also *Couderc and Hachette Filipacchi Associés v France* (2015) App no 40454/07.

[52] *Magyar Helsinki Bizottsag v Hungary* (2016) 71 EHRR 2, para 168.

prior and indirect censorship set out in Article 13 of the American Convention. As noted earlier, the IACtHR offers a strong protection of the right to privacy which includes protection against the invasion of privacy by third parties. In *Fontevecchia and D'Amico v Argentina*, the IACtHR held that 'the State has an obligation to guarantee the right to privacy through positive action, which may involve, in certain cases, the adoption of measures to ensure the protection of privacy against interference by public authorities as well as private individuals or institutions, including the media'.[53] The Court is thus prepared to extend its protection of privacy beyond the state–individual relationship, and has expressed particular sensitivity for the need to do so in the digital age. Nevertheless, the IACtHR has so far generally continued to affirm the Convention's absolute prohibition of prior censorship, which has pushed it to find remedial ways of addressing violations of privacy, such as the affirmation of the 'right of reply' and the legality of subsequent civil sanctions, rather than ordering the prior suppression of information present in the public domain.[54] Operating in a context of post-dictatorial transition for a number of countries in its region, the IACtHR is more sceptical than the ECtHR about the choice of remedies by its contracting states, and has been more prescriptive than its European counterpart in this context, particularly in cases where states have resorted too quickly to the removal or banning of information.[55] Still, in light of the strong terms in which informational self-determination has now been protected in the *CAJAR* judgment including, in certain instances, the right to erasure, it is likely that if faced with a case concerning publication of data following covert surveillance, the IACtHR would take a stricter approach towards the availability of this data in the public domain altogether.

3.4 Surveillance and Monitoring of Private Individuals by Public and Private Actors

The ECtHR has recognised that surveillance and monitoring can have considerable repercussions for individuals even outside the context of press freedom, and has generally given a narrow margin of appreciation to states in respect of the necessity of collecting, storing, and distributing identifiable data, such as a person's image. It has treated the proportionality of these measures stringently, particularly in cases where the interference with privacy was covert. For example, in *Perry v United Kingdom*, the police had covertly videotaped the applicant whilst he was at the police station and used the videotape in the prosecution

[53] *Fontevecchia and D'Amico v Argentina* IACHR Series C no 238 (2011), para 49. See also *Escher v Brazil* (n 19), para 115.

[54] See, eg, *Moya Chacón v Costa Rica* IACHR Series C no 451 (2022).

[55] A Huneeus, 'Courts Resisting Courts: Lessons from the Inter-American Court's Struggle to Enforce Human Rights' (2011) 44 *Cornell International Law Journal* 493, 496.

against him. The Court held that there had been a violation of Article 8 of the ECHR, as there had been no indication that the applicant had had any expectation that footage would be taken of him in the police station. The interference in question had also not been in accordance with the law, because the police had failed to obtain the applicant's consent, to inform him that the tape was being made; and to inform him of his rights in connection with these actions. The Court's case law in respect of other forms of tracking, including geolocation tracking, has been comparatively less stringent but still entails a high justificatory threshold.[56]

Similarly, the Court has taken a strict approach to covert monitoring and surveillance in cases concerning individuals' intimate privacy by private actors regardless of subsequent disclosure (albeit that subsequent disclosure/publication is an aggravating factor). In this regard, the ECtHR has stipulated that both gender-based cyberviolence and the intimate filming of minors are severe violations of Article 8 that must be criminalised under domestic law.[57]

The ECtHR has also extended its protection of privacy to public and private workplaces, although its approach in this field has been more mixed.[58] While this topic is dealt with more extensively in subsequent chapters, it is worth briefly laying down a few introductory examples that set the comparative picture in this field. In *Antović and Mirković v Montenegro*, the ECtHR found a violation of the right to private life of two lecturers who had been filmed whilst teaching at a public university, as the video surveillance had not been in accordance with the law, even though it had been communicated to the individuals in question.[59] By contrast, in *López Ribalda and Others v Spain*, the Court applied these criteria strictly in a situation involving the covert video-surveillance of employees, which led to their dismissal. The applicants, who worked in a private supermarket and were suspected of theft, were subjected to covert video surveillance by the employer to establish their misconduct. The Court found that there had been no violation of Article 8, as the Spanish courts had carefully balanced the rights of the applicants and those of the employer and had thoroughly examined the justification for the video-surveillance. The key argument made by the applicants was that they had not been given prior notification of the surveillance despite the fact that the law provided for this. However, the ECtHR found that domestic courts had not exceeded their margin of appreciation in finding the monitoring proportionate and legitimate in these circumstances, which concerned a

[56] See, eg, *National Federation of Sportspersons' Associations and Unions (FNASS) and Others v France* (2018) App nos 48151/11 and 77769/13; *Ben Faiza v France* (2018) App no 31446/12.

[57] *Khadija Ismayilova v Azerbaijan* (2019) App nos 65286/13 and 57270/14; *Volodina v Russia (No 2)* (2021) App no 40419/19; *Söderman v Sweden* (2013) 58 EHRR 36.

[58] For a fuller analysis see E Frantziou, 'The Right to Privacy While Working from Home: Why Employee Monitoring Infringes Art 8 ECHR' (*UK Labour Law Blog*, 5 October 2020). Available at: https://uklabourlawblog.com/2020/10/05/the-right-to-privacy-while-working-from-home-wfh-why-employee-monitoring-infringes-art-8-echr-by-eleni-frantziou/.

[59] *Antović and Mirković v Montenegro* (2017) App no 70838/13, para 59.

quasi-public space where only a limited expectation of privacy arose and where a competing right (the employer's right to property) was at issue alongside Article 8.[60] A similar approach was followed in the context of a dismissal following the collection of geolocation data through a monitoring device installed in the applicant's vehicle in *Florindo de Almeida Vasconcelos Gramaxo v Portugal*.[61] It is unclear whether the less stringent treatment of surveillance is attributable to the fact that the employer in these scenarios was acting in a purely private capacity, whether the decisions are underpinned by an implicit 'threshold' assessment (ie an assumption that the surveillance or sanctions suffered were less serious), or by a combination of these factors.

In addition to physical workplace surveillance systems, the ECtHR has held that digital communications monitoring by employers can violate Article 8 of the ECHR and has, in this regard, treated public and private employers in a similar manner. For example, in *Bărbulescu v Romania*, it held that an individual could not be dismissed simply because he had accessed social networks during working hours, which the employer discovered following surveillance of his online activity. The Court also held that states had to demonstrate that an adequate legislative framework was in place to guarantee the protection of privacy in the workplace, and that national courts had struck a fair balance between the interests of the employer and those of the employee.[62] Similarly, in *Melike v Turkey*, the ECtHR emphasised that the mere fact of liking political comments on Facebook outside of work cannot lead to a person's dismissal, thereby suggesting that communications monitoring, even of publicly accessible online posts, may violate privacy.[63]

While neither the Inter-American nor African systems have specific case law addressing the effects of online surveillance by private parties, certain parallels can be found in the case law of the IACtHR. Beyond its broad analysis of Article 11 IACHR as comprising both public and private acts, as well as its recent affirmation of informational self-determination as an autonomous right, the Inter-American system has also affirmed that atypical sanctions, such as employer disciplinary measures and private reprimands affecting one's career prospects, can violate the American Convention.[64] The jurisprudence of the ECtHR and the IACtHR therefore have in common the need to protect privacy in a range of social relations, including the relationship between employer and employee.

[60] *López Ribalda and Others v Spain* (2019) 71 EHRR 7, paras 118–25.
[61] *Florindo de Almeida Vasconcelos Gramaxo v Portugal* (2022) App no 26968/16.
[62] *Bărbulescu v Romania* (n 16), para 121.
[63] *Melike v Turkey* (2021) App no 35786/19. See also *Danileț v Romania* (2024) App no 16915/21.
[64] *Urrutia Laubreaux v Chile* IACHR Series C no 409 (2020) (it should be noted, however, that in this case the claimant was a judge and, as such, a public employee).

4 Comparative Reflections on the Approach of Regional Human Rights Courts Regarding Digital Monitoring

As highlighted in the introduction, an analysis of the common patterns and differences between regional human rights systems is important when assessing the extent to which applicable international standards can capture, through litigation, the challenges of surveillance and monitoring in the digital age. But can these systems offer coherent responses to this relatively new and distinctly difficult to regulate field of privacy litigation? The answer to this question is not straightforward. While the preceding sections have shown elements of progress with regard to violations of rights in the digital age in regional human rights law, they also reveal deficiencies that are worth considering when assessing the current state and possible future development of digital monitoring in regional human rights law. More specifically, the case law of all three regional systems can be understood as being defined by a focus on mass forms of monitoring and surveillance; a lower standard of protection from monitoring by private, as opposed to state, actors; and an open-ended approach to the justifications of monitoring.

All three systems show awareness of and concern for state abuses of power in the field of mass, indiscriminate or generalised surveillance operations, typically employed in the context of counter-terrorism. Regional human rights law sets out safeguards against arbitrariness and emphasises the need for 'lawful' monitoring, in the sense of monitoring that is duly detailed in laws of sufficient quality and transparency. However, there is much greater disparity between the three systems when it comes to the targeting of specific individuals, particularly when monitoring and surveillance are conducted by private actors, rather than by state authorities.

In this regard, the case law of the ECtHR is the most detailed, having considered private violations of rights in cyberspace as well as the implications of cyber-attacks and digital monitoring for individuals' private lives on numerous occasions. As the ECtHR's former president Síofra O'Leary has pointed out in her extra-judicial writing, the ECtHR is acutely actor-aware, adapting its approach according to the actor who violates privacy in the digital era.[65] ECtHR case law in this field is more prescriptive and clear in the context of negative violations of rights and where state attribution is easy to establish (eg, cases where an internet service provider is statutorily obligated to collect and store data, which may then be shared with state actors).[66] By contrast, the ECtHR appears less inclined to intervene in cases of private data violations. For example, its approach is less consistent when it comes to ordering the correction or erasure of private data published as a result of monitoring. Further, while the Court has accepted the existence of liability through positive obligations for instances of purely private

[65] S O'Leary, 'Balancing Rights in a Digital Age' (2018) 59 *Irish Jurist* 59, 72–74.

[66] See *Big Brother Watch* (n 28); *Vladimir Kharitonov v Russia* (2020) App no 10795/14.

monitoring, in recent years it has been open to a range of justifications for the monitoring that may have included economic considerations, particularly in the field of employment monitoring. In this context, as well as in respect of the interaction with Article 10 on free speech, the ECtHR has resorted to the use of a balancing terminology that indicates a degree of reticence in accepting the value of information per se. This suggests that the ECtHR is holding onto its traditional stance regarding non-intervention in private matters (understood as matters concerning private law, such as employment contracts, rather than, eg, the criminal law) as well as expressing, more generally, a harm or seriousness driven approach to violations of privacy, rather than accepting 'self-determination' in the sense of control over one's data as a core element of Article 8, despite its occasional references to this notion.[67]

In the same vein, the case law of the African Court and Commission shows a broader hesitancy in accepting data violations as a self-standing harm. This is, of course, largely conditioned by the absence of a specific protection of privacy in the African Charter. The peripheral role of African judicial and quasi-judicial rights enforcement mechanisms that can be gleaned from the above analysis nevertheless suggests that the hurdle of litigating privacy in the digital age in the African system through other provisions, such as dignity and collective rights, may be greater than previously suggested in the academic literature, albeit that this may change as the jurisprudence starts to multiply in future.[68] While the ACHPR's emphasis on equality can be a source of inspiration for the other two systems, which have not yet addressed monitoring through this lens in their state surveillance case law, the absence of directly relevant case law is a cause of concern, particularly in view of the large-scale digital shutdowns that African states have experienced, often in the context of political turbulence.

The silence of the African system and relative reticence of the European system can be contrasted with the case law of the IACtHR, which is framed more expansively and clearly than that of the ECtHR in the context of personal data, while also eschewing some of the limitations of the latter with regard to the divide between private and public violations of rights. The IACtHR is the only one of the three courts to recognise 'informational self-determination' as a self-standing right, and the IACHR can thus be considered the only system (among those under consideration) where the protection of privacy has actively developed with the digital age to cover issues of data protection as a matter of personal autonomy, rather than emphasising the severity of the consequences of data disclosure or interception. This clearer stance on private data does, however, raise questions about how the IACtHR will manage private violations of rights going forward and

[67] On the concept of informational self-determination as a justificatory premise of privacy in human rights law, see F Thouvenin, 'Informational Self-Determination: A Convincing Rationale for Data Protection Law?' (2021) 12 *Journal of Intellectual Property, Information Technology and E-Commerce Law* 246.

[68] See, eg, Jimoh (n 20).

whether and how it can continue to maintain the absolute protection from prior and indirect censorship mandated by Article 13 of the IACHR and its prior jurisprudence. It is to be hoped that lessons in this respect will generally not be taken from the ECtHR's approach: as highlighted in the preceding analysis, this does not currently offer adequate answers regarding the core of the right to privacy, particularly in cases that concern personal data, while the use of the balancing method gives rise to an over-broad and inconsistent scope for justifying interferences with digital privacy.[69] At the same time, as more case law reaches the IACtHR, certain choices will unavoidably have to be made about whether it is possible to continue to embrace stricter standards with regard to both privacy and free speech and, particularly, whether all actors should benefit equally from these protections.

5 Conclusion: Between Convergence and Evasion in the Protection from Digital Monitoring Through Regional Human Rights Standards

This chapter has shown that, on the one hand, there can be real and effective protection of individuals in specific contexts within regional systems of rights protection. For example, there is broad parity between the three systems regarding the need to justify surveillance measures appropriately, despite accepting the necessity of state surveillance measures in principle. There is also a growing convergence on issues of data access and balancing privacy with freedom of expression. On the other hand, while regional human rights law can offer some insights as to how digital monitoring may be brought within existing human rights structures, there remain important challenges in capturing the specificities of the digital age, especially with regard to the conduct of private actors and the nature and scope of the justifications that can be adduced to accept monitoring/surveillance. More generally, it can be observed that regional human rights jurisprudence has remained rather limited, indirect and, to a certain extent, modest. So far, only the case law of the ECtHR has directly addressed the consequences of monitoring an individual's online footprint for an individual's private life, and it has done so within a line of case law displaying important contradictions and lacking clear overarching principles. Indeed, if we compare the above-mentioned cases with sub-regional human rights law, such as the European Union's *Costeja Gonzalez* and *Schrems* cases – rightly dubbed the 'online privacy revolution' – one would get the impression that the main event is taking place elsewhere.[70] This is not an isolated phenomenon. For instance,

[69] F Brimblecombe, 'The Public Interest in Deleted Personal Data? The Right to Be Forgotten's Freedom of Expression Exceptions Examined Through the Lens of Article 10 ECHR' (2020) 23(10) *Journal of Internet Law* 1, 16–17.

[70] Case C-131/12 *Google Spain v AEPD and Mario Costeja González*, ECLI:EU:C:2014:317, [2014] 3 CMLR 50; Case C-362/14 *Maximillian Schrems v Data Protection Commissioner* ECLI:EU:C:2015:650,

despite the absence of relevant case law at the ACtHPR, the ECOWAS Court has issued important decisions on privacy protection that largely mirror those of the European Court of Justice.[71] And while in the Inter-American context there has been a bolder development of privacy in the digital age, the IACtHR's case law has also largely followed the emergence of extensive and directly applicable obligations on data access and disclosure through *habeas data*, which are specialised *amparo* (constitutional lawsuit) proceedings found in several constitutions in the region.[72]

It follows that, although some regional human rights laws offer principles to protect people from digital monitoring, solutions still tend to be local and more limited in scope. There remains a lack of unified, comprehensive efforts to treat monitoring as one of the key human rights challenges in the digital age. This is regrettable as, while the standards set by national and supranational courts can have a positive indirect effect on regional human rights litigation, they have neither the jurisdictional reach of the ECHR, IACHR and ACHPR nor their normative power as authoritative interpreters of human rights. By contrast, when the findings of regional human rights courts converge, they have been shown to bring about real and rapid changes in the behaviour of global players which, in this context, may include internet service providers, search engines and online media.[73] The comparative case law analysed in this chapter shows that this power could be exercised not by rupture, but by a more confident and explicit evolution and adaptation of privacy principles to the digital environment. For this to be rendered possible, though, a more concrete exploration across all three systems of the origins and level of harm that is required for a privacy violation to be understood as a human rights violation is necessary. Why are monitoring and surveillance infringements of privacy? Does anything change if we are monitored personally or as part of a wider measure? Does it matter if we are monitored by a private individual, instead of a state authority/government agency? Addressing these questions through litigation will be central to the development of a more coherent regional human rights jurisprudence that can carry prior principles concerning due justification, attribution and balancing into the digital age.

[2016] 2 CMLR 2; L Bershidsky, 'The EU Sets Off an Online Privacy Revolution' (*Bloomberg*, 16 December 2015). Available at: www.bloomberg.com/view/articles/2015-12-16/the-eu-starts-a-data-privacy-revolution.

[71] *Amnesty International Togo and Others v Republic of Togo* ECOWAS ECW/CCJ/JUD/09/20 (2020).

[72] See, for a detailed examination: A Carías, *Constitutional Protection of Human Rights in Latin America: A Comparative Study of Amparo Proceedings* (Cambridge, Cambridge University Press, 2008).

[73] On the transformative nature of positive human rights obligations for non-state actors in the context of global constitutionalism, see S Fredman, *Human Rights Transformed: Positive Rights and Positive Duties* (Oxford, Oxford University Press, 2001), especially ch 2.

3

Electronic Monitoring of Migrants

VIRGINIA MANTOUVALOU*

> I felt like an animal. You know these tags I watch on documentaries, they are tagging animals and they are controlled. They are watched from everywhere. … The animal is the one who is suffering, but they are tongueless, they can't express their pain. So this has really, this tag like sank in me so bad.[1]

1 Introduction

Electronic monitoring has been used extensively in criminal justice in the United Kingdom (UK) and many other legal orders.[2] In recent years, this type of monitoring has also been employed in immigration, a practice that is less well-known. In this context, the measure is typically imposed on individuals not by a court order but by an administrative decision, without close scrutiny of its necessity and implications for the lives of those monitored. In political rhetoric, electronic monitoring is presented as an acceptable and effective measure that pursues a legitimate aim, that of immigration control. The idea that the expansive use of electronic monitoring through invasive technologies is acceptable is due to a broader set of 'hostile environment' policies, that are ostensibly directed against irregular migrants,

* I am grateful to all participants at the conference on 'Electronic Monitoring' at the University of Amsterdam in September 2024, and particularly to the organisers, Jeevan Hariharan and Hadassa Noorda. Many thanks are also due to Hugh Collins and Natalie Sedacca for comments on a draft.

[1] Interview reported in the Report by J Hynes and M Leslie, for Bail on Immigration Detention, Medical Justice and Public Law Project, *'Constantly on Edge': The Expansion of GPS Tagging and the Roll-Out of Non-Fitted Devices* (2023) 25.

[2] For an overview and analysis, see M Nellis, 'Electronic Monitoring Around the World' (2021) *Oxford Research Encyclopedia of Criminology and Criminal Justice.* Available at: htpps://oxfordre.com/criminology/display/10.1093/acrefore/9780190264079.001.0001/acrefore-9780190264079-e-642.

making the UK an unappealing destination for migrants more generally.[3] In this context, electronic monitoring is often perceived as a less problematic way to control immigration if compared to other measures. It is therefore accepted by many as a suitable alternative to even more restrictive practices that are proposed and at times implemented, such as immigration detention and collective expulsions.[4]

However, an increasing number of organisations have raised the alarm about the practice of electronic monitoring, explaining the severe impact that it has on the personal and social lives of those affected, and their physical and mental health.[5] 'Net-widening' is an additional effect of electronic monitoring that requires careful consideration, as the practice may increase the numbers of individuals who are controlled through a variety of measures.[6] Electronic monitoring, alongside other hostile environment policies, create structures of oppression that are state-mediated.[7] Iris Marion Young explained that 'oppression designates the disadvantage and injustice some people suffer not because a tyrannical power coerces them, but because of the everyday practices of a well-intentioned liberal society'.[8] Indeed, laws on electronic monitoring may have the appearance of legitimacy as an exercise of border control powers, so they may seem acceptable in a liberal state as a more limited type of intrusion than other restrictions. However, if we consider them more closely, we see that they marginalise people who may already be vulnerable and render them powerless, while also normalising their dehumanisation.[9]

This chapter, first, presents briefly electronic monitoring in criminal justice. It turns secondly to the practice of monitoring of migrants on bail and asylum seekers under the UK Immigration Act 2016, which has been expanded significantly from 2020 onwards. It considers the legislation, the technology used and its effects on individuals. Thirdly, I turn to legal challenges of electronic monitoring that demonstrate some of the problems associated with the measure and underline

[3] For discussion of the policies, see M Griffiths and C Yeo, 'The UK's Hostile Environment: Deputising Immigration Control' (2021) 41 *Critical Social Policy* 521. On the harmful effects of the policies in the employment context, see N Sedacca, 'Migrant Work, Gender, and the Hostile Environment: A Human Rights Analysis' (2024) 53 *Industrial Law Journal* 63.

[4] On problems of immigration detention, see, eg, the reports of Bail for Immigration Detention. Available at: www.biduk.org/pages/62-bid-research-reports; see also C Costello, 'Immigration Detention: The Grounds Beneath Our Feet' (2015) 68 *Current Legal Problems* 143. Collective expulsions of migrants are prohibited under art 4 of Protocol 4 of the European Convention on Human Rights.

[5] See especially, Bail on Immigration Detention, Medical Justice and Public Law Project, *Every Move You Make: The Human Cost of GPS Tagging in the Immigration System* (2022); and Hynes and Leslie (n 1).

[6] The concept of net widening was first introduced by Stanley Cohen to illustrate the risks of criminal law reform: S Cohen, *Vision of Social Control: Crime, Punishment and Classification* (Cambridge, Polity Press, 1985) 41.

[7] On state-mediated structural injustice, see V Mantouvalou, *Structural Injustice and Workers' Rights* (Oxford, Oxford University Press, 2023) Ch 2.

[8] IM Young, 'Five Faces of Oppression' in GL Henderson and M Waterstone (eds), *Geographic Thought: A Praxis Perspective* (New York, Routledge, 2008).

[9] ibid. Young discusses marginalisation and powerlessness as two instances of oppression.

its effects on human rights. While my primary focus is on the UK, the use of electronic monitoring in immigration is increasing and should be scrutinised in other legal orders.[10]

2 Electronic Monitoring in Criminal Justice

Electronic monitoring has been used for decades in criminal justice and is described as 'a way of supervising offenders in the community whilst they are on bail, serving a community sentence or after release from prison'.[11] Together with other non-custodial sentences, tagging as a sentence imposed either instead of or in addition to imprisonment is viewed by many as a viable alternative to imprisonment. It has been well documented that prisons can cause significant harm to those who are incarcerated, with numerous human rights bodies having ruled that prisons violate the human rights of those held within them.[12] There are strong calls for abolition of prisons, for the radical reduction of the prison population and the improvement of prison conditions.[13]

Community sentences, such as electronic monitoring, on the other hand, appear to impose fewer restrictions on people's physical freedom, as they are not locked up but live in the community. This means that they can maintain aspects of their personal and family life, which they would have been unable to do in prison. However, community sentences contribute towards what is described as 'net-widening', namely giving these sentences to offenders who might otherwise receive

[10] The US example is discussed later on in this chapter. On Canada, see C Gidaris, 'Rethinking Confinement through Canada's Alternatives to Detention Program' (2020) 1 *Incarceration* 1; J Bongiorno, 'The Electronic Shackling of Migrants' *Maisonneuve* (Montreal, 4 January 2022). Available at: https://maisonneuve.org/article/2022/01/4/electronic-shackling-migrants/; on Australia, see L Rivas, H McNeill and M Randolph, 'Deter, Detain, Deport and Demonise: Should Others Follow the Australian Crimmigration Model?' (2025) *Australian Journal of International Affairs*. Available at: www.tandfonline.com/doi/full/10.1080/10357718.2025.2515388#abstract; see also the High Court ruling *YBFZ v Minister for Immigration, Citizenship and Multicultural Affairs* [2024] HCA 40; for further plans to introduce electronic monitoring see the announcement of the Greek government that it will be using electronic monitoring in the context of immigration: 'Migrants on deportation list to wear ankle monitors, Greek government says' *AP* (New York, 11 August 2025). Available at: https://apnews.com/article/migrants-greece-asylum-ankle-monitorsdeportations-88075c2ed95dfb6b20a34638bb9dc9c4; see also the debates in New Zealand: G Bonnett, 'Electronic monitoring of asylum seekers and new rules for dawn raids being considered' *RNZ* (Wellington, 30 June 2025). Available at: www.rnz.co.nz/news/political/565495/electronic-monitoring-of-asylum-seekers-and-new-rules-for-dawn-raids-being-considered.

[11] M Nellis, 'Surveillance, Stigma and Spatial Constraint: The Ethical Challenges of Electronic Monitoring' in M Nellis, K Beyens and D Kaminski (eds), *Electronically Monitored Punishment: International and Critical Perspectives* (London, Willan, 2013).

[12] See S Snacken, 'Human Dignity and Prisoner Rights in Europe' (2021) 50 *Crime and Justice* 301; see also D van Zyl Smit and S Snacken, *Principles of European Prison Law and Policy* (Oxford, Oxford University Press, 2011).

[13] A Davis, *Are Prisons Obsolete?* (New York, Seven Stories Press, 2003); T Shelby, *The Idea of Prison Abolition* (Princeton, Princeton University Press, 2022).

lighter or no sentences, thus expanding control by the criminal justice system.[14] In the context of criminal justice, Noorda has examined the restrictions imposed by electronic monitoring to freedom insightfully, explaining that it can be viewed as part of what she has described as 'exprisonment' – practices that do not impose incarceration, but which still restrict individual freedom very heavily.[15] Electronic monitoring in criminal justice has also been described as 'e-carceration', a term that emphasises that technological tools that monitor the location of people in criminal justice are not necessarily a less-restrictive alternative to imprisonment, but more of an alternative *form* of imprisonment.[16]

Alongside prison, electronic monitoring and other community sentences can have serious human rights implications, including severe restrictions on the right to private life, the right to work and may also amount to inhuman and degrading treatment.[17] Whether they are proportionate and suitable sentences when someone has been convicted of a crime or a suitable measure for people charged with a crime when there is at risk of absconding is a major debate. Supranational human rights organisations, such as the United Nations and the Council of Europe have scrutinised community sentences in criminal justice, including electronic monitoring. In addition to the general rules on community sentences adopted by these organisations, the Council of Europe also developed a specific Recommendation on electronic monitoring in 2014, which underlined concerns, including restrictions on private and family life, and recommended principles to govern its use.[18] The provisions of these documents shed light on the challenges of community sentences and what needs to be done so that they can be compatible with human rights law.

As we see, even though there is a turn towards the expansive use of electronic monitoring in criminal justice to avoid prison overcrowding and reduce the cost and effect of imprisonment, the measure still raises serious concerns for those monitored.[19]

[14] See Cohen (n 6).

[15] On exprisonment, see H Noorda, 'Preventive Deprivations of Liberty: Asset Freezes and Travel Bans' (2015) 9 *Criminal Law and Philosophy* 521; H Noorda, 'Exprisonment: Deprivations of Liberty on the Street and at Home' (2023) 42 *Criminal Justice Ethics* 1.

[16] J Kilgore, E Sanders and K Weisburd, 'The Case Against E-Carceration' *Inquest* (30 July 2021). Available at: https://inquest.org/the-case-against-e-carceration/.

[17] V Mantouvalou and H Noorda, 'Non-Custodial Sentences and Human Rights' (2024) *European Human Rights Law Review* 228; D van Zyl Smit, 'Community Sanctions and European Human Rights Law' in L Zedner and J Roberts (eds), *Principles and Values in Criminal Law and Criminal Justice: Essays in Honour of Andrew Ashworth* (Oxford, Oxford University Press, 2012) 191.

[18] United Nations Standard Minimum Rules for Non-custodial Measures, known as the 'Tokyo Rules', General Assembly resolution 45/110 of 14 December 1990; Council of Europe, Recommendation of the Committee of Ministers to the Member States on the European Rules on Community Sanctions and Measures, revised 2017 (CM/Rec(1992)16-rev); Council of Europe, Recommendation of the Committee of Ministers to the Member States on electronic monitoring (CM/Rec(2014)4).

[19] See, eg S Kotecha, '"More offenders could be tagged", as Minister insists he's "not soft on crime"' *BBC* (London, 8 May 2025). Available at: www.bbc.com/news/articles/c7050ex1zjjo.

3 Electronic Monitoring in Immigration

Electronic monitoring within the immigration context presents greater challenges. This is due to the application of criminal justice measures in immigration proceedings, despite the absence of a criminal conviction or sentence. It should be understood under the broader description of 'crimmigration' which refers to the convergence between immigration and criminal law, one illustration of the hostile environment.[20] Immigration is increasingly being considered as tantamount to criminality and electronic monitoring is a perfect instantiation of how crimmigration operates. The question that arises is the following: how is it permissible and lawful to monitor a person constantly, when this is not even punishment for an offence committed based on a court decision with all the safeguards that this would entail? To illustrate the problem, this section focuses primarily on the development of the electronic monitoring schemes of migrants in the UK.

The legal basis for imposing electronic monitoring on migrants in the UK was first the Asylum and Immigration (Treatment of Claimants) Act 2004, which provided that this measure could be imposed on individuals on immigration bail who were viewed as being at high risk of harm, reoffending or absconding.[21] It was further extended in the UK Immigration Act 2016, which is widely known for significantly bolstering hostile environment policies. In addition to individuals on immigration bail, paragraph 2(3) of Schedule 10 to the Immigration Act 2016 brought in a duty on the Secretary of State to electronically monitor those who are subject to a deportation order or deportation proceedings.[22] The legislation also contains two exceptions: one is when the imposition of monitoring would be impractical and the second one is when the imposition of the condition would be contrary to the European Convention on Human Rights (ECHR).[23]

In recent years, the scheme has been expanded in several ways. From 2020, this monitoring became more intrusive than it was before. This was because of a change from radio frequency monitoring to Global Positioning System (GPS) monitoring. GPS constantly monitors the person's location via satellites that send their geolocation data to the authorities. Since 2021, the Home Office has a duty to conduct this monitoring on many more people who are on immigration bail than previously. In addition to this monitoring under the Immigration Act, the Home Office introduced a pilot programme to monitor the location of more people seeking asylum. According to the scheme's guidance, this would affect those who arrived in the UK through 'unnecessary and dangerous routes'. This programme was in force for 18 months, between June 2022 and December 2023. Published

[20] J Stumpf, 'The Crimmigration Crisis: Immigrants, Crime, and Sovereign Power' (2006) 56 *American University Law Review* 367; for an example of this in the UK, see L Zedner, 'The Hostile Border: Crimmigration, Counter-terrorism, or Crossing the Line on Rights' (2019) 22 *New Criminal Law Review* 318.

[21] Asylum and Immigration (Treatment of Claimants) Act 2004, s 36.

[22] Immigration Act 2016 (IA 2016), Sch 10, para 2(1)(e).

[23] IA 2016, Sch 10, para 2(5).

policy on GPS monitoring requires regular reviews of the circumstances under which the monitoring has been imposed.[24]

Thousands of people have been tagged in the UK. For instance, between January and November 2023, about 3,900 individuals were tagged, while GPS monitoring of those on immigration bail increased by 56 per cent in 2023.[25] Data for 2024 showed that electronic monitoring increased – an increase driven by the use of this measure on people on bail and on migrants.[26] According to the same Ministry of Justice data, 4,371 migrants were fitted with an electronic device between 2023 and 2024, which presented a 24 per cent increase when compared to the previous year and a steady increase from 2021.[27]

With the election of a Labour government in summer 2024, some hostile policies on immigration and asylum seekers were discontinued, such as the 'Rwanda scheme', which proposed that asylum seekers be sent to Rwanda to have their asylum claims heard, and the detention of migrants in barges while their asylum applications were pending.[28] However, policies such as GPS-tagging remained in place, despite a Home Office evaluation, published in January 2025, which found that GPS-tagging of asylum seekers did not affect compliance, when compared with traditional reporting that did not involve electronic monitoring.[29] Ministry of Justice data of 2025 showed that 33 per cent of individuals under GPS-monitoring are under immigration orders and also demonstrated a general upwards trend in electronic monitoring.[30] This trend is set to continue according to new laws and policies announced by the Labour government.[31]

The Border Security, Asylum and Immigration Act 2025 further expands the powers of the electronic monitoring of migrants. Section 46 gives the Home Secretary the power to impose highly restrictive conditions on any person with

[24] Guidance on 'Immigration Bail Conditions: Electronic Monitoring'. Available at: www.gov.uk/government/publications/offender-management/immigration-bail-conditions-electronic-monitoring-em-expansion-pilot-accessible.

[25] Hynes and Leslie (n 1) at 2 and 10.

[26] Ministry of Justice, 'Electronic Monitoring Statistics Annual Publication' (18 July 2024). Available at: www.gov.uk/government/statistics/electronic-monitoring-statistics-annual-publication-march-2024/electronic-monitoring-statistics-annual-publication-march-2024.

[27] ibid.

[28] On this, see the Supreme Court decision *AAA (Syria) & Ors, R (on the application of) v Secretary of State for the Home Department* [2023] UKSC 42 (15 November 2023), [2023] UKSC 42; Home Office, 'Vessel to accommodate migrants' (5 April 2023). Available at: www.gov.uk/government/news/vessel-to-accommodate-migrants; see also M Davidson, 'Floating Prisons and Ex-military Bases: Large Asylum Accommodation Sites Harm Health' (2023) 382 *British Medical Journal* 1874.

[29] Home Office, 'GPS expansion pilot evaluation' (12 January 2025). Available at: www.gov.uk/government/publications/gps-expansion-pilot-evaluation/gps-expansion-pilot-evaluation#:~:text=Key%20findings.%20This%20report%20suggests%20that%20GPS,and%20August%202023%20presented%20a%20similar%20picture.

[30] Ministry of Justice, 'Official Statistics, Electronic Monitoring MI Publication, England and Wales: June 2025' (28 August 2025). Available at: www.gov.uk/government/statistics/electronic-monitoring-mi-publication-june-2025/electronic-monitoring-mi-publication-england-and-wales-june-2025#statistician-s-comment-data-quality.

[31] R Webster, 'The Growth of Electronic Monitoring' (29 August 2025). Available at: www.russellwebster.com/the-growth-of-electronic-monitoring/.

limited leave to enter or remain in the UK, including electronic tagging. Section 55 gives courts the power to impose electronic monitoring in the context of a Serious Crime Prevention Order. These are court orders used to protect the public by preventing, restricting or disrupting a person's involvement in serious crime by imposing various conditions on the individual. Crimes for which these orders can be imposed include money laundering and drug trafficking. The imposition of this order is based on a test of whether it is 'appropriate' to protect the public on the civil, rather than criminal, standard of proof. Under this section, monitoring is permitted for up to twelve months, and it is possible to have indefinite extensions.

As in the context of criminal justice, the government's position is that tagging as a measure to control immigration is acceptable as it is less intrusive compared to other schemes that were put in place by the previous Conservative government. There are severe criticisms of the institution of immigration detention, which is used widely in Europe and the US and is described as a 'thriving business', while people being held on a barge or being deported to Rwanda have obvious human rights implications.[32] The argument is that electronic monitoring should be used as an immigration control mechanism to avoid these harsher measures. However, it is wrong to take the extreme practices of detention in barges and the Rwanda scheme as a baseline when considering the fair treatment of people who seek asylum and other migrants on bail. The fact that consecutive UK governments, as well as governments in other legal orders, support and expand this kind of scheme does not mean that electronic monitoring of migrants is humane and should be viewed as acceptable for being a lesser evil.

4 Monitoring Technology and its Effects

To illustrate the restrictions of freedom imposed by electronic monitoring and to challenge the assumption that its widespread use is an acceptable measure, we need to understand further the devices and technology employed and their effects on people's lives. Two types of GPS monitoring are used in this context. First, there is an ankle tag. This sends constant information about an individual's location.The second type of device is a non-fitted device. Individuals need to carry this device with them constantly; when they hear a beeping signal (several times every day), they must immediately place their finger on it. Through their fingerprint, individuals share with the authorities biometric information many times every day allowing the authorities to obtain information about their location. Fitted devices are worn by people for periods of three to twenty-four months, and non-fitted devices for eighteen months to indefinitely. Other potential technological tools considered for this monitoring include smart watches with facial recognition and apps accessed through smart

[32] See L Arbogast, *Migrant Detention in the European Union: A Thriving Business* (MIGREUROP, 2016) 17; see *AAA (Syria) & Ors* (n 28).

phones.[33] In addition, further tracking measures discussed recently include devices placed under people's skin, which have been described as 'alarmingly dystopian'.[34]

Research conducted by expert organisations on public and immigration law revealed the extensive and at times devastating impact of the measure.[35] Reports explained that GPS monitoring has a number of effects, including that it creates stigma, makes people refrain from normal daily activities, and leads to isolation; for those who have children, it has a serious impact on their relationship with their children as, for example, they cannot explain to them why they are tagged and cannot participate in family activities; it is connected to mental health problems because of its indefinite nature; it creates physical discomfort and pain; and it has technical problems, which may mean that the monitoring device requires charging every few hours in a way that interferes with basic activities or that it does not function properly for long periods of time.

Interviewees in the study 'Every Move You Make' explained that they cannot participate in some social and family activities in a public space, with some of them referring to swimming. One of them said, for instance:

> Every week you know me and my kids were going for swimming, but after that I've never been. My kids asking me, 'Going swimming, going swimming?', you know, when I've been there once but people asking questions and look at me like big criminal.[36]

Another interviewee explained the effect of social isolation because of tagging as follows:

> I'm looking over my shoulder every time, everywhere I go. It's made me pull out of a lot of things. I can't hang out with my friends because I know I've got a tag. I know somehow somewhere, it might show, so I'm isolating myself because of that. Because I know the tag might show and a lot of people will start asking ... So you know, people have weddings and ... I'm like nah, I just pull out. Of course, people get to know, but I don't want to put it in their faces and tell them nah I'm on a tag.[37]

Further evidence of social isolation was described as follows:

> I used to be very sociable, got a group of friends and that. Now, the majority, when they know that I'm on the tag, they're avoiding me, for no particular reason. ... They [friends] don't want to associate with myself ... I'm getting emotional because it's so hard.[38]

[33] As discussed here 'Equality impact assessment: GPS non-fitted devices (accessible) (7 October 2025). Available at: www.gov.uk/government/publications/offender-management/equality-impact-assessment-gps-non-fitted-devices-accessible.

[34] R Booth, 'Tech Firms Suggested Placing Trackers Under Offenders' Skin at Meeting with Justice Secretary' *The Guardian* (London, 1 July 2025). Available at: www.theguardian.com/society/2025/jul/01/tech-firms-suggested-placing-trackers-under-offenders-skin-at-meeting-with-justice-secretary.

[35] *Every Move You Make* (n 5): Hynes and Leslie, above n 1.

[36] ibid at 25 (initials of interviewees removed).

[37] ibid 24.

[38] ibid 28.

Another interviewee experienced embarrassment because of the association of the tag with criminality:

> I tried to hide it as much as I can but sometimes the trousers go a little bit up and it might show and you can just see people looking at you ... but I don't make that quick thing of hiding it, I just let it be and you know put it away in my own time because I don't want people to think 'Oh if I've got a tag, let me hide it or move away from there', then they will definitely start thinking there is a criminal thing going on.[39]

Additional problems were reported because the tag had to be charged frequently and made noises if it ran out of battery, while the mental effect of the tag was described as torture:

> It's on my leg and as soon as I see this it's a constant reminder that you know, you might be taken away from your family, and so psychologically it's every time I see it ... So it's got that cycle now of wanting to charge at 2 o'clock, waking me up all the time. But I don't have a problem with that it's just the psychological thing it's crazy, every time I see it and I'm just thinking they're going to take me from my daughter any minute now ... it's torturing really ... Any time now, they can just come to anywhere I am and scrape me up, and take me to a detention centre. And constantly it just makes you think like, I wonder if they're going to come here if I'm at my mum's house, I wonder if they're going to come here.[40]

Some of the people tagged explained that the tag made them feel suicidal.[41] The profound and severe impact of electronic monitoring on people's mental health has also been analysed in academic literature.[42]

The physical effects of the tags, which are heavy objects that are sometimes tightly fitted, included eczema, and an effect on the ability to sleep as, at times, the tag vibrated in the middle of the night.[43] Further challenges were created because of mechanical problems with the tag, which people had to charge constantly. These led to disruptions during basic social activities, such as attending a friend's birthday or sleeping.[44] One interviewee explained that

> [e]ven when you sleep it takes 4 hours to charge, you cannot be comfortable in bed, you got that thing dangling around your leg with wires and all that. When you move the charger gets disconnected, starts vibrating, making noise and... it's a torture, it's a torture. I don't even know how to put it into words. After all the detention ... the end of that they say, That's not enough, you know have to be on a monitor for life. What for?[45]

Interviewees also reported difficulties in challenging the tagging, but also explained that there were additional reporting requirements to the Home Office,

[39] ibid 26.
[40] ibid 27, 29.
[41] ibid.
[42] See M Bhatia, 'Racial Surveillance and the Mental Health Impacts of Electronic Monitoring on Migrants', (2021) 62 *Race & Class* 18.
[43] *Every Move You Make* (n 5) at 31.
[44] ibid 32, 33.
[45] ibid 44.

despite the fact that their location should be known to the authorities via the tag; concerns were also expressed about the collection and use of personal data by the Home Office and its subcontractors.[46]

The focus of 'Constantly on Edge' was on non-fitted devices– those that can be carried (rather than fitted around the ankle). The study explained that non-fitted devices are as stigmatising and they interfere heavily with normal daily activities. In public spaces, the vibration may disturb others and make the person feel shame.[47] Further issues arising with non-fitted devices include significant stress due to regular alerts from the device and a feeling that one is constantly being watched, which impacts their mental health. Interviewees explained that they had to scan their finger up to 10 times a day, at different points every day, within a 60-second slot after the beeping sound.[48] One interviewee said:

> You got to be, like focused on this click and immediately it has to be like a part of you. It needs to be very close to you all the time. Even if you like, for example, go to shower. [...] It has still to be close to you. Because you don't know when it might come, there is no certain appointments for this. So you can't even have a chilled out, relaxed shower when you're wearing this. How could they think of doing this to *people*.

One interviewee described that being monitored by a non-fitted device felt like 'torture in the habits', because of its affect on their mental health and everyday life, while others emphasised the psychological impact of feeling thay they were under constant surveillance.[49]

A separate concern arises from the use of artificial intelligence (AI) tools by the Home Office in the process of electronic monitoring for immigration control.[50] First, there is the 'Identify and Prioritise Immigration Cases' tool, which is used on individuals subject to detention and removal under the Immigration Act 2016 and other legislation. This tool prioritises cases and makes recommendations on issues such as detention, removal and access to services and benefits. Second, the 'Electronic Monitoring Review Tool' produces recommendations on GPS tracking as a condition of immigration bail according to paragraph 4 of Schedule 10 to the Immigration Act 2016. This tool is used in quarterly reviews of electronic monitoring by the Home Office that aim to establish if the measure remains appropriate. Using an automated harm score it decides the minimum period that an individual should be subject to a fitted or non-fitted device. It also generates recommendations on whether someone should remain subject to a fitted device or be transitioned to a non-fitted one.

[46] ibid 36, 38–39.
[47] Hynes and Leslie (n 1) at 21.
[48] ibid 22–24.
[49] ibid 24, 25.
[50] See Privacy International, 'Submission to the Information Commissioner: 'Request for Assessment of Processing Operations by the Secretary of State for the Home Department ("Home Office")' (18 August 2025). Available at: privacyinternational.org/sites/default/files/2025-08/18.08.2025%20Privacy%20International%20complaint%20against%20Home%20Office%20algorithmic%20tools%20%5Bpublic%20version%5D.pdf.

The most recent expansion of electronic monitoring under section 46 of the Border Security, Asylum and Immigration Act 2025 gives the Home Secretary the power to impose highly restrictive conditions on anyone with limited leave to remain in or enter the UK, including electronic tagging. During the drafting of the legislation, this was described by Amnesty International as 'an extraordinary overreach of power'.[51] It was also heavily criticised by the Public Law Project as discriminatory, disproportionate and unjustified.[52]

The electronic monitoring of migrants has also been implemented in the US. In this context, too, the practice has been heavily criticised for invading privacy and for causing physical harm and mental health problems to people who may already be traumatised and other related effects.[53] Electronic monitoring schemes in the immigration system have been criticised as being much more intrusive than other alternatives to immigration detention and have been described as 'digital cages'.[54] An extensive empirical study that focused on the use of ankle tags found that it has a devastating impact on individuals, including serious effects on their physical and mental health, social isolation, work opportunities, and family and other personal life.[55] It also found that it is deployed in a discriminatory manner and that it is not effective.[56]

Even though the electronic monitoring of migrants may at first appear to be less intrusive than immigration detention and other measures targeting migrants, upon closer inspection we see that it has severe effects on all aspects of people's personal and social lives, it marginalises them and makes them feel powerless. Furthermore, as is the case with schemes used as alternatives to imprisonment in criminal justice, it leads to net-widening in the sense that it does not reduce the numbers of people who would be in immigration detention, but that it increases the numbers of individuals who are controlled through a variety of measures.[57] In terms of meeting the alleged aim of the schemes, which is to reduce absconding, further questions arise both because the rate of absconding was already extremely low, and because recently published data suggest that GPS tagging does not affect compliance.[58] Along the lines of findings in the context of criminal justice, it emerges that this is really not an alternative to detention, but an alternative form of detention. As Bhatia and Canning put it, electronic monitoring 'is neither a "soft"

[51] Amnesty International, 'Written Evidence to the Joint Committee on Human Rights' para 12.2. Available at: https://committees.parliament.uk/writtenevidence/139645/pdf/.

[52] Public Law Project, 'Written Evidence to the Joint Committee on Human Rights', Available at: https://committees.parliament.uk/writtenevidence/140223/pdf/.

[53] American Bar Association, *Commission on Immigration, 'Electronic Monitoring of Migrants: Punitive Not Prudent'* (2024).

[54] FE Marouf, 'Alternatives to Immigration Detention' (2017) 38 *Cardozo Law Review* 2141; S Sherman-Stokes, 'Immigration Detention Abolition and the Violence of Digital Cages' (2024) 95 *University of Colorado Law Review* 219.

[55] T Giustini et al, 'Immigration Cyber Prisons: Ending the Use of Electronic Ankle Shackles' (2021) *Faculty Online Publications* 3. Available at: larc.cardozo.yu.edu/faculty-online-pubs/3.

[56] ibid.

[57] This point is also underlined in the American Bar Association report (n 53) at 16 and 29.

[58] *Every Move You Make* (n 5) at 18; Home Office (n 29).

nor a humane option. It brings prisons to individual homes and living spaces, and makes every moment lived under the watchful eye of the state'.[59] Even though electronic monitoring may have an appearance of legitimacy, and may even be thought of as a humane way to control immigration, it is a measure that oppresses people, and may also violate human rights, as the section which follows shows.

5 Human Rights

In recent years, UK courts and other bodies have examined cases involving the human rights of people electronically monitored in the immigration system. The UK Information Commissioner (ICO), the regulator for data protection that monitors compliance with legislation including the Data Protection Act 2018 and the General Data Protection Regulation, found that the practice is contrary to data protection laws, which protect aspects of the right to private life.[60] Moreover, there have been successful legal challenges in courts and tribunals assessing the compatibility of the electronic monitoring of migrants with human rights law.

In addition, parliamentary committees examining the expansion of electronic monitoring during the drafting of the Border Security, Asylum and Immigration Act 2025 also questioned its compatibility with the ECHR. Some of the issues raised involve the right to private life of people monitored, such as their personal and family interactions, sexual relations, and the collection and processing of personal data. This electronic monitoring is so extensive, that it not only has implications for an individual's private life, but it affects other human rights, including the right to work, freedom of association and freedom of religion. other aspects can have such a severe effect on individuals that they can be classified as inhuman and degrading treatment.

5.1 ICO

The first successful legal challenge was in March 2024, when the ICO issued an enforcement notice and a warning to the Home Office in relation to the Electronic Monitoring Expansion Pilot involving asylum seekers.[61] The ICO, John Edwards, stated:

[59] M Bhatia and V Canning, 'Exponential Expansionism: Key Contemporary Challenges to Immigration Detention Abolitionism' in M Bosworth et al (eds), *Handbook on Border Criminology* (Cheltenham, Edward Elgar Publishing, 2024) 328, 334.

[60] Reg (EU) 2016/679 of the European Parliament and of the Council of 27 April 2016 on the protection of natural persons with regard to the processing of personal data and on the free movement of such data, and repealing Directive 95/46/EC [2016] OJ L119/1.

[61] See 'ICO finds the Home Office's pilot of GPS electronic monitoring of migrants breached UK data protection law' (1 March 2024). Available at: https://https://ico.org.uk/about-the-ico/media-centre/news-and-blogs/2024/03/ico-finds-the-home-office-s-pilot-of-gps-electronic-monitoring-of-migrants-breached-uk-data-protection-law/.

> Having access to a person's 24/7 movements is highly intrusive, as it is likely to reveal a lot of information about them, including the potential to infer sensitive information such as their religion, sexuality, or health status. Lack of clarity on how this information will be used can also inadvertently inhibit people's movements and freedom to take part in day-to-day activities.

If such information were to be mishandled or misinterpreted, it could potentially have harmful consequences to people and their future. The Home Office did not assess those risks sufficiently, which means the pilot scheme was not legally compliant.[62]

The ICO explained that the pilot failed to assess the intrusiveness of the monitoring with people's privacy, given that they were constantly monitored and their geolocation data was tracked. He emphasised that for such intrusive tracking to be justified, there must be a very strong reason. In addition, the ICO found that no consideration was given to the fact that many of the people monitored under this scheme were vulnerable because of their immigration status, the dangerous trips that they had undertaken, and possible language barriers. Finally, the ICO raised concerns about the fact that, even though the scheme was discontinued in December 2023, the Home Office and third-party organisations would continue to have access to the personal information collected, unless this data is deleted or anonymised.

In August 2025, the organisation Privacy International issued a new formal complaint to the ICO about the use of automated tools in the context of electronic monitoring of migrants.[63] According to this complaint, the 'Identify and Prioritise Immigration Cases' and the 'Electronic Monitoring Review' tools are problematic and breach a number of provisions of data protection law, for reasons such as the lack of transparency in the collection and retention of data, the extensive use of this data, including sensitive personal data, and the limited human involvement, even though these tools make decisions of great significance for the lives of those affected, including detention, deportation and electronic monitoring through GPS tags.[64] This new legal challenge before the ICO will further test the impact of new technologies on privacy rights of individuals in the immigration or asylum systems.[65]

[62] ibid.

[63] See 'Privacy International issues complaint to the UK regulator regarding the deployment of two algorithms for immigration purposes suspected of failing to adequately comply with data protection law' (15 August 2025). Available at: https://privacyinternational.org/press-release/5640/privacy-international-issues-complaint-uk-regulator-regarding-deployment-two.

[64] For a summary of the legal challenges against the schemes, see Complaint, para 15.

[65] For broader analysis of this issue in the context of strategic litigation by civil society organisations, see F Palmiotto and D Ozkul, 'Climbing a Wall: Strategic Litigation Against Automated Systems in Migration and Asylum' (2024) 25 *German Law Journal* 935.

5.2 Electronic Monitoring in Courts

In addition to the ICO findings on data protection, the first two cases on electronic monitoring have also been heard in UK courts and tribunals. These challenged aspects of electronic monitoring imposed as a condition for immigration bail. Courts found several problems with the schemes.

5.2.1 Nelson

Mark Nelson, a Jamaican national who was a car mechanic and father of five, was in prison where he was held for having committed offences of possession with intent to supply a class B drug, abstracting electricity, and two offences of racially aggravated harassment.[66] When he was due to be released, a deportation order was made, which he challenged. He was released while on bail subject to restrictions and was fitted with an electronic monitoring device while awaiting deportation. The imposition of electronic monitoring was a condition for his release from detention (rather than part of his sentence for the crimes that he had committed). Nelson challenged his GPS tagging under Article 8 of the ECHR that protects the right to private life.

Article 8 states: '[e]veryone has the right to respect for his private and family life, his home and his correspondence'. The second paragraph permits restrictions insofar as there is a legitimate aim and the restriction is proportionate to the aim pursued.[67] Nelson claimed that his tagging was unlawful for over a year, given that the Home Office did not review it in a lawful or timely way and that, for a period of six months, it was not functioning properly. The Upper Tribunal (Immigration and Asylum Chamber) found that Nelson's tagging constituted an unlawful interference with his right to private life. The legal basis for this finding was that, in the view of the Tribunal, the Home Secretary had failed to comply with their own policy of reviewing the monitoring regularly. It explained that:

> the requirement for there to be regular reviews, is an integral part of the legal framework governing the imposition and continuation of electronic monitoring. […] The legislative regime specifies that the electronic monitoring condition should not continue if its continuation would be either impractical or in breach of the human rights of the bailed person. Neither of those considerations are static, and the existence of those exceptions is undoubtedly an important feature which underpins the need for the policy.[68]

The lack of regular reviews in this case undermined the lawfulness of the continuing imposition of the condition.

[66] *R (on the application of Nelson) v Secretary of State for the Home Department* [2024] UKUT 00141 (IAC).

[67] ECHR, para 8(2) states: 'There shall be no interference by a public authority with the exercise of this right except such as is in accordance with the law and is necessary in a democratic society in the interests of national security, public safety or the economic well-being of the country, for the prevention of disorder or crime, for the protection of health or morals, or for the protection of the rights and freedoms of others.'

[68] *Nelson* (n 66) at para 64.

In addition, the fact that the device was not sending a GPS signal for a period of six months, a situation about which the Home Office had been informed, also made the tagging unlawful. Wearing the tag for a long period of time during which it was not functional rendered it incompatible with Article 8 of the ECHR, given that it was disproportionate or incompatible with the aims of the legislation. During the period when the tag was not functional, there was inadequate justification for the interference with private life, and 'appropriate steps should have been taken far sooner to either repair or replace the tag so that the applicant would have been wearing it for the purpose intended'.[69] However, the requirement that Nelson continues wearing the tag was ruled to be proportionate and therefore lawful by the Tribunal. In reaching this decision the Tribunal took note of a number of factors, including the aims of immigration control and the effects of tagging on the mental health of the claimant. It described this finding as 'very finely balanced'.[70]

5.3 ADL and Others

A further legal challenge succeeded in May 2024 in the case of *ADL and Others v Secretary of State for the Home Department*, which involved both fitted and non-fitted GPS devices.[71] In this case, the four claimants were: a 26-year-old Portuguese national, Fabio Dos Reis, who had criminal convictions including drug-related convictions and whose monitoring condition continued even though his deportation order had been revoked; a 36-year-old Jamaican national who had learning difficulties, had been convicted for crimes including attempted robbery, and had been recognised as a victim of modern slavery (BNE); a 25-year-old Sudanese national who had been subjected to detention and torture in Sudan and was recognised as a victim of human trafficking (ADL), and finally a 59-year-old Nigerian national who was subject to female genital mutilation as a child (PER), with four children and health problems. All claimants had been fitted with GPS tracking when they were released from detention as part of their bail conditions, and not as part of a sentence for a crime committed. Through these devices their geolocation information was recorded on a daily basis about once a minute. The devices send information to the relevant Home Office team if there is tampering with the device, a flat battery, or an unsuccessful verification through the system of a non-fitted device.

The High Court found that the authorities had acted unlawfully under several aspects of domestic law, and contrary to the right to private life under Article 8 of the ECHR. In the case of ADL, the Court ruled that he had been tracked unlawfully throughout the period of his tracking both because the relevant reasons for his tracking had not been considered and because it later became disproportionate. The retention of his data was also unlawful. In relation to Dos Reis, it was ruled that he was tracked unlawfully for the period after his deportation order

[69] ibid para 69.
[70] ibid, para 77.
[71] *ADL and Others v Secretary of State for the Home Department*, [2024] EWHC 994 (Admin).

was revoked. All data collected had to be deleted after he regularised his immigration status. BNE was unlawfully tracked for a period of one month, when his tracking was disproportionate and the data collected during that period had to be deleted. Finally, PER was unlawfully tracked in the initial period of his monitoring, because the relevant factors had not been considered.

These cases illustrate some of the intrusions of privacy experienced by people through electronic monitoring and suggest that the use of tagging is often performative. This point emerges in a particularly striking way when the tag is not working but it is not removed: the measure often seeks to symbolise toughness towards immigration and satisfy populist sentiments, while it does not meet any purpose other than the oppression of the claimants. This leads to violations of human rights law.

5.4 Parliamentary Committees

The expansion of powers to monitor migrants was also scrutinised by parliamentary committees in the context of the passing of the Border Security, Immigration and Asylum Act 2025. The UK Joint Committee on Human Rights was highly critical of both section 46 that gives further powers to the Home Secretary, and section 55 that gives courts the power to order electronic monitoring in the context of Serious Crime Prevention Orders.[72]

In relation to section 46, the Committee noted that the imposition of electronic monitoring (as well as curfews and confinement) on people who have not committed a criminal offence may violate Article 5 of the ECHR (right to liberty and security).[73] Article 5 of the Convention protects liberty in a narrow sense, namely physical liberty.[74] It establishes a right to liberty and security but also provides a list of exceptions, when deprivation of liberty is permitted. These include the deprivation of liberty after conviction, as well as deprivation of liberty for non-compliance with a court order, or for fulfilment of an obligation prescribed by law. However, physical liberty cannot be entirely separated from a wider understanding of liberty: liberty to participate in society (eg to pursue a profession or education, and to engage in social life).[75] The Joint Committee explained that this provision can be violated even if someone is not incarcerated, if the restrictions on their liberty are very severe.[76] In addition, it added that the restrictions through

[72] Joint Committee on Human Rights, *Legislative Scrutiny: Border Security, Asylum and Immigration Bill*, Fourth Report of Session 2024-25, HL Paper 143/HC (2025) 789.

[73] ibid para 143.

[74] *Engel and others v The Netherlands* (1979-1980) 1 EHRR 647, at 58.

[75] On notions of liberty under the Convention, see SW Stark, 'Deprivations of Liberty: Beyond the Paradigm' (2019) *Public Law* 380.

[76] *Secretary of State for the Home Department v JJ* [2007] UKHL 45; *Secretary of State for the Home Department v AP* [2010] UKSC 24; see also *Guzzardi v Italy* App No 7367/76, Judgment of 6 November 1980.

electronic monitoring are such that they may also violate the right to private life and the right to freedom of association.[77]

The Joint Committee also noted that in parliamentary debates the Minister for Border Security and Asylum said that 'the powers will be used only in cases involving conduct such as war crimes, crimes against humanity, extremism or serious crime, or where the person poses a threat to national security or public safety'.[78] However, the Committee explained that section 46 is much broader than that,[79] and rightly underlined that when there is evidence of such egregious crimes, the individual has to be investigated and prosecuted.[80] The Joint Committee concluded that section 46 providing for electronic monitoring, geographical exclusions, and curfews, should be set out clearly in the Bill and should be limited to instances involving the commitment of serious crimes of the kind that the Minister mentioned in parliamentary debates. Given the severe restrictions of rights of people affected by these measures, the Committee also recommended that the exercise of the powers under clause 43 should be subject to judicial scrutiny.[81]

Moreover, the Joint Committee examined section 55 that gives courts the power to impose electronic monitoring in the context of a Serious Crime Prevention Order.[82] It explained that this gives this power when there are 'reasonable grounds' that the Order will protect the public and that the imposition of the order will be an 'appropriate' measure. The Committee noted here that this power is clear and sufficiently prescribed and that it pursues a legitimate aim. However, it also noted that the correct test to be applied by courts is whether the measure is necessary to pursue the stated aim, and whether it is proportionate, in line with the second paragraph of Article 8 of the ECHR and not just whether it is 'appropriate'.[83]

The Select Committee on the Constitution examining section 46 also noted that the powers of the Secretary of State are particularly broad.[84] It raised concerns about this 'broad and subjective power'.[85] It recommended 'narrowing the power to impose "such other conditions as the Secretary of State thinks fit" and that safeguards on the use of the power should be included on the face of the Bill'.

[77] JCHR (n 72) at para 143.
[78] ibid para 145.
[79] ibid para 145.
[80] ibid para 148.
[81] ibid para 149.
[82] ibid para 159.
[83] ibid para 161.
[84] House of Lords, Select Committee on the Constitution, *Border Security, Asylum and Immigration Bill, 10th Report of Session 2024–25 (2025).*
[85] ibid para 26.

5.5 Further Human Rights Implications

The cases, reports and other materials presented in the above section focused primarily on violations of the right to private life under Article 8 of the ECHR and other legislation through the monitoring, including collection and retention of personal data, as well as restrictions of the right to liberty under Article 5 of the ECHR. Other aspects of the electronic monitoring of migrants, such as its effects on the physical and mental health and the humiliation experienced by individuals, may amount to inhuman or degrading treatment under Article 3 of the ECHR. This provides that '[n]o one shall be subjected to torture or to inhuman or degrading treatment or punishment'. Article 3 contains an absolute prohibition, which means that there is no test of proportionality to assess the necessity of the treatment.

According to well-established case law of the European Court of Human Rights (ECtHR), for Article 3 to be breached, the conduct in question has to reach a 'minimum level of severity'.[86] In order to assess this threshold, the Court takes into account factors such as the duration and physical or mental effects of the treatment, as well as the sex, age, and health of the victim.[87] For instance, the ECtHR has said that 'the nature, duration and severity of the ill-treatment to which the applicant [is] subjected and the cumulative negative effects on his health are sufficient to be qualified as inhuman and degrading'.[88] This minimum level of severity may be reached in the case of some individuals who are monitored, when there is evidence that they cannot undertake everyday activities, that they are experiencing the treatment as degrading in their social circle, and when the measure also has severe effects on their physical and mental health.[89] People who are tagged may already have unaddressed mental health issues, which may be worsened by the tagging process itself.[90] Additionally, this practice may negatively impact their physical health.[91] It may be alleged that these measures have a legitimate aim, as we saw, for instance, in the reasoning of the Tribunal in *Nelson*,[92] and that they do not aim to humiliate deliberately. However, even if they do not intend to humiliate, they can still constitute a violation of article 3 of the ECHR if they reach the level of severity required for the provision to be breached.

The ECtHR has not yet examined electronic monitoring for criminal justice or immigration control purposes. Yet, given the connections between imprisonment and exprisonment (to use Noorda's term), we can extend principles that the Court has developed on detention to electronic monitoring in the community.[93] In this way, we can identify circumstances under which electronic monitoring may constitute inhuman and degrading treatment, for instance, in case law on detention and mental health. To give an example, in *Romanov v Russia*, the Court ruled that the conditions

[86] *Ireland v UK* App No 5310/71, Judgment of 18 January 1978, para 162.
[87] ibid.
[88] *Dybeku v Albania* App No 41153/06, Judgment of 18 December 2007, para 51.
[89] See eg, the discussion in *Nelson*, para 6, and *ADL*, para 75.
[90] *Every move you make*, above n 5, see especially 28–30, 34, 44.
[91] ibid 30–31.
[92] *Nelson*, para 71.
[93] See Noorda (n 15); see also the discussion in Mantouvalou and Noorda (n 17).

of detention of the applicant for a lengthy period of time had severe effects on him and constituted inhuman and degrading treatment, even though there had been no indication that there was an intention to humiliate and debase him.[94] In *Dybeku v Albania*, the Court decided that there was a violation of Article 3, as the nature of the applicant's psychological situation made him more vulnerable than other detainees and the conditions of his detention exacerbated his distress, anguish and fear.[95] Extending principles from this line of cases to the electronic monitoring of migrants, it can be argued that when electronic monitoring is imposed on people who suffer from mental health conditions, lasts for lengthy periods and exacerbates their condition, it may amount to inhuman and degrading treatment.

Moreover, evidence shows that migrants under electronic monitoring have difficulty finding work both because of the stigmatising effect of ankle tags and because of practical difficulties created by non-fitted devices, such as the fact that they need to be charged regularly and for many hours. For instance, an interviewee with an ankle tag explained in the Report 'Every Move You Make':

> I've tried to apply for a few jobs and even though the Home Office have stated I'm allowed to work and I have all my rights. A few weeks ago, I tried to volunteer at a charity shop, he just looked at my ankle monitor and asked me, 'What is that?'... In his mind he already wrote me off. The other job, I had an interview and such but they didn't contact me back because of the tag on my ankle, they just look at that and I suffer from prejudice. They just think if I have a tag on me I must have committed a grievous crime for me to be put on a GPS tag.[96]

The inability to find work further contributes to people's marginalisation and powerlessness.

While the right to work is not explicitly safeguarded by the ECHR, it has occasionally been recognised within the context of the right to private life under Article 8 of the Convention.[97] As previously indicated, Article 8 does not establish an absolute entitlement. Restrictions on the right to private life, including the right to work as an element of that right, may be imposed provided they are prescribed by law, serve a legitimate purpose, and are necessary and proportionate in relation to the objective pursued. Elements of the restrictions of the right to work that have been documented in reports, case law and other materials may fail to meet article 8 requirements, in line with the findings in *Nelson* and *ADL*. The right to work of migrants who are under electronic monitoring is limited, and this limitation may be found to violate the ECHR as a disproportionate restriction. Similar findings can be made in relation to the right to associate under Article 11 of the ECHR and freedom of religion under Article 9, which are both qualified provisions where restrictions are permitted only if there is a legitimate aim and insofar as they are necessary and proportionate to the aim pursued.

[94] *Romanov v Russia* App No 63993/00, Judgment of 20 October 2005, para 80.
[95] *Dybeku v Albania* App No 41153/06, Judgment of 18 December 2007, paras 51–52.
[96] *Every Move You Make* (n 5) at 25; see also the discussion in Giustini et al (n 55) at 3.
[97] *Sidabras and Dziautas v Lithuania* App Nos 55480/00 and 59330/00, Judgment of 27 July 2004.

Finally, organisations and scholars considering electronic monitoring of migrants have explained that it can be discriminatory on the basis of immigration status or race.[98] This can violate Article 14 of the ECHR that provides that '[t]he enjoyment of the rights and freedoms set forth in this Convention shall be secured without discrimination on any ground such as sex, race, colour, language, religion, political or other opinion, national or social origin, association with a national minority, property, birth or other status'. Race as a prohibited ground of discrimination is mentioned explicitly in Article 14, which is an open-ended provision. In addition, the ECtHR has ruled that immigration status is a prohibited ground of discrimination, and explained that differential treatment on this ground has to be subject to a test of proportionality.[99] In *Bah v UK*, the issue involved differential treatment in relation to housing benefits, and the Court accepted that the authorities may have a margin of appreciation on immigration status, particularly so in relation to welfare benefits.[100] In the cases of electronic monitoring, on the other hand, any margin of appreciation should be very limited given that it does not involve access to welfare benefits. Article 14 is not a free-standing provision. It can only be violated in conjunction with another Convention right. The interferences and possible violations of provisions, such as Articles 3, 8, 9 and 11 of the ECHR, discussed earlier in this section, can be viewed not only as stand-alone violations but also as possible violations of Article 14 together with these provisions.

6 Conclusion

The quote in the introduction of this piece illustrates the dehumanisation experienced by migrants that has become increasingly normalised. This has had a pervasive effect on people's minds and affects what legal measures they perceive as acceptable for the purpose of immigration control. Electronic monitoring may appear to be legitimate as it is less extreme than physical detention and mass deportations. Yet mass monitoring has a serious impact on individuals who may already be traumatised and contributes towards their oppression. The constant electronic monitoring of asylum seekers, victims of modern slavery and other migrants for long periods of time affects their mental and physical health, isolates and stigmatises them.

Iris Marion Young said that, when faced with structural oppression, it is not sufficient to amend the laws or get rid of the rulers.[101] She was right that the oppression of racialised and other groups is deeply entrenched in many aspects of culture. However, changes in the legal framework can contribute towards challenging these oppressive structures. The criminalisation of immigration instantiated in this chapter through the measure of electronic monitoring is a set of legal rules that must be challenged as they violate fundamental principles of human rights law.

[98] Bhatia (n 42); Privacy International complaint to the ICO, above n 63.
[99] *Biao v Denmark* App No 38590/10, Judgment of 24 May 2016.
[100] *Bah v UK* App No 56328/07, Judgment of 27 September 2011; ibid, para 47.
[101] Young (n 8).

PART II

The Digitally Monitored Worker

4

Managerial Authority and the Boundaries of Legitimate Workplace Monitoring

JOE ATKINSON*

1 Introduction

In the early nineteenth-century New Lanark mills established by the socialist Robert Owen, workers' speech, task performance and behaviour were all closely observed by supervisors who recorded this information in 'books of character', and placed colour-coded 'silent monitors' above individuals' workstations to indicate their past conduct.[1] Monitoring also extended to workers' behaviour away from the factory, to enforce rules of 'morality' such as church attendance and prohibitions on the use of foul language. As is clear from this example, workers have long been subject to intrusive monitoring by employers, to an extent that would not be countenanced in any other area of their lives.[2] Indeed, some degree of monitoring and oversight is inherent in capitalist employment relationships, as the conflicting interests of capital and labour mean that employers need to monitor workers to ensure compliance

* My thanks to Jeevan Hariharan and Hadassa Noorda for helpful comments on an earlier draft and all their work in bringing this project to fruition, as well as to the participants of the Digital Monitoring workshop held at the University of Amsterdam and Netherlands Institute for Advanced Study for the insightful discussion.

[1] G Cole, *The Life of Robert Owen*, 2nd edn (London, Macmillan, 1930) 104.

[2] Monitoring is defined here as the observation or collection of data, D Lyon, *Surveillance Society: Monitoring Everyday Life* (Buckingham, Open University Press, 2001). On this view, monitoring encompasses 'surveillance'. The alternative approach is to distinguish the two concepts, so that surveillance is limited to certain problematic or excessive forms of monitoring. Such a distinction is unhelpful for present purposes, however, where the focus is precisely on this boundary between legitimate and illegitimate exercises of managerial authority to monitor; H Collins, 'Is the Contract of Employment Illiberal?' in H Collins, G Lester and V Mantouvalou (eds), *Philosophical Foundations of Labour Law* (Oxford, Oxford University Press, 2018).

with their instructions, and that workers are not attempting to increase their share of surplus value by shirking. The hierarchical nature of capitalist production similarly means that employer attempts to co-ordinate production and maximise output necessarily rely on the collection of extensive information about worker performance.

It is therefore no surprise that invasive monitoring remains a feature of many workplaces today. One aspect of this monitoring that has changed significantly, however, is the replacement of human oversight by digital systems which collect (and analyse) vast amounts of worker data. These technologies have transformed the nature and extent of employers' monitoring power. Moreover, digital monitoring is now inseparably linked to the emergence of 'algorithmic management' technologies that use the data collected from monitoring to undertake or support managerial functions. These changes highlight the inadequacies of existing employment law frameworks, which are premised on more limited forms of supervision by human managers and largely play a facilitating rather than constraining role over monitoring.

This chapter considers how employment law should respond to employers' new digitally enabled monitoring capabilities. It adopts a novel approach to this question, which centres on the normative foundations and extent of employers' legitimate authority to monitor workers. The analysis is largely focused on English law, but the normative discussion is of a more general application. Although counteracting and constraining managerial power is a central concern of labour law, the theoretical underpinnings of this authority remain underexplored, and the literature that does exist is yet to consider the justification of employer authority in the context of worker monitoring.[3] This chapter examines some leading potential justifications of managerial authority and argues these cannot provide a basis for employers' current default legal power to monitor their workers. There is, therefore, a need to better align the boundaries of lawful and legitimate managerial authority to monitor.

The argument proceeds as follows. Section 1 briefly sets out employers' legal power to monitor their workers which remains the default position at common law despite being subject to some important limits. Section 2 then gives an overview of how digital technologies have transformed worker monitoring, and their impacts on workers' rights, wellbeing and working conditions. These developments should prompt us to question the appropriateness and extent of employers' default monitoring authority. Section 3, therefore, seeks to identify the boundaries of legitimate worker monitoring through an assessment of the normative foundations

[3] For some recent explorations see E Anderson, *Private Government: How Employers Rule Our Lives (and Why We Don't Talk about It)*, The University Center for Human Values Series (Princeton, Princeton University Press, 2017); G Racabi, 'Abolish the Employer Prerogative, Unleash Work Law' (2022) 43 *Berkeley Journal of Employment and Labor Law* 79; A Bogg and C Estlund, 'Between Authority and Domination: Taming the Managerial Prerogative' 44 *Comparative Labour Law and Policy Journal* 237; V De Stefano and N Countouris, '"Lifting the Private-Law Veil": Employer Authority and the "Contractual-Coating" of Worker Subordination' 44 *Comparative Labour Law and Policy Journal* 274.

of managerial authority. It argues that the leading justificatory accounts of this authority, grounded in property, consent and instrumental considerations, cannot justify employers' default discretionary power to monitor. Rather, employers' authority must be constrained in this context if it is to be legitimate. Following this, section 4 identifies strategies for aligning lawful and legitimate powers to monitor, including rights to a collective voice over its form and extent, as well as a right to a justification for monitoring.

2 Default Authority to Monitor

Employment law plays a dual role in both establishing employers' hierarchical power and extensive control over workers, while also seeking to protect workers from the worst excesses and negative consequences of that power.[4] In fulfilling its protective function, however, employment law has generally not sought to constrain employer decision-making over core aspects of production, including their power to oversee workers.[5] Although not unlimited, the default allocation of authority to determine the location, timing, processes, outputs, and oversight of production all lie with the employers, unless otherwise stated by contract or statute. The legal source of these powers is not immediately obvious. Certainly, they are not conferred by statute and are often simply assumed by courts to be an inherent and necessary feature of employment relationships.[6] Given this, and the necessity of managerial oversight for production, it is perhaps no surprise that worker monitoring is regarded as part of employers' broad authority to organise their business as they see fit.

Historically, the high degree of managerial authority conferred on employers is a remnant of the master and servant relationship, with De Stefano and Countouris locating the historical origins of this power in public rather than private law frameworks.[7] Despite this history, the employment contract is now the primary legal mechanism used to give effect to employer authority and control over workers. The superior bargaining position of employers means that they will usually draft employment contracts unilaterally and offer them to workers on a take-it-or-leave-it basis. This enables them to include binding express terms that empower them to monitor workers however they choose, or to incorporate monitoring

[4] This is sometimes described as 'managerial prerogative', but managerial authority is preferred here.

[5] Bogg and Estlund (n 3); E Tucker, 'Somethings Old, Somethings New and a Lot That's Blue: Political Economic Reflections on Worker Subordination and the Law in Contemporary Capitalism' (2024) 44 *Comparative Labour Law and Policy Journal* 327.

[6] Racabi (n 3).

[7] S Deakin and F Wilkinson, *The Law of the Labour Market: Industrialization, Employment, and Legal Evolution* (Oxford, Oxford University Press, 2005) ch 2; V De Stefano et al, 'Does Labour Law Trust Workers? Questioning Underlying Assumptions Behind Managerial Prerogatives' (2024) 53 *Industrial Law Journal* 206; De Stefano and Countouris (n 3).

policies contained in company handbooks that can be unilaterally varied on an ongoing basis.

Moreover, even where employment contracts do not expressly confer monitoring powers, employers will nevertheless have broad authority to monitor workers due to the default implied terms read into employment contracts by the courts. The implied terms of obedience and co-operation, for instance, mean that employees will be legally bound by employer instructions to comply with company monitoring policies and adopt any new technologies as required.[8] Refusal will likely amount to a breach of contract, allowing the worker to be dismissed without notice. The contract of employment thus puts workers in a position of legal subordination, including in respect of the mechanisms used to monitor them at work.

Employers, as private individuals, have a general residual liberty at common law to act in any way they choose, provided it is not otherwise prohibited by law.[9] They therefore enjoy a broad freedom to choose how to organise their business and production processes, which extends to what digital systems to adopt to manage and oversee these production processes. Both the firm and these digital systems are regarded as employers' property in respect of which they can exercise their general liberty. However, this liberty is conceptually and legally distinct from employers' right to exercise control over workers. It is the employment contract which establishes this authority, and grounds the legal power of employers to compel workers to submit to monitoring.

There are some important limits to employers' monitoring power within employment law. Worker monitoring may amount to unlawful discrimination, for example, if it is introduced because of a protected characteristic, or puts a group sharing a protected characteristic at a particular disadvantage.[10] Where monitoring is used as part of an unfair disciplinary process that leads to dismissal it might give rise to a claim for unfair dismissal.[11] Claims for constructive unfair dismissal might also be available where monitoring is in breach of an express or implied contract term; in particular, where monitoring is so invasive, or adopted in such a manner, that it is incompatible with the implied term of trust and confidence. In all these instances, however, the starting point remains that monitoring is a lawful exercise of employer authority. Employer decisions and policies relating to monitoring are binding under the contract of employment by default, unless and until they are challenged under one of these frameworks. Importantly, it is workers who bear the heavy burden of challenging the legitimacy of monitoring, rather than monitoring being presumptively illegitimate unless and until employers can justify it.

Other limits on employer monitoring are found outside employment law; most significantly data protection law. At least in principle, the General Data Protection

[8] *Cresswell v Board of Inland Revenue* [1984] 2 All ER 713.
[9] As articulated in *Wheeler v Leicester CC* [1985] UKHL 6, [1985] AC 1054, per Browne-Wilkinson LJ.
[10] Equality Act 2010, s 19; Equality Act 2010, s 13.
[11] J Atkinson, 'Workplace Monitoring and the Right to Private Life at Work' (2018) 81 *MLR* 688.

Regulation (GDPR) and United Kingdom (UK) GDPR reverse employer's default power to monitor, as the collection and processing of workers' personal data is prohibited unless a lawful basis can be identified. In addition to having an identifiable lawful basis, the collection and processing of workers' personal data must comply with key principles such as transparency, purpose limitation and data minimisation.[12] Workers also have certain rights as data subjects, including to be informed of data collection and processing, and not be subjected to decisions based on fully automated processes.[13] The application of these data protection frameworks in the workplace has led to victories for workers, who have been able to challenge some employer monitoring practices as disproportionate or unjustifiably intrusive.[14]

Data protection law is not specifically targeted or designed to address worker monitoring, however, and imposes only a limited constraint on employers' power to monitor.[15] To start, some worker monitoring will not be covered by data protection law because the data collected falls outside the definition of personal data, such as where individual workers cannot be identified from the data. Second, the legitimate interests of employers, for instance in efficient production, harmonious industrial relations, or reputation management, are a legitimate ground for data collection and a wide range of monitoring will be lawful on this ground.[16] Additionally, crime prevention is now a 'recognised legitimate interest' in the UK, meaning that no balancing exercise is needed if data collection is carried out for this purpose.[17] As a result, worker monitoring that is intended to identify or prevent fraud or criminal damage to employer property can now be conducted with a minimal threshold for lawfulness.

In addition to these substantive weaknesses, there are procedural factors which make data protection law ineffective in curbing employers' power to monitor in practice. For example, the initial assessment of whether worker monitoring has a lawful purpose and complies with the relevant GDPR principles is carried out by employers. The lack of guidance or oversight of these employer assessments creates a risk of partiality, and of data protection being regarded as merely a tick-box exercise. The lawfulness of these initial decisions is then difficult for workers to challenge due to the complexity of the legal frameworks and monitoring

[12] General Data Protection Regulation, arts 5–6.

[13] General Data Protection Regulation, ch 3.

[14] See examples in G Zanfir-Fortuna and T Troester-Falk, 'Processing Personal Data on the Basis of Legitimate Interests under the GDPR' (Future of Privacy Forum, 2018); A Aloisi, 'Regulating Algorithmic Management at Work in the European Union: Data Protection, Non-Discrimination and Collective Rights' (2024) 40 *International Journal of Comparative Labour Law and Industrial Relations* 37.

[15] The shortcomings of data protection law in the employment context are set out fully in E Albin, 'The Three-Tier Structural Legal Deficit Undermining the Protection of Employees' Personal Data in the Workplace' (2025) 45 *Oxford Journal of Legal Studies* 81; A Aloisi, A Joppe and H Abraha, 'From "General" to "Context-Specific" Data Protection for Workers: Insights from the EU Rules on Platforms, Algorithmic Management and AI Systems' (2025) 16 *European Labour Law Journal* 538.

[16] See examples in Zanfir-Fortuna and Troester-Falk (n 14).

[17] Data (Use and Access) Act 2025, amending Annex 1 UK GDPR, s 5.

technologies involved, and the fact that data protection claims cannot be brought before an employment tribunal. There is also a serious lack of effective enforcement by some Data Protection Authorities in the employment context.[18] This includes the UK's Information Commissioner's Office, which appears unable or unwilling to investigate and issue penalties for data protection breaches by employers.[19]

These critiques aside, data protection law does not fundamentally challenge employers' common law authority to monitor workers. Their instructions and monitoring policies remain presumptively contractually binding. It is true that employees' implied duty of obedience is subject to the caveat that instructions must be lawful and reasonable, suggesting that there may be no contractual duty to comply with instructions to submit to monitoring that breaches data protection law.[20] This is far from guaranteed, however, as, in some cases, the courts have found that refusing to comply with an instruction to act unlawfully is a breach of contract.[21] Moreover, even if the instruction ultimately lacks binding contractual force, the initial starting point of default authority to monitor remains, and the burden lies on the worker to displace this.

3 The Digital Transformation of Monitoring

As is evident from the New Lanark example, extensive worker monitoring predates digitalisation. Intense methods of surveillance were developed in the slave plantations that fuelled the industrial revolution, and extensive monitoring was relied on to enforce the strict 'factory discipline' of early industrialisation in the UK.[22] Given this, moving from human oversight to monitoring via digital technologies might be thought to pose few new challenges for employment law. Despite some continuities, however, digital technologies have had a revolutionary effect on monitoring practices, resulting in new harms and detrimental impacts for workers.

The digital transformation of monitoring is itself a longstanding process, with email monitoring and digital CCTV (closed-circuit television) having existed in workplaces and been the subject of labour scholarship for decades.[23] But monitoring capabilities have advanced dramatically in recent years, largely due to the

[18] H Abraha, 'A Pragmatic Compromise? The Role of Article 88 GDPR in Upholding Privacy in the Workplace' (2022) 12 *International Data Privacy Law* 276.

[19] For details of ICO enforcement see 'Enforcement Action' (*Information Commissioner's Office*). Available at: https://ico.org.uk/action-weve-taken/enforcement/.

[20] *Donovan v Invicta Airlines* [1970] 1 Lloyd's Rep 486.

[21] *Buckoke v Greater London Council* [1971] Ch 655, [1971] 2 All ER 254.

[22] C Rosenthal, 'Slavery's Scientific Management: Masters and Managers' in S Beckert and S Rockman (eds), *Slavery's Capitalism: A New History of American Economic Development* (Philadelphia, University of Pennsylvania Press, 2016); S Pollard, 'Factory Discipline in the Industrial Revolution' (1963) 16 *The Economic History Review* 254.

[23] FHR Hendrickx (ed), *Employment Privacy Law in the European Union: Surveillance and Monitoring* (Antwerpen, Intersentia, 2002); S Wallach, 'The Medusa Stare: Surveillance and Monitoring of Employees and the Right to Privacy' (2011) 27 *International Journal of Comparative Labour Law and Industrial Relations* 189–219.

emergence of artificial intelligence (AI) driven monitoring tools, and 'algorithmic management' systems that can translate the vast amounts of worker data collected into usable evaluations or recommendations for employers. Although not exhaustive, this section sets out how these digital systems are driving qualitative and quantitative changes in worker monitoring, and their detrimental impacts for workers.

3.1 The New World of Digital Monitoring

The transformative effect of digital surveillance technologies can be demonstrated by comparing employer monitoring capabilities before and after they emerged.[24] Workers' attendance and hours, for instance, would previously have been tracked by manually signing in/out or the use of punch cards. They can now be monitored automatically through a combination of biometric access points, heat and motion sensers at workstations, and facial recognition CCTV which provide employers with more accurate and granular information.

Digital tools have also fundamentally altered the supervision and assessment of performance. Workers' activity and task performance would historically have been assessed periodically, perhaps at the end of each shift, with a single human manager overseeing a group of workers. In contrast, almost every aspect of workers' performance, activity and behaviour can now be tracked and analysed in real time by digital systems, in a manner equivalent to having a manager constantly watching each individual worker.

The specific technologies used to monitor workers' performance will vary with the type of work being performed. Software packages and applications sometimes known as 'bossware' can track office workers on a minute-by-minute basis by logging their keystrokes, taking screenshots or photographs using laptop webcams, and tracking internet usage along with electronic communications and any other activity on employer-owned computer systems.[25] Workers will often be unaware which, if any, such tools are being used to monitor them, and even

[24] The examples of digital monitoring discussed below are examined extensively in VI Gonzalez et al, 'Digital Monitoring, Algorithmic Management and the Platformisation of Work in Europe' (Publications Office of the European Union 2025); Eurofund, 'Employee Monitoring and Surveillance: The Challenges of Digitalisation' (Luxembourg, Publications Office of the European Union, 2020); K Ball, 'Electronic Monitoring and Surveillance in the Workplace' (Luxembourg, Publications Office of the European Union, 2021); RA Bales and KVW Stone, 'The Invisible Web at Work: Artificial Intelligence and Electronic Surveillance, Under the Labor Laws' (2020) 41 *Berkeley Journal of Employment and Labor Law* 1; I Ajunwa, K Crawford and J Schultz, 'Limitless Worker Surveillance' (2017) 105 *California Law Review* 735; Big Brother Watch, 'BossWare: The Dangers of High-Tech Worker Surveillance & How to Stop Them' (Big Brother Watch, 2024); A Paliokaitė et al, *Study Exploring the Context, Challenges, Opportunities, and Trends in Algorithmic Management* (Luxembourg, Publications Office of the European Union, 2025).

[25] DB Ferreira and EA Gromova, 'The Bossware Era and the E-Panopticon: Current Technologies and Legal Challenges' (2025) *Industrial Law Journal* (advance access online). Available at: https://doi.org/10.1093/indlaw/dwaf006.

standard systems such as Microsoft Outlook, Teams and Zoom collect extensive worker data and generate performance reports for employers.[26]

The location and task performance of warehouse, logistics and customer-facing workers can similarly be monitored much more closely by digital tools than would ever have been possible by human managers. Amazon workers wear devices which track their location and 'pick rate' in real time, identifying the precise amount of time taken for each individual task as well as how long workers spend interacting with colleagues or taking bathroom breaks.[27] Location tracking in real time via GPS (Global Positioning System) is now ubiquitous in delivery and logistics work, with sensors monitoring driving speed and style and internal cameras trained on drivers, including sometimes where vehicles are used for personal rather than work purposes.[28] Retail and customer service workers may be subjected to AI-powered CCTV or voice recording systems capable of tracking and analysing task performance, and giving feedback and instructions in real time.[29]

Monitoring workers away from the workplace is difficult without digital tools, as it relies on peer reporting or human surveillance. In contrast, automated social media monitoring tools mean employers can keep tabs on workers' behaviour and acts of expression away from the workplace. The widespread dual use of laptops, phones and vehicles for work and personal purposes can also result in location and communication monitoring being applied in people's personal lives outside of working time.[30]

These are just some of the most common forms of digital surveillance at work. More extreme technologies continue to be developed, such as wearable devices that monitor workers' physiological state (heart rate, hydration levels etc), systems which record voice patterns and muscle movements to identify workers' concentration levels, sentiments or emotional states, and even the microchipping of workers.[31]

Digital monitoring thus enables supervisors to track their workforces' location, activity and communications in real time, creating *quantitative* and *qualitative* changes to previously analogue oversight. Quantitively, monitoring is applied

[26] 'Technology Managing People – The Worker Experience' (London, Trades Union Congress, 2020); Z Doffman, 'Microsoft Teams Starts Telling Your Boss Where You Are—Now Just 8 Weeks Away' *Forbes* (Jersey City, 4 December 2025). Available at: www.forbes.com/sites/zakdoffman/2025/12/04/microsoft-teams-update-tells-your-boss-where-you-are-just-8-weeks-away/.

[27] M Molè, 'Commodified, Outsourced Authority: A Research Agenda for Algorithmic Management at Work' (2024) 17(2) *Italian Labour Law e-Journal* 169.

[28] Big Brother Watch (n 24); I Ajunwa, 'Algorithms at Work: Productivity Monitoring Applications and Wearable Technology as the New Data-Centric Research Agenda for Employment and Labor Law' (2018) 63 *Saint Louis University Law Journal* 21.

[29] J Atkinson and P Collins, 'Artificial Intelligence and Human Rights at Work' in A Quintavalla and J Temperman (eds), *Artificial Intelligence and Human Rights* (Oxford, Oxford University Press, 2023).

[30] V Mantouvalou and M Veale, 'Bring Your Own Device — Now Hand It Over! Rescuing Workers' Privacy During Data Searches' (2025) 45 *Comparative Labor Law & Policy Journal* 487. See N Zekić, 'Employee Monitoring and the Right to Disconnect: What is at Stake?' in H Noorda and J Hariharan (eds), *Digitally Monitored: Freedom, Surveillance and the Law* (London, Bloomsbury Publishing, 2026).

[31] Eurofund (Paliokaitėn 24).

more frequently, to collect more information, from a larger group of workers, than ever before. Although digital monitoring has existed for decades it has sharply increased in recent years.[32] In part, this is due to the relative affordability and accessibility of advanced monitoring tools. Employers may have always wanted to subject their workforce to intensive surveillance but have previously been limited by cost and practical considerations.[33] Increased demand for worker monitoring is also the result of the emergence of platform work and shift to working from home caused by the COVID-19 pandemic, both of which require employers to manage and co-ordinate large-scale remote workforces.[34]

Qualitatively, digital technologies enable entirely new categories of data to be collected. Rather than relying on external observable behaviours, monitoring can now be aimed at workers' internal physical (heart rate, tiredness and stress levels etc) and psychological states (sentiments, beliefs and preferences, concentration levels etc), as well as their social interactions and relationships. Another important aspect of this change is the move from discrete to continuous forms of monitoring. The shift from periodic snapshots to the ongoing collection of information in real time might appear to be merely a quantitative extension of existing monitoring practices. However, continuous monitoring changes the very nature of surveillance. There is a clear difference in kind rather than extent, for example, between monitoring how many deliveries a worker made in a shift, and the minute-by-minute tracking of their location, driving speed, communications and physical condition.

3.2 Monitoring and Algorithmic Management

To fully understand the digital transformation of monitoring it is important to grasp the close link between these forms of monitoring and the emergence of 'algorithmic management'. These are algorithmic systems capable of using the vast amounts of worker data collected via digital monitoring to undertake or support managerial functions.[35] Algorithmic management can be deployed at all stages of the employment relationship, from hiring and the allocation of work, performance evaluations and remuneration levels, right through to disciplinary matters and dismissal. As part of this, these systems can combine multiple sources of data

[32] M Hickok and N Maslej, 'A Policy Primer and Roadmap on AI Worker Surveillance and Productivity Scoring Tools' (2023) 3 *AI and Ethics* 673, 675; Institute for the Future of Work, 'Final Report of the Pissarides Review into the Future of Work and Wellbeing' (London, Institute for the Future of Work, 2025).

[33] See M Molè, 'Labour is Not a Commodity, Employer Authority is? The Consumption of Digital Monitoring at Work and its Regulation' in H Noorda and J Hariharan (eds), *Digitally Monitored: Freedom, Surveillance and the Law* (London, Bloomsbury Publishing, 2026).

[34] Ball (n 24).

[35] A Mateescu and A Nguyen, 'Explainer: Algorithmic Management in the Workplace' (New York, Data & Society Institute, 2019).

collected via monitoring to reveal, infer, or predict additional categories of information about workers that have not been observed directly, such as their personal beliefs and characteristics, whether they are likely to leave the company or be a trade union member.

There is a symbiotic relationship between algorithmic management and extensive digital monitoring of workers. Without these systems employers would only be able to make limited use of the data collected through monitoring, so would have little incentive to take on the costs associated with these technologies. Conversely, algorithmic management relies on large scale collection of worker data to function, and by its very nature is surveillance management. Given this, it would be a mistake to attempt to understand, or regulate, either digital monitoring or algorithmic management in isolation from the other.

3.3 Impacts on Workers

For employers at least, the benefits of monitoring appear clear. More worker data allows them to co-ordinate production more effectively, and the increased information asymmetries further strengthen their bargaining position and levels of control over workers. There is some evidence, however, that introducing ever more extensive and intensive monitoring will not benefit employers. Monitoring that is unwanted or resented by workers can lead to higher rates of misconduct or other 'unproductive' behaviours, and monitoring that is harmful to workers' health or wellbeing is likely to impact their commitment and performance at work, with knock on effects for economic productivity and higher turnover rates.[36]

Digital monitoring may also have some benefits for workers. These systems may be able to improve working conditions by identifying health and safety risks, for example, and employer analysis of workers' personal interactions and communications may enable them to combat discrimination and harassment. Data collected from worker surveillance can also be valuable for holding employers to their contractual and statutory obligations. For instance, having records of precise hours worked makes it easier for workers to calculate and claim entitlements relating to pay and working time.

But these potential benefits are far outweighed by the negative impacts and risks that digital monitoring poses to workers' rights, autonomy, and wellbeing. Most obviously, monitoring poses an acute threat to worker privacy across multiple dimensions.[37] Workers' informational privacy, meaning their ability to

[36] J Atkinson and J Evans, 'Negotiating the Future of Work: Legislating to Protect Workers from Surveillance' (London, IPPR, 2025).

[37] Otto identifies seven dimensions of worker privacy, all of which are plausibly threatened by digital monitoring: 'privacy of the person, privacy of behaviour and action, privacy of communication, privacy of data and image, privacy of thought and feeling, privacy of location and space, and privacy of association', M Otto, 'Privacy at Work and the Right to Private Life Outside Work' in G Davidov, B

control information relating to them, is threatened where employers collect, store or process, data without their knowledge or full understanding.[38] The complex and frequently concealed nature of digital monitoring poses a higher risk to this dimension of privacy than traditional managerial oversight. Further threats to informational privacy arise where algorithmic tools are used to infer or predict information about workers that has not been collected directly.

Hariharan and Noorda argue that, in some circumstances, monitoring also unjustly threatens workers' physical privacy, meaning 'sensory intrusions into our *bodies* and *personal space*'.[39] Location tracking, sound or visual recordings, wearables collecting biometric data and heat sensors are all examples of tools capable of violating workers' physical privacy by observing their bodily presence and activity. Another dimension of privacy at stake, and the counterpart to physical privacy risks, is workers' psychological or mental privacy. Although not currently widespread, digital systems now exist which aim to detect workers' emotional and psychological states, for example through the analysis of minute muscle movements, speech patterns, or even their brainwaves.[40] Such tools have the potential to infringe upon the inner sanctum of their personal thoughts, beliefs and sentiments, and so might also be framed as threatening workers' right to freedom of thought.[41]

A further set of impacts that could be seen as undermining privacy concern workers' 'relational' or 'expressive' privacy, meaning their ability to form and develop personal relationships and express personal views.[42] However, these are perhaps better understood as threats to the rights of free association and expression. Just as it is important to resist a 'reductive' view of worker privacy, that is overly focused on 'personal data/information protection', it is also important to recognise that human rights other than privacy are at stake in worker monitoring.[43] Where workers are aware (or suspect) that their acts of expression and association are being monitored they will think twice about exercising these rights

Langille and G Lester (eds), *The Oxford Handbook of the Law of Work* (Oxford, Oxford University Press, 2024).

[38] Control over one's personal information is thus treated as an element of the right to privacy here. The relationship between data protection and privacy is not straightforward, however, as data protection has also been recognised as a free-standing fundamental right in art 8 of the EU Charter of Fundamental Rights and Freedoms. The UK courts have also found the Charter right to data protection 'clearly goes further' than the right to privacy under art 8 of the ECHR, *R (Davis & Watson) v Secretary of State for the Home Department* [2015] EWHC 2092 (Admin), [2016] 1 CMLR 13, [80].

[39] J Hariharan and H Noorda, 'Imprisoned at Work: The Impact of Employee Monitoring on Physical Privacy and Individual Liberty' (2025) 88 *MLR* 333. A similar distinction between physical and informational privacy is made in NA Moreham, 'Beyond Information: Physical Privacy in English Law' (2014) 73 *CLJ* 350.

[40] V De Stefano, '"Masters and Servers": Collective Labour Rights and Private Government in the Contemporary World of Work' (2020) 36 *International Journal of Comparative Labour Law and Industrial Relations* 425.

[41] Atkinson and Collins 'Artificial Intelligence' (n 29).

[42] JW DeCew, *In Pursuit of Privacy: Law, Ethics, and the Rise of Technology* (Ithaca, Cornell University Press, 1997) 69–70.

[43] Otto (n 37); Atkinson and Collins (n 29).

in ways that may be viewed negatively by employers. Worker surveillance therefore has a 'chilling effect' on rights beyond privacy, in a manner which Fussey and Murray describe as a 'compound human rights harm'.[44]

Hariharan and Noorda make a similar point regarding workers' right to liberty, rightly pointing out that surveillance can have a chilling effect on their freedom of movement.[45] But there is no reason to confine this analysis to liberty rights: the same equally applies to the exercise of workers' other rights. Rights that seem particularly vulnerable to the chilling effect of employer surveillance are expressions of unpopular opinions or beliefs, and acts of political association or trade union organising. The chilling effects on these rights threaten workers' moral agency by making them less free to make 'agentic choices' out of fear of retaliation, and undermine the functioning of democratic processes that rely on their free exercise.[46]

This potential chilling effect is well understood and acknowledged in respect of state surveillance, but often overlooked in the employment context.[47] The chilling effect of employer monitoring may be more significant than state surveillance, however. The more personalised and granular nature of control exercised, combined with weaker oversight of employers than that provided by administrative law, means there is greater likelihood of offending an employer and triggering a negative response when exercising one's human rights.

In addition to undermining human rights at work, digital surveillance has adverse effects on workers' wellbeing and conditions and threatens the normative goals of labour law. Monitoring tools allow employers to exercise increasingly close control over the pace and performance of work, limiting the scope for workers to exercise autonomy over these matters. This lack of autonomy undermines the value of work as a means of self-realisation, increases the risk of personal domination of workers by employers, and may prevent workplaces from fulfilling their potential as sites of meaningful citizenship.[48] Being subject to continuous and intensive monitoring has a detrimental effect on worker stress levels and trust within the employment relationship, and often leads to the intensification of work, with negative consequences for workers' physical and mental health.[49]

[44] P Fussey and D Murray, *Facial Recognition Surveillance: Policing and Human Rights in the Age of Artificial Intelligence* (Oxford, Oxford University Press, 2025) ch 3.

[45] Hariharan and Noorda 'Imprisoned at Work' (n 39).

[46] S Tsuruda, 'Working as Equal Moral Agents' (2020) 26 *Legal Theory* 305.

[47] See eg R O'Fathaigh, 'Article 10 and the Chilling Effect Principle' (2013) 3 *European Human Rights Law Review* 304.

[48] H Collins, 'Is There a Human Right to Work?' in V Mantouvalou (ed), *The Right to Work: Legal and Philosophical Perspectives* (Oxford, Hart Publishing, 2015); J Atkinson and P Collins, 'Worker Voice and Algorithmic Management in Post-Brexit Britain' (2023) 29 *Transfer: European Review of Labour and Research* 37; C Estlund, *Working Together: How Workplace Bonds Strengthen a Diverse Democracy* (Oxford, Oxford University Press, 2003).

[49] 'Technology Managing People – The Worker Experience' (n 26); A Todolí-Signes, 'Making Algorithms Safe for Workers: Occupational Risks Associated with Work Managed by Artificial Intelligence' (2021) 27 *Transfer: European Review of Labour and Research* 433.

Where digital monitoring is integrated into algorithmic management software this has further negative effects on workers' rights, voice, and conditions.[50] The symbiotic nature of monitoring and algorithmic management makes it artificial to consider these impacts as distinct from those of monitoring. The use of opaque and complex algorithmic tools to undertake or support managerial functions make it harder for workers to have any say in workplace governance, or to understand and contest decisions. This further reduces workers' capacity for autonomy and moral agency at work. As these systems are generally designed exclusively to maximise economic output and productivity, they also raise the prospects of unfair or arbitrary decision-making that does not take appropriate account of workers' interests. For instance, algorithmic decision-making has repeatedly been shown to be discriminatory, due to both design choices and because they replicate historical inequalities captured in their training data.[51]

The threat to decent working conditions posed by intensive monitoring is compounded by algorithmic management. These systems facilitate the growth of precarious work, such as platform work or zero hours contracting, and often contribute to the deskilling of jobs by breaking them down into discrete tasks that are more easily technologically overseen and managed. The risks of work intensification and to worker health created by digital surveillance are further heightened if human decision-making is replaced by algorithmic systems. The digital transformation of monitoring, and the closely linked emergence of algorithmic management practices, thus has radical implications for the world of work.

4 Legitimate Managerial Authority

The digital transformation of monitoring calls into question employers' current default legal authority to monitor. The harms and risks of digital monitoring should prompt us to (re)consider when, and on what basis, worker monitoring should be legally permissible. It is suggested that a valuable way of approaching this question is to examine the justification and normative foundations of managerial authority more generally, in order to determine the extent of employers' authority in the specific context of monitoring. Despite a central goal of labour law being to protect workers against abuses of managerial power, the underlying foundations of this authority are underexamined. As a result, employer authority is 'primarily assumed rather than proved, and asserted rather than defended'.[52] But

[50] J Atkinson and P Collins, *Algorithmic Management and a New Generation of Rights at Work* (London, Institute of Employment Rights, 2024).

[51] C O'Neil, *Weapons of Math Destruction: How Big Data Increases Inequality and Threatens Democracy* (London, Allen Lane, 2016); J Buolamwini and T Gebru, 'Gender Shades: Intersectional Accuracy Disparities in Commercial Gender Classification', in SA Friedler and C Wilson (eds), *Conference on Fairness, Accountability and Transparency* (New York, PMLR, 2018).

[52] Racabi (n 3); C Sunstein, 'Human Behavior and the Law of Work' (2001) 87 *Virginia Law Review* 205.

it is vital to understand these foundations if we are to determine where to place the legal limits on employers' managerial power.

This section examines the leading potential foundations for employers' authority and concludes they only provide a basis for limited employer power to monitor workers. Authority is taken here to mean practical authority, meaning that employers' instructions to submit to monitoring are reasons for action that impose duties on workers to comply.[53] Employer instructions have authority in this sense when they provide content-independent and exclusionary reasons for action, meaning their normative force does not depend on their merits and they pre-empt (at least some) other reasons for action.[54] The focus is on legitimate managerial authority, meaning employers' normative power to give instructions or make decisions that impose duties on workers, rather than the extent of their effective or accepted (de facto) authority.[55] Authority is legitimate where 'there really is a sufficient reason for its subjects to subordinate themselves to it' even if they disagree with the orders being given.[56]

This understanding of authority is drawn from the political philosophy literature. When examining the foundations of managerial authority one might likewise start with theories of political authority and apply them to employers in place of the state. This strategy relies on an analogy between the firm and state which is commonly made by those arguing in favour of workplace democracy, who claim that democracy is essential for legitimate workplace authority just as it is for legitimate state authority.[57] Although contested, the firm-state analogy can undoubtedly provide valuable insights for labour law.[58] However, there are also important differences between the two contexts which complicate the translation of legitimate authority from the state to employers.[59] State-centric justifications of authority may therefore provide limited assistance in understanding managerial authority.[60] This is evident for functionalist theories for example, that view political authority as justified where it furthers morally mandatory goals such as

[53] In contrast to theoretical, or epistemic authority, which merely provides reason for belief, T Christiano and S Sciaraffa, 'Authority' (*The Stanford Encyclopedia of Philosophy*, 7 October 2025). Available at: https://plato.stanford.edu/archives/win2025/entries/authority/.

[54] This understanding is widely adopted from J Raz, *The Morality of Freedom* (Oxford, Oxford University Press, 1986) ch 3. One factor that distinguishes political from managerial authority is that the categories of reason that are excluded by legitimate political authority are more extensive than by legitimate managerial authority.

[55] Christiano and Sciaraffa (n 53).

[56] C McMahon, 'Managerial Authority' (1989) 100 *Ethics* 33, 34.

[57] R Dahl, *A Preface to Economic Democracy* (Berkeley, University of California, 1985); H Landemore and I Ferreras, 'In Defense of Workplace Democracy: Towards a Justification of the Firm–State Analogy' (2016) 44 *Political Theory* 53.

[58] I González-Ricoy, 'Little Republics: Authority and the Political Nature of the Firm' (2022) 50 *Philosophy & Public Affairs* 90.

[59] Bogg and Estlund (n 3).

[60] As with the justification of authority at the international or global level, S Canduzzi, 'Theories of Normative Legitimacy Beyond the State and the Role of Their Conceptual Dimension: Methodological Insight from Raz's Service Conception of Authority' (2025) *Res Publica*. Available at: https://doi.org/10.1007/s11158-025-09742-x.

freedom or democratic governance, because managerial authority is not necessary for any such morally mandatory goal.[61]

The most influential theory of political authority is the service conception developed by Joseph Raz. The core of this account is the normal justification thesis (NJT), which states that authority is justified if

> *the alleged subject is likely to better comply with the reasons which apply to him … if he accepts the directives of the alleged authority as authoritatively binding and tries to follow them, rather than by trying to follow the reasons which apply to him directly.*[62]

Although generally discussed in relation to political authority, the NJT is in fact intended as 'general explanation of all practical authorities' rather than being specific to the state.[63] This suggests it might provide a valuable framework for understanding the justification and extent of managerial authority. Bogg and Estlund consider this, but reject the NJT as a justification for managerial power, because employers are accountable to capital and must exercise this power to seek profits rather than serving workers' interests.[64] In the vast majority of cases, it is certainly difficult to see how obeying employer orders will lead workers to act in line with right reasons more often than acting on those reasons directly. Employer instructions will often conflict with workers' moral agency and important moral reasons they have for acting.[65]

This dismissal of the NJT's potential to ground managerial authority might be too quick, however. The NJT provides a piecemeal approach to justifying legitimate authority, meaning the legitimacy of managerial authority must be considered for each employer individually. Even within capitalist employment relations, therefore, it might be possible for some employers to adopt business models and policies that mean they manage the firm in a way that meets the NJT, and thus exercise legitimate authority. The requirements of the NJT are more likely to be met where firms don't adopt the traditional capitalist model; such as worker owned firms, co-operatives, or those with extensive worker co-determination. The NJT might therefore be used to argue in favour of promoting corporate law frameworks such as these that facilitate legitimate managerial authority. For the vast majority of existing employment relationships, however, it seems that we must either reject the service conception of authority or conclude that these employers exercise merely de facto, rather than legitimate, authority.

[61] Christiano and Sciaraffa (n 53); The instrumental justification of managerial authority considered below is not functionalist in this sense, because the goal of maximal economic efficiency is not a *morally mandatory* goal.

[62] Raz (n 54) at 53.

[63] J Raz, 'Comments and Responses' in LH Meyer, SL Paulson and T Pogge (eds), *Rights, Culture, and the Law: Themes from the Legal and Political Philosophy of Joseph Raz* (Oxford, Oxford University Press, 2003) 263.

[64] Bogg and Estlund (n 3).

[65] McMahon (n 56); Tsuruda (n 46).

Other conceptions of political authority might fare better in justifying managerial authority, such as those grounded in associational obligations.[66] But rather than examining the place of managerial authority within leading philosophical accounts, the approach taken here is to examine prominent foundational ideas within labour law scholarship. Namely employers' property rights, worker consent, and instrumental justifications. It is argued, however, that these cannot provide employers with unfettered default authority to monitor workers.

4.1 Property Rights

It is often thought that employers' authority to manage workers and the workplace, including their default power to introduce digital monitoring, must flow from their ownership of the firm. The basic premise is ownership implies a right to control that which is owned. Employers' ownership of the firm therefore implies 'the sole right to determine all matters concerning the operation of the enterprise' including 'rights to the managerial control over the people carrying out the production process'.[67] On this view, the digital systems used to monitor and manage workers form part of the firms' property, which employers have unilateral authority to adopt and implement as they choose.[68]

The idea that property rights provide the foundation for managerial authority seems plausible because there is a close connection between ownership and control within many theories of property rights. The most absolute articulation of this is by Blackstone, who described ownership as the 'sole and despotic dominion which one man claims and exercises over the external things of the world, in total exclusion of the right of any other'.[69] Waldron similarly views ownership as meaning that 'society will uphold [the owners] decision as final when there is any dispute about how the object should be used'.[70] Although ownership is now frequently conceived as a bundle of property rights which may be divided between several parties rather than sole dominium, there remains a close association between property and control in recent theories.[71] Under the liberal theory of property advanced by Dagan and Samet, for instance, property 'implies private control', and

[66] See, eg Plato, *Euthyphro, Apology, Crito*, FJ Church (trans) (London, Macmillan, 1948); R Dworkin, *Law's Empire* (Cambridge MA, Harvard University Press, 1986).

[67] CW Summers, 'Employment at Will in the United States: The Divine Right of Employers' (2000) 3 *University of Pennsylvania Journal of Labor and Employment Law* 65; D Ellerman, 'Fallacies about Corporations: Comments on "Democratizing the Corporation"' (2023) 51 *Politics & Society* 225.

[68] Albin (n 15).

[69] W Morrison (ed), *Blackstone's Commentaries on the Laws of England Volumes I-IV*, Vol II (London, Routledge-Cavendish, 2001) 3.

[70] J Waldron, *The Right to Private Property* (Oxford, Oxford University Press, 1990) 47.

[71] G Gaus, 'Property' in D Estlund (ed), *The Oxford Handbook of Political Philosophy* (Oxford, Oxford University Press, 2012).

confers 'some measure of private authority over resources: a normative power to determine what others may or may not do with the resource'.[72]

The view that authority to govern the workplace, and determine the systems used to oversee workers, logically follows from employers' ownership of the firm is deeply embedded in the psyche of labour law. As Klare says, a 'pervasive' belief exists, 'that it is simply inherent in the nature of private property that management is endowed with ultimate decision making authority'.[73] Critics of employment law similarly equate ownership with control, and frame legal protections against unfair dismissal or of worker voice as interferences with employers' rights to manage the workplace conferred by ownership of the means of production.[74] Sanjukta Paul describes this view of property as being part of labour law's distinctive theory of the firm, with Ellerman locating its roots in Marx's idea of the 'rights of capital'.[75] It is likely also the historical legacy of the origins of the employment relationship, when employers were thought to have property rights in workers' labour.[76]

The connection between employers' property rights and managerial control is reflected in many of the substantive rules of employment law.[77] Outside of specific statutory exceptions, employer property is strongly protected from the harms of industrial action, as well as through the denial of any right of trade unions access to employer property for organising purposes. The restriction of mandatory topics for collective bargaining to the narrow issue of workers' terms and conditions of employment similarly embodies a reluctance to interfere with employers' ability to control the firm as their property.[78] More broadly, the background assumption that employers are entitled to direct the enterprise by virtue of their property rights leads courts to view legal 'incursions on managerial prerogative with suspicion and to construe them narrowly'.[79]

[72] H Dagan and I Samet, 'The Beneficiary's Ownership Rights in the Trust Res in a Liberal Property Regime' (2023) 86 *MLR* 701; H Dagan and I Samet, 'Express Trust: The Dark Horse of the Liberal Property Regime' in S Degeling, J Hudson and I Samet (eds), *Philosophical Foundations of the Law of Express Trusts* (Oxford, Oxford University Press, 2023).

[73] KE Klare, 'Workplace Democracy & Market Reconstruction: An Agenda for Legal Reform' (1988) 38 *Catholic University Law Review* 1, 86.

[74] H Collins, V Mantouvalou, and G Lester, 'Introduction: Does Labour Law Need Philosophical Foundations' in H Collins, V Mantouvalou, and G Lester (eds), *Philosophical Foundations of Labour Law* (Oxford, Oxford University Press, 2018) 26. See, eg, R Epstein, 'In Defense of the Contract at Will' (1984) 51 *University of Chicago Law Review* 947.

[75] S Paul, 'Labor Law, Ownership, and the Firm' (2025) 99 *Chicago-Kent Law Review* 177; Ellerman (n 67).

[76] RJ Steinfeld, *The Invention of Free Labor: The Employment Relation in English and American Law and Culture, 1350–1870* (Chapel Hill, University of North Carolina Press, 1991) 54–60; C Mummé, 'Property in Labour and the Limits of Contract' in U Mattei and J Haskell (eds), *Research Handbook on Political Economy and Law* (Cheltenham, Edward Elgar Publishing, 2015).

[77] C Estlund, 'Labor, Property, and Sovereignty after Lechmere' (1994) 46 *Stanford Law Review* 305; J Tomassetti, 'Managerial Prerogative, Property Rights, and Labor Control in Employment Status Disputes' (2023) 24(1) *Theoretical Inquiries in Law* 180; Paul (n 75).

[78] Trade Union and Labour Relations (Consolidation) Act 1992, Sch A1.

[79] Tomassetti (n 77) at 188; ACL Davies, 'Judicial Self Restraint in Labour Law' (2009) 38 *Industrial Law Journal* 278.

Despite being widely taken for granted, property rights alone are insufficient to ground managerial authority. Indeed, ownership of the means of production is neither necessary nor sufficient to justify managerial authority. Not *necessary* because those individuals that own the firm are often not the same as those who exercise managerial authority. One example of this might be thought to be the distinction between the shareholders, who own the firm, and managers who direct and monitor workers. It is possible, however, to view managers as the agents of the shareholders, who are exercising authority on their behalf and ultimately accountable to them. Other instances of employers having rights that fall short of ownership are more difficult to explain. Employers may be renting or leasing the means of production, for example, or have a mere licence of use but, nevertheless, exercise authority over workers. It is also possible for an employer to exercise managerial authority without owning any property other than the capital used to pay wages. It is far from clear how the property rights to purely financial capital can ground rights to control and monitor workers in such cases.

Property rights are also not *sufficient* in themselves to establish managerial authority. An inherent and default authority to control is not a feature of (even unified) ownership under any plausible theory of property.[80] In many cases this is because the foundational values that justify property are themselves incapable of generating duties of worker obedience. Under accounts that ground property rights in their contribution to human freedom or flourishing, for instance, the duties correlating to property rights must not undermine those same values, with significant limits therefore needed on the extent of managerial power.[81]

More generally, the bundle of rights and duties that do plausibly make up the content of property rights are not capable of justifying managerial authority. The right of owners to use and dispose of their property as they see fit, for example, might mean that employers are free to organise production processes as they choose, including which tools and digital systems to adopt as part of this. But this is a far cry from having any authority to require that workers comply with these production processes or subject themselves to digital monitoring. Consider the analogy of owning a laptop. The owner's property rights mean they can use the laptop however they choose, including installing systems that monitor how the laptop is being used. But they have no right or authority to require that any third party actually uses the laptop. To think otherwise in the context of ownership of the firm would amount to employers having a right to forced labour. At most, ownership can confer a negative veto over how property is used by others rather than any positive right to command.[82]

[80] The focus here is on theories which view property rights as genuine pre-legal moral entitlements, but this point also holds for conventionalist theories of property, as in L Murphy and T Nagel, *The Myth of Ownership: Taxes and Justice* (Oxford, Oxford University Press, 2002).

[81] H Dagan, *A Liberal Theory of Property* (Cambridge, Cambridge University Press, 2021); GS Alexander, *Property and Human Flourishing* (New York, Oxford University Press, 2018) ch 7.

[82] Ellerman (n 67) at 3; C McMahon, *Authority and Democracy: A General Theory of Government and Management* (Princeton, Princeton University Press, 1994) 16.

This negative veto over property use, otherwise known as a 'right to exclude', is often seen as the core of ownership and property rights.[83] Although it cannot ground legitimate managerial authority in itself, it may indirectly enable employers to exercise control over workers in practice. This is because a right to exclude implies the ability to choose the conditions on which to permit access and the uses that property can be put to by others. Employers' ownership of the firm therefore means they can grant or deny workers access to the means of production, i.e. to work and income which is essential for their survival and flourishing. This creates a position of unequal bargaining power, where employers are ordinarily able to dictate the terms on which workers access employment, including a condition that employers have the authority to monitor workers. In the context of ownership of the firm, the right to exclude also effectively amounts to a right for employers to dismiss workers, and the express or implicit threat of dismissal will similarly enable them to exercise control over workers.

Even if employers have legitimate, rather than *de facto* authority in these circumstances, something which is questioned below, this is not grounded solely on employers' property rights. Consider again the analogy of laptop ownership. The owner may set conditions on its use by third parties, such as charging a certain fee or that the users' activity will be tracked via digital systems. However, they still lack any authority to demand third parties actually use the laptop in accordance with these conditions. Ownership may plausibly confer a normative power to determine what others *may or may not* do with one's property, but this is not the same as the power to determine that they *must* make this use of it. It is a 'fundamental myth' that property rights in the firm imply a right to manage or to monitor workers.[84] Something more is needed to ground this authority.

4.2 Worker Consent

The leading candidate of what is required to move from property rights to managerial authority is the consent or agreement of the workers subject to that authority. Consent based theories of authority are common in the philosophical literature, where consent is 'widely considered capable of grounding political legitimacy and obligation, provided it is given under morally permissible conditions'.[85] We shall return to this important proviso below. Consent intuitively offers an even stronger basis for managerial than political authority as there is an actual and identifiable agreement between employer and employee. The core idea being that 'By giving

[83] J Penner, *The Idea of Property in Law* (Oxford, Oxford University Press, 1997) 71.

[84] A Dorfman, 'Private Ownership and the Standing to Say So' (2014) 64 *University of Toronto Law Journal* 402; Ellerman (n 67).

[85] See Christiano and Sciaraffa (n 53); G Çapar, 'The Service Conception, Specification Problem and Its Moral Foundations' (2025) *Res Publica*. Available at: https://doi.org/10.1007/s11158-025-09738-7.

full consent, workers "authorise" management to govern them'.[86] Consent-based accounts of employer authority also seem particularly well suited to justify worker monitoring, where one of the main threats is to privacy. As privacy is often understood in terms of the ability to exercise control over one's body, information and personal life, it seems that no privacy harm can arise where workers consent to monitoring.[87]

Consent might most straightforwardly ground employers' authority to monitor where this forms part of the parties' express agreement, as embodied by the contract of employment. Such consent could take the form of express terms setting out a power to monitor, or incorporation of a company handbook that contains a monitoring policy. In the absence of specific provisions relating to monitoring powers there may be more general express terms conferring authority on employers to make decisions relating to work organisation that encompasses a power to monitor. Such agreements seem prima facie sufficient to legitimise monitoring, provided one accepts that individuals may voluntarily impose obligations on themselves and alienate their autonomous judgement to employers on certain matters.[88] In short, it appears the principle of *volenti non fit injuria* applies where workers have expressly agreed to monitoring.[89]

However, even if digital monitoring is expressly authorised by workers there are good reasons to doubt the weight that should be given to this consent, which mean that consent does not have the same 'moral magic' as in other contexts.[90] Labour law scholars have consistently questioned the possibility of free and meaningful consent within the employment context due to the unequal power relation between employers and workers.[91] In their pioneering work on industrial democracy, Beatrice and Sidney Webb point out that the pressing needs of labour compared to capital, information asymmetries, and lack of outside options available to workers due to an oversupply of labour, all create a situation where workers must generally accept the first job offered to them on terms dictated by the employer.[92] This is compounded by the comparative freedom of movement

[86] A Fox, *History and Heritage: The Social Origins of the British Industrial Relations System* (London, Routledge, 1985) 67.

[87] As argued by B Kobayashi and L Ribstein, 'Privacy and Firms' (2002) 79 *Denver Law Review* 526.

[88] Against the anarchist position of RP Wolff, *In Defense of Anarchism* (New York, Harper & Row, 1970). McMahon argues on similar grounds that consent can only establish 'minimal legitimacy' for managerial authority because workers cannot subordinate their moral judgements to employers: McMahon (n 56) at 36.

[89] P Pettit, 'Employment Without Domination' in I González-Ricoy and JL Marti (eds), *Workplace Republicanism* (forthcoming). Available at: https://papers.ssrn.com/sol3/papers.cfm?abstract_id=5043067.

[90] Bogg and Estlund (n 3). Citing HM Hurd, 'The Moral Magic of Consent' (1996) 2 *Legal Theory* 121.

[91] P Davies and M Freedland (eds), *Kahn-Freund's Labour and the Law*, 3rd edn (London, Stevens & Sons, 1983) ch 1; G Morris, 'Fundamental Rights: Exclusion by Agreement?' (2001) 30 *ILJ* 49; S Bagenstos, 'Consent, Coercion, and Employment Law' (2020) 55 *Harvard Civil Rights–Civil Liberties Law Review* 409; M Niezna and G Davidov, 'Consent in Contracts of Employment' (2023) 86 *MLR* 1134; M Niezna, 'Consent to Labour Exploitation' (2024) 53 *Industrial Law Journal* 3.

[92] S Webb and B Webb, *Industrial Democracy* (London, Longmans, Green & Co 1902) 658–61.

enjoyed by capital over labour in an era of globalisation.[93] The traditional narrative of labour law takes this inequality of power as its starting point and raison d'être; with labour law existing to provide a countervailing force to the superior position of employers.[94]

This unequal power dynamic has significant implications for the value of worker consent. Workers have little genuine opportunity to refuse the express terms laid down by employers, and consent loses 'a great deal of its moral force' due to a lack of alternative options.[95] In reality, therefore, freedom of contract is 'more of a verbal symbol than a social fact' in the employment context.[96] More recently, Anderson has echoed these insights in arguing that employers' authority is not based on any genuine 'meeting of minds'.[97] That employment contracts usually lack 'the sort of equality and voluntariness that is required to morally vindicate the content of the agreement' means that the legitimacy of employer authority cannot be determined simply 'by pointing to the fact that the existing rights and duties have been agreed to by the parties'.[98]

A second set of concerns about the value of worker consent relate more specifically to digital monitoring. Workers are frequently unaware of whether they are being digitally monitored by their employer. Even if they are aware, they are unlikely to know the specific forms that monitoring takes, how these systems operate, or the precise purposes they are used for. Given this, it is hard to see worker consent to broad monitoring authority as sufficiently informed to be meaningful. In addition, there are problems with relying on an individualistic model of consent to digital monitoring.[99] These technologies are often embedded in algorithmic management systems that process data on individual workers to make assessments and decisions about others. Data aggregation may also infer or reveal facts about individual workers that they have not voluntarily disclosed. Workers may therefore be assessed or managed based on monitoring that they have not personally consented to. A focus on individual worker consent cannot account for these relational dimensions and harms of digital monitoring. An individualised model of consent to monitoring is also fundamentally at odds with the collective nature of labour law, where collective voice and decision-making over monitoring is needed to counteract the superior bargaining power of employers.[100]

[93] H Arthurs, 'Who's Afraid of Globalization? Reflections on the Future of Labour Law' in JDR Craig and SM Lynk (eds), *Globalization and the Future of Labour Law* (Cambridge, Cambridge University Press, 2006).

[94] The leading articulation being Davies and Freedland (n 91).

[95] A Marmor, 'The Dilemma of Authority' (2010) *USC Law Legal Studies Paper* No 10–6, fn 28.

[96] Niezna (n 91); Davies and Freedland (n 91) at 25.

[97] E Anderson, 'Equality and Freedom in the Workplace: Recovering Republican Insights' (2015) 31(2) *Social Philosophy and Policy* 48.

[98] T Campbell, 'Should Managers Talk About Rights?' (2003) 3(2) *Philosophy of Management* 3.

[99] I Cofone, *The Privacy Fallacy: Harm and Power in the Information Economy* (Cambridge, Cambridge University Press 2023); Aloisi, Joppe and Abraha (n 15).

[100] H Abraha, 'Regulating Algorithmic Employment Decisions through Data Protection Law' (2023) 14 *European Labour Law Journal* 172.

These doubts about the value of worker consent are reflected in some aspects of labour and data protection law. When determining employment status, for instance, the UK Supreme Court has made clear that it is the reality of the relationship that matters, and the written contractual agreement of the parties should not be taken as the starting point.[101] This is a necessary response to employers' ability to insert sham terms in employment contracts by virtue of their superior bargaining position. In data protection law, although consent is a lawful basis for processing, UK and European level guidance make it clear that the unequal power relations that exist in employment mean that consent is not an appropriate basis for collection and processing of worker data.[102] More generally, the very existence of statutory employment rights, and fact that workers are not generally free to waive these minimum standards, are an acknowledgment of the shortcomings of worker consent and that the world of work cannot be governed solely via freedom of contract.

Rather than seeing the validity of worker consent as a binary matter, Davidov and Niezna suggest that consent is better understood as existing on a spectrum in the employment context.[103] Elsewhere, Davidov also makes a helpful distinction between 'core' terms of the employment contract, that are more likely to be subject to negotiations and should therefore be given more weight, and 'periphery' terms that are unilaterally dictated by employers and should therefore be given less.[104] Express terms authorising monitoring are likely to fall into this latter category, implying that limited weight should be given to worker consent in this context. These insights suggest that there is point at which worker consent should cease to be given any weight, so that apparent consent to monitoring may be insufficient to establish legitimate monitoring authority.

If consent is to plausibly justify employers' authority to monitor, workers must 'really consent to the degree of managerial discretion that is actually exercised'.[105] Achieving this will require supportive legal frameworks that move worker consent to monitoring along the spectrum of validity and turn them from periphery to core terms which are subject to negotiation. Central to this will be mechanisms that ensure consent to monitoring is freely given and adequately informed, including a system of social security which make non-consent (ie exit) a viable option. Vehicles providing for collective worker voice over monitoring will also be crucial, both for enabling negotiations with employers on a more equal footing, and for addressing the relational nature of privacy.

Moreover, in labour law as in other areas of life, there are some things that the law rightly does not recognise people as capable of consenting to. The law sets a

[101] *Uber v Aslam* [2021] UKSC 5, [2021] 4 All ER 209.

[102] Opinion 2/2017 on data processing at work, adopted on 8 June 2017; ICO, 'Employment Practices and Data Protection: Monitoring Workers' (2023).

[103] Niezna and Davidov (n 91). See also S Bajaj and P Tomlin, 'Consenting Under Coercion: The Partial Validity Account' (2024) 74 *The Philosophical Quarterly* 709.

[104] G Davidov, 'A Theory of the Contract of Employment' (2025) *Industrial Law Journal*. Available at: https://doi.org/10.1093/indlaw/dwaf031.

[105] Pettit (n 89).

minimum floor of working conditions and standards, such as minimum wages, rest periods and safety standards. These are generally non-waivable standards that workers cannot consent to work below. There must similarly be minimum standards in the context of monitoring, which identify those forms of monitoring that workers cannot consent to.

Even if such legal frameworks exist, however, many employment relationships will simply lack any express worker consent to monitoring – whether via a specific monitoring term or a more general conferral of managerial authority. Despite this, employers will nevertheless have the power to monitor workers by virtue of the implied terms of worker obedience and co-operation read into the contract. It is hard to see how consent can be the foundation of employers' monitoring power in these circumstances. The only way that this might be possible is by relying on tacit rather than express consent or by moving from actual (subjective) to implied or hypothetical consent.

Workers might be said to tacitly consent to digital monitoring by remaining in their job when they are aware of the monitoring. This is certainly how courts sometimes approach employer attempts to unilaterally vary the contract, where an employee may be taken to agree to the new terms if they continue to work without protesting the change.[106] A similar claim is sometimes made in respect of political authority, namely that continuing to live in a country amounts to tacit consent to the state's authority.[107] One issue with these arguments is that the high costs of non-consent, i.e. of resigning or leaving the country, make it hard to ascribe much moral weight to this 'consent'.[108] Moreover, in the many instances where workers don't know that they are subject to digital monitoring, or the details of how these systems are being used, they cannot be seen as even tacitly consenting to such monitoring.

Workers might alternately be taken to impliedly consent to monitoring, or be deemed to have so consented, simply by entering the employment relationship. This might be possible, for instance, if workers' implied duties of obedience and co-operation are viewed as obligations that are necessarily inherent in the employment relationships. On this view, these duties are obligations of 'role morality' inherent in the employment relationship, that are given effect by the courts via the law of implied terms.[109] In which case workers can be seen as having voluntarily accepted these obligations when they chose to enter the employment relationship.

[106] *Daley v Strathclyde* [1977] IRLR 414; *cf Abrahall v Nottingham City Council* [2018] EWCA Civ 796, [2018] ICR 1425.

[107] Christiano and Sciaraffa (n 53).

[108] D Hume, 'Of the Original Contract' in A MacIntyre (ed), *Hume's Ethical Writings* (London, University of Notre Dame Press, 1965).

[109] J Andre, 'Role Morality as a Complex Instance of Ordinary Morality' (1991) 28 *American Philosophical Quarterly* 73; J Atkinson, '*Johnson v Unisys Ltd* (2001): A Compelling Constitutional Vision of Common Law and Statute?' in J Adams-Prassl, A Bogg and ACL Davies (eds), *Landmark Cases in Labour Law* (Oxford, Hart Publishing, 2022).

Viewing terms implied into contracts 'in law' as legal instantiations of obligations of role morality makes sense, given that these terms are implied into specific categories of contract. As such, they are obligations associated with particular contractual relationships or roles. It is also a good explanatory 'fit' with how these terms are characterised and regarded by the courts themselves. Namely, as duties which are inherent in the nature of the relationships in question.[110] The default terms implied into employment contracts, or those for sale or lease, can therefore be seen as attempting to articulate the inherent obligations that parties take on when they enter into these relationships.

Of course, this leaves unanswered the question of *why* employer authority, including the power to monitor workers, is inherent in employment relationships. Answering this requires some substantive normative argument beyond worker consent. Attempts to ground managerial authority in hypothetical consent, for instance by arguing that workers are under an obligation to consent to monitoring because no reasonable person could refuse it, likewise face the challenge of explaining why this failure to consent to authority is invalid.[111]

In sum, consent may provide employers with legitimate authority to monitor where there is express agreement to this authority, under conditions which make this consent valid and meaningful. Absent such consent, however, attempts to rely on deemed or hypothetical consent need to provide some further substantive reasons for why the law is justified in treating them *as if* they had consented to such authority.

4.3 Instrumental Benefits

The most common justification of managerial authority outside of property and contract is instrumental. More specifically, the economic benefits of employer control are said to justify the allocation of default authority to employers. Unilateral co-ordination by employers maximises efficiency and economic output because it allows flexibility and responsiveness, supports specialisation and the division of labour, and can resolve any disputes and conflicts of interests.[112] As a result, hierarchical capitalist production is more dynamic than alternative economic models and will lead to higher overall societal welfare.[113]

Bogg and Estlund agree with Elizabeth Anderson that these benefits are sufficient to justify a measure of managerial authority, provided it is subject to limits that reduce the risks of interpersonal domination to an acceptable level.[114] In a

[110] *Scally v Southern Health and Social Services Board* [1992] 1 AC 294. For discussion see H Collins, 'Implied Terms: The Foundation in Good Faith and Fair Dealing' (2014) 67 *Current Legal Problems* 297.

[111] See analogously in respect of political authority, DM Estlund, *Democratic Authority: A Philosophical Framework* (Princeton, Princeton University Press, 2009).

[112] FW Taylor, *Shop Management* (New York, Harper & Brothers, 1919) 43–45; McMahon (n 56); Anderson (n 3).

[113] Bogg and Estlund (n 3).

[114] ibid.

similar vein, Collins argues that employees' duties of obedience and co-operation implied into the contract of employment are best seen as grounded in economic and policy goals.[115] These arguments are founded on Coase's theory of the firm, which posits that hierarchical employment relations exist because they reduce transaction costs and so are more efficient than concluding multiple arm's-length contracts.[116]

Provided the economic advantages of managerial authority are accepted, they provide a plausible reason for the law to confer default power on employers to manage and oversee workers within the boundaries of consensual employment relations.[117] However, meaningful consent to participate in employment relations remains a vital counterpart to these benefits, as grounding managerial authority solely in its economic benefits opens the door to justifying forced labour or other exploitative working arrangements.

Under this instrumentalist justification, the legitimacy of managerial authority does not arise from the employment relationship itself. It is instead derivative of state authority. Employers have the authority to monitor workers only because a legal rule gives them this power and this rule originates from a state that itself exercises legitimate authority.

One important implication of this consequentialist justification is that the scope of employers' authority, including to monitor workers, must be limited. On this view managerial authority is merely a rule of legal policy, based on economic factors. As such, the substance of the rule must take appropriate account of competing values and policy issues if it is to be legitimate. Crucially, the economic considerations underpinning employer authority cannot ride roughshod over workers' human rights, which are supposed to be resistant to economic trade-offs. As reflected in the European Court of Human Rights' jurisprudence on positive obligations, where workers' human rights are at stake the domestic rules of employment law must strike a fair balance between competing rights and interests, and employers must not be legally permitted to disproportionately interfere with workers' Convention rights.[118] It can likewise be argued that the scope and content of managerial authority must be compatible with other values such as freedom from domination and workers' moral agency.[119] More generally, if employers' legal power to monitor is justified by its positive consequences, the rule also needs to take account of the risks and harms that flow from it. Employers' managerial authority should therefore

[115] Collins 'Implied Terms' (n 110).

[116] RH Coase, 'The Nature of the Firm' (1937) 4 *Economica* 386.

[117] For a critical assessment of this assumption, see J Tomassetti, 'The Powerful Role of Unproven Economic Assumptions in Work Law' (2022) 3(1) *Journal of Law and Political Economy* 49.

[118] L Lavrysen, *Human Rights in a Positive State: Rethinking the Relationship Between Positive and Negative Obligations Under the European Convention on Human Rights* (Cambridge, Intersentia, 2016); V Mantouvalou, 'The Human Rights Act and Labour Law at 20' in A Bogg, A Young and J Rowbottom (eds), *The Constitution of Social Democracy: Essays in Honour of Keith Ewing* (Oxford, Hart, 2020); J Atkinson, 'Taking Human Rights Seriously at Work: The Past, Present and Future of Employment Law' (2025) *Industrial Law Journal*. Available at: https://doi.org/10.1093/indlaw/dwaf033.

[119] As argued, respectively, by Bogg and Estlund (n 3); Tsuruda (n 46).

not extend to forms of monitoring with no economic benefit, where this could be achieved in ways that have fewer negative impacts on workers, or where its benefits are clearly outweighed by these negative impacts.

If the legitimacy of capitalist production is accepted, as is the working premise here, then some degree of worker oversight must be accepted as inevitable due to the inherent conflicts of interests that exist between labour and capital. At the same time, if employers' authority to monitor is a policy-based rule, created by the state rather than reflecting a pre-legal obligation, it is clear that these monitoring powers must be subject to limits. The key question, then, is what should these limits be?

Bogg and Estlund identify three types of limit that might be needed for different aspects of managerial authority (eg dismissal or monitoring).[120] First, mandatory standards that prohibit certain decisions without the possibility of justification, second, the exclusion of prohibited reasons (ie discrimination and victimisation) for otherwise presumptively legitimate employer actions, and finally, the need for certain decisions to be affirmatively justified if they are to be legitimate. Employers will enjoy a broad area of discretionary decision-making other than where these three types of limits apply. The final category reverses the normal default of employer authority, as it imposes the initial burden on employers to give adequate reasons for their actions. Bogg and Estlund suggest this requirement of affirmative justification should only be required for a relatively limited set of managerial decisions. Namely, where there is a threat of personalised domination, and an immediate and serious adverse economic impact on workers. They identify disciplinary dismissals as the 'clearest case' for applying a justification requirement and are generally sceptical of extending it to other areas of managerial authority.[121] They believe a wider requirement for justification would be unduly burdensome on employers, and so ultimately deny society the welfare gains of managerial authority. For example, they specifically reject a justification requirement for the adoption of new technologies because this would 'undercut the reasonably efficient pursuit of the organization's mission'.[122] On this approach, monitoring should generally fall into the area of employers' discretionary authority, with prohibited-reason (ie discrimination) protections applying where monitoring significantly impacts workers' basic needs and interests.

Although Bogg and Estlund's analysis of when managerial decisions need affirmative justification is developed within a neo-republican framework it is not conceptually tied to this. Their requirement of a threat of interpersonal domination can relatively easily be extended to include threats to human rights or other important values. The proposed requirement of financial harm is troubling, however, as there is no reason why protection from financial impacts should be prioritised over non-monetary harms on workers. A better approach is to require

[120] Bogg and Estlund (n 3) at 262–66.
[121] ibid 267.
[122] ibid.

that employers provide a positive justification for monitoring where it has significant detrimental impacts on workers' human rights or basic interests, with workers ultimately having the ability to test the adequacy of this justification in a public forum. The impact of some forms of monitoring may fall short of this threshold, but many of the invasive digital systems used to monitor workers would stand in need of justification. Reliance on general claims about the costs of this underplay the significant harms that can result from digital monitoring. The power of the employers to monitor must be compatible with the human rights of the workers and strike a fair balance with competing policy considerations if it is to be a legitimate exercise of state authority. Reversing the default authority to monitor and providing workers with a right to a justification for harmful monitoring practices will help ensure these boundaries are maintained.

5 Aligning Legitimate and Lawful Monitoring Authority

It has been argued that legitimate managerial authority to monitor may be grounded in express consent, provided this is sufficiently free and informed to be meaningful. Alternatively, the instrumental benefits of employer power might justify de facto managerial authority to monitor even where no such consent is present, provided that the scope of this authority is subject to limits that render it compatible with workers' human rights and other fundamental values. There will be various ways of designing legal frameworks that appropriately take account of and reflect these boundaries. This section briefly sets out some measures that could be adopted in the UK to better align employers' legal authority to monitor with the scope of legitimate managerial authority.

Ensuring that workers collectively have a voice regarding employer monitoring practices and policies is an important means of securing meaningful consent. Collective representation and negotiation with employers counteracts the inequality of power that arises when individual workers interact with employers. Collective worker voice can also take account of the relational nature of digital monitoring in ways that individualised models of consent cannot.

In the UK, collective worker voice over monitoring should therefore be strengthened by integrating monitoring into existing collective bargaining and consultation frameworks. The forms and purposes of worker monitoring should be expressly listed as a potential topic for collective bargaining and trade disputes, and as a mandatory topic for bargaining under the statutory trade union recognition procedure.[123] New consultation rights over the use of monitoring technologies that are broadly analogous to those that exist for collective redundancies should be introduced, with employers also required to seek to reach an agreement with workers and to involve them in assessments of the impact of surveillance tools on

[123] Atkinson and Evans 'Negotiating the Future of Work' (n 36) at 12.

human rights and working conditions.[124] Workplace technology representatives should be established to serve as a focal point for these consultations, something that is particularly important in the majority of private sector workplaces that lack a significant trade union presence.[125]

These collective bargaining and consultation frameworks must be supported by more extensive transparency and information rights. Workers and their representatives need information about employers' existing and proposed use of surveillance technologies to effectively engage in negotiations and consultation, and for consent to monitoring to be meaningful. This should include rights to detailed information on the forms of surveillance proposed, the data gathered and the purposes for which it will be used, as well as the employers' reason for introducing the monitoring and why they view it as necessary and proportionate. These transparency obligations could be part of the bargaining and consultation provisions proposed above. Or they could be introduced as part of a wider requirement for employers to undertake and publish detailed impact assessments before introducing monitoring systems, with workers and their representatives having the opportunity to be involved in the process. Whichever option is preferred, the intertwined nature of monitoring and algorithmic management means that any new bargaining, consultation and information rights should also be extended to these management systems rather than being restricted to monitoring tools.[126]

In addition to mechanisms that facilitate genuine consent, there is a need for workers to be able to contest worker monitoring and ask for it to be justified. One way of achieving this would be to introduce a right to a justification for why monitoring has been introduced, with the ability for workers to contest the justification offered where monitoring adversely affects them. This would remove the default authority to monitor currently enjoyed by employers, and place the burden on them to establish good reasons for their decisions in this context in a similar manner as currently exists for the law of unfair dismissal, while ultimately providing them with a wide area of freedom to introduce forms of digital monitoring that don't overstep the boundaries of legitimacy.

Finally, there is a need for some hard limits to be drawn on the types of digital monitoring technologies that should be permissible. Some categories of monitoring technology should be classed as 'automatically unfair', in the same way that some categories of dismissal are deemed automatically unfair and not open to justification.[127] There is an emerging consensus in technology regulation of the need for prohibitions of this kind.[128] There is not space here for a detailed consid-

[124] ibid.

[125] Atkinson and Evans (n 36); Atkinson and Collins (n 48).

[126] Atkinson and Evans (n 36).

[127] Atkinson and Collins (n 29).

[128] Reflected in, eg, the Regulation (EU) 2024/1689 of the European Parliament and of the Council of 13 June 2024 laying down harmonised rules on artificial intelligence and amending Regulations (EC) No 300/2008, (EU) No 167/2013, (EU) No 168/2013, (EU) 2018/858, (EU) 2018/1139 and (EU) 2019/2144 and Directives 2014/90/EU, (EU) 2016/797 and (EU) 2020/1828 (Artificial Intelligence Act)

eration of what should fall into the category of automatically unfair monitoring technologies. However, these prohibited uses of technology can be identified by reference to the normative foundations of employers' monitoring power. Namely, those monitoring practices that the law should not recognise as being possible to consent to, or that cannot plausibly be justified by reference to their economic benefits given their adverse impacts on workers' human rights or other fundamental values.

6 Conclusion

Digital technologies have radically transformed the extent and granularity of worker monitoring and enabled the widespread introduction of surveillance-driven algorithmic management systems. These changes have significant implications for workers' human rights and wellbeing at work. This chapter has sought to reorient debates on workplace monitoring by centring the notion of legitimate managerial authority. Examining the normative foundations of managerial authority reveals that the current legal default, under which employers are allocated power to monitor, cannot be justified. At most, the combination of employers' rights in property and contract and the instrumental benefits of managerial authority can ground a qualified power to monitor. The legitimacy of monitoring is conditional on the existence of meaningful worker consent and its compatibility with workers' human rights and other fundamental values.

Reforms are therefore needed to help ensure that the scope of employers' lawful authority to monitor tracks the scope of their legitimate authority in this context. This involves a shift away from viewing monitoring as part of employers' default discretionary authority that is inherent in the employment relationship. Central to this alignment will be strong collective voice over monitoring, extensive information rights, prohibitions of automatically unfair monitoring technologies and an individual right to a justification.

[2024] OJ L2024/1689, Art 5; Directive (EU) 2024/2831 of the European Parliament and of the Council of 23 October 2024 on improving working conditions in platform work [2024] OJ L2024/2831, Art 7; V Dubal, 'Data Laws at Work' (2024) 134 *The Yale Law Journal Forum* 405; J Adams-Prassl et al, 'Regulating Algorithmic Management: A Blueprint' (2023) 14 *European Labour Law Journal* 124.

5

Employee Monitoring and the Right to Disconnect: What is at Stake?

NUNA ZEKIĆ

1 Introduction

One of the main positive aspects of technological progress has been the improved access to information and communication. Through various digital devices, we can easily connect with others and have instant access to myriad amounts of information and data. This convenient connection and availability extends to employment relations. Most workers can stay in contact with their employers, colleagues and clients outside the traditional working space and hours. Many employees now regularly work from home or other places. They carry or are surrounded by devices, which make it possible for them to be permanently connected to their employer, colleagues or clients.

Even though technology makes it possible to work remotely and flexibly, which can have clear advantages for workers and their employers alike, research shows that the use of such technology can have negative consequences as well. Workers see the intensity of their work increasing and they feel they must be available for continuous work communication. The most significant change has been the blurring of the divide between working time and private time.

Workers are, in addition, exposed to digital monitoring. The technological devices that make remote work possible, also – either secretly or openly – track the movements or behaviour of their users. Many employers already make use of algorithmic management and monitoring tools, such as software that keeps track of employees' online activities, GPS (global positioning system) tracking in company cars, and portable devices that track physiological and biomechanical status. The expectation is that the digital monitoring of workers will only increase.

One of the ways to remove oneself from this (constant) digital connection and monitoring is to *disconnect*. To simply switch off the devices that keep workers connected to their digital workspace and to remain 'offline'. The 'right to disconnect' is a concept which is increasingly on the radar of policy and lawmakers. Several countries have introduced a 'right to disconnect', while in others the added value of such a right is still very much a subject for debate.

This contribution addresses the connection between digital monitoring in the modern workplace and the right to disconnect. By linking the nature of the right to disconnect to the technological processes used to keep workers tethered to their jobs outside of their working place and hours, this chapter highlights the fundamental questions and tensions which are raised when thinking about disconnection from the digital sphere at work. It explores the discussion on the right to disconnect and examines to what extent workers already have this right. In addition, it analyses the extent to which this right serves as a solution to constant monitoring.

First, the chapter highlights how technology and digital devices make it possible for workers to be constantly connected to their work and to be available to the employer either more or less voluntarily or at the request of the employer outside the regular working hours (section 2). This so-called hyperconnectivity also makes digital monitoring even more intrusive. Next, the two legal frameworks that are supposed to protect the workers from adverse consequences are analysed to find out whether the workers have a right to disconnect: The working time legislation (section 3) and the laws on privacy protection (section 4). Is it true that workers can already choose to disconnect? Is new legislation not required? It is argued that neither the existing working time laws nor the laws on privacy protection give enough protection to workers who wish to disconnect from their 'digital workspace', especially non-standard workers who are only implicitly obliged to remain connected. Finally, (in section 5) it explores what the added value would be of a new right to disconnect.

2 Hyperconnectivity at the Modern Workplace

Due to digitalisation the modern workplace is changing. Digital technology has made it possible for workers in many occupations to work *remotely*, for example from home instead of the office, and to work *flexibly*, i.e. outside the traditional or the contractual 'office hours'. The COVID-19 pandemic has only accelerated the movement to teleworking – working remotely while communicating with work via digital devices. Flexible working and teleworking have undoubtably brought benefits to employers and workers alike. They have allowed workers previously not or under-employed to take on paid work, a situation employers benefit from as well. Being able to work 'anytime and anywhere' has helped many workers to better combine work and private life, even though for parents, the positive impact of telework can only be felt if it is supported by sharing care responsibilities between the parents and by equal access to telework.[1] Otherwise, women end up carrying a much greater load. Still, in general, with the ability to work remotely, workers can save on commuting time or take a more interesting job further away from home, because they don't have to come into the office every day. At the same time, employers can save on office space and offer flexible and remote working as an employment benefit.

However, 'working anytime, anywhere' raises concerns about the possible negative impacts on workers' lives. This contribution focuses on the two main risks for workers: health and safety and privacy.[2] These categories each have their own distinct legal frameworks; both are essential for human dignity. As the modern workplace evolves, some core principles of worker protection are once again taking centre stage.

There are health and safety concerns associated with the 'digital workplace'. First, it seems that despite the (old) promise of technology making work easier and reducing working time – or even replacing some jobs all together –research suggests that flexible working results in employees working more hours than they are contractually obliged to.[3] Moreover, technological devices can increase the intensity of work during working hours, resulting in a higher workload, because workers need to process more data and are often expected to communicate with clients and colleagues instantly.[4] Mobile instant messaging can foster collaboration, teamwork and productivity, but instant communication can also fuel the expectation that workers are always accessible and that it should not take them long to respond. Continuous notifications on mobile phones and laptops of new incoming messages can cause a sense of urgency and a need for an immediate response.[5] Workers may feel they are constantly connected to and available for work, since their employer, clients, and co-workers can contact them via digital devices at any time. Besides the feeling of being constantly connected and available for work, continuous information flow through IT (information technology) can

[1] See, eg H Chung, *The Flexibility Paradox: Why Flexible Working Leads to (Self-)Exploitation* (Bristol, Policy Press, 2022); T Bazzani, 'Telework and Right to Disconnect' in F Hendrickx and C Hiessl (eds), *The Meaning of Work: A Labour Law Perspective*, Bulletin of Comparative Labour Relations Vol 119 (Alphen aan den Rijn, Kluwer Law International, 2025) 106.

[2] Other risks can be identified as well. For instance, in terms of electronic surveillance, Ball describes different psycho-social risks such as decreased job satisfaction, decreased organisational commitment, increased counterproductive work behaviours/resistance, increased stress and increased turnover propensity. See K Ball, *Electronic Monitoring and Surveillance in the Workplace: Literature Review and Policy Recommendations* (Luxembourg, Publications Office of the European Union, 2021) 68–70.

[3] See eg Chung 2022 (n 1).

[4] A Bencsik and T Juhasz, 'Impact of Technostress on Work-Life Balance' (2023) 19 *Human Technology* 41, 43.

[5] N Blabst and S Diefenbach, 'WhatsApp and Wellbeing: A Study on WhatsApp Usage, Communication Quality and Stress' in L Hall et al (eds), *Proceedings of the 31st International BCS Human Computer Interaction Conference* (Sunderland, BCS, The Chartered Institute for IT, 2017).

also lead to an information overload, leading to difficulties to cope, a state that is also referred to as *technostress*.[6]

The new way of working has caused the boundaries of working time and private life to blur, which might be the most impactful effect on workers lives.[7] Without such boundaries the work–life balance may be disrupted leading work to encroach on personal time leaving less time and attention for leisure, wellbeing, and personal and social interests. Furthermore, as mentioned above, there can be negative consequences on equality between the genders, because of its disproportionate impact on workers with caring responsibilities, who still tend to be women. Finally, working time regulation, which aims primarily to protect workers' health and safety from excessive work demands, is less effective when the boundaries between work and private life are blurred. This will be elaborated on below.

The blurring of the work and non-work divide extends to the sphere of privacy as well.[8] Most employers feel the need to monitor work performance especially when employees work remotely and can set their own working hours. The fact is that employers generally determine which equipment, including ICT (information and communications technology) and other digital tools, are given to the workers to allow them to do their jobs. Usually, employers will consider that it is at their discretion what software is installed on those devices; this can be software that is able to track or monitor the usage of the equipment. While monitoring employees who work from home (or elsewhere, eg in their car), employers can collect data not only about their work performance but their *personal* lives as well. Employees routinely use their company-provided devices both for work and personal activities.[9] They usually do not know to what extent their usage is being monitored. In this way, it is easy for employers to gather information on everything the employee does on the employer-provided device.

In addition, the commercialisation and adoption of so-called 'wearables' are rapidly expanding and entering the work-sphere. These are portable electronic devices that are worn on the body or attached to garments or other clothing accessories. These are capable of the real-time and continuous monitoring of each worker's physiological and biomechanical status as well as their near environment.[10] They can detect and measure not only the worker's movement but

[6] TS Ragu-Nathan et al, 'The Consequences of Techno-Stress for End Users in Organizations: Conceptual Development and Empirical Validation' (2008) 19 *Information Systems Research* 417.

[7] Bencsik and Juhasz (n 4) at 41–61.

[8] V Mantouvalou and M Veale, 'Blurred Boundaries: Rescuing Workers' Privacy in the Process of Searching Data and Devices' (*UK Labour Law Blog*, 27 November 2023). Available at: https://uklabourlawblog.com/2023/11/27/blurred-boundaries-rescuing-workers-privacy-in-the-process-of-searching-data-and-devices-by-virginia-mantouvalou-and-michael-veale/.

[9] L Eisenstadt, 'Data Analytics and the Erosion of the Work/Nonwork Divide' (2019) 56 *American Business Law Journal* 445, 469.

[10] S Marassi and J Bolte, 'Wearable Technology to Monitor Workers' Health and Safety: Benefits, Risks, and Legal Considerations' in F Hendrickx and C Hiessl (eds), *The Meaning of Work: A Labour Law Perspective*, Bulletin of Comparative Labour Relations Vol 119 (Alphen aan den Rijn, Kluwer Law International, 2025) 180–88.

also, for instance, their heart rate, breathing rate, brain activity, perspiration, blood pressure, skin temperature, as well as any environmental parameters (eg chemical, and physical agents such as hazardous substances and ultraviolet (UV) radiation).[11] An increasing number of employers in the United States (US), where healthcare insurance often runs through employment, provides these devices to their employees as part of their 'wellness programs'.[12] It appears that employers are primarily using the data to demonstrate to insurance companies and investors that their workers have improving health, as Eisenstadt observes. However, the data could obviously be used in other ways as well: 'It is not difficult to imagine an employer relying on physiological data gathered during an employee's nonwork time to make decisions about his future in the workplace.'[13]

Indeed, wearables are often introduced as measures to *protect* workers' health and safety, because they can conduct real-time, continuous, and remote measurements and monitoring, enabling employers to adopt tailored measures to prevent and reduce occupational risks.[14] However, they are increasingly used in warehouses, logistic centres, and call centres to monitor workers' productivity by tracking the amount of work and the pace at which workers are required to perform their tasks.[15] Thus, in addition to the privacy aspect, there are health and safety risks associated with wearables. Marassi and Bolte explain how, given their nature (wearables are electrical devices, equipped with batteries and sensors), the use of such devices can pose potential risks to workers' physical safety in the event of malfunction but also to their mental health, because their use can induce stress and anxiety.[16]

That being said, the potential intrusion on workers' privacy is alarming.[17] The simple consequence of the growing use of such fast-emerging technologies by employers is that a wide array of (personal and sensitive) data about the workers ánd their surrounding environments can easily become available to the employer. In addition, machine-learning algorithms and (big) data analytics can be used to process data, potentially connecting different data sets. Employers can aggregate and analyse massive quantities of data. For example, algorithms scan through (large amounts of) employees' writing, extract patterns in the wording that indicate emotions, and track trends across the workforce.[18] This can be on internal company networking platforms or internal company surveys, but there are also programs that can, for example, mine data from employees' social media accounts

[11] Marassi and Bolte (n 10) at 181.
[12] Eisenstadt (n 9) at 478–80.
[13] ibid at 480.
[14] Marassi and Bolte (n 10) at 189.
[15] See, eg PV Moore, *Data Subjects, Digital Surveillance, AI and the Future of Work* (Brussels, European Parliamentary Research Service, 2020).
[16] Marassi and Bolte (n 10) at 191–92.
[17] See the first chapter of this volume by H Noorda and J Hariharan, 'Introduction: The Nature, Scope and Legal Complexity of Digital Monitoring' in H Noorda and J Hariharan (eds), *Digitally Monitored: Freedom, Surveillance and the Law* (London, Bloomsbury Publishing, 2026).
[18] Eisenstadt (n 9) at 471.

and then analyse the information for use by the employer.[19] When workers use laptops with surveillance software installed for personal use, employers can come to know about workers' 'off-duty hobbies, consumer preferences, and political views'; but also, as Eisenstadt warns, whether they are 'contemplating becoming pregnant or concerned about developing diabetes'.[20]

Employers can use this data for their at-work decisions, but they can also use the data in their capacity as a businesses seeking to make a profit. Eisenstadt rightly argues that the new ways employers can collect, analyse, and use employees' off-duty data constitutes a dramatic increase in the process of erosion of the work/non-work divide.

3 Working Time Regulation

3.1 Regulation and Its Aim

It is time to turn to the two legal frameworks that are supposed to protect workers from these adverse consequences as described above to analyse whether they contain a right to disconnect. For labour law scholars analysing whether a worker can choose to disconnect to avoid constant digital monitoring, one of the first starting points would be working time regulation. Relatively strong working time regulation has existed in the European Union (EU) for some time. In fact, working time limitations are to be found in the earliest parts of employment law in many countries. Moreover, limitation of working time is not confined to labour law; it has also been identified as a *human right* and is included in several human rights instruments. For example, different Conventions and Recommendations of the International Labour Organization (ILO) refer to working hours, eg the 1919 Hours of Work (industry) Convention (No 1). Article 2 of the Council of Europe's Revised European Social Charter (ESC) calls for 'reasonable daily and weekly working hours', weekly rest periods and a minimum of four weeks annual holiday with pay. Article 24 of the Universal Declaration of Human Rights (UDHR) is perhaps the most clear and concise stating: 'Everyone has the right to rest and leisure, including reasonable limitation of working hours and periodic holidays with pay.'[21] However, not every country has codified a right to rest. By contrast, the US Fair Labor Standards Act (FLSA) gives *some* employees the right to a bonus salary for working overtime, but the Act does not guarantee workers a minimum number of rest days, as does the EU Working Time Directive (WTD).[22]

[19] ibid 472–75.

[20] ibid 446.

[21] See, eg N Bueno, 'The Right to Rest and to the Limitation of Working Hours' in H Cantú Rivera (ed), *The Universal Declaration of Human Rights: A Commentary* (Leiden, Brill Nijhoff, 2024).

[22] The FLSA exempts numerous classes of workers from the Act's overtime protections, see, eg Eisenstadt (n 9) at 466; Directive 2003/88/EC of the European Parliament and of the Council concerning certain aspects of the organisation of working time [2003] OJ L299/9.

An important reason for limiting working hours is the protection of workers' health and safety. In particular, structural overtime or frequent night work, with its related lack of recovery time, threatens the health and safety of workers. Consequently, the health and safety of the public may be put at risk when overtired workers perform their work. Furthermore, the consequences of 'unhealthy work' hours are usually borne by the general public.[23] The issue of health and safety remains a prominent rationale for policies aimed at keeping working time within its legal limits. Indeed, improving workers' health and safety is the main objective of the WTD. Therefore, working time regulation is, in many countries, part of *public* labour law and accompanied by both public and private enforcement. Thus, working time regulation is not underpinned by the idea of interpersonal justice alone, it also serves the public interest. This is reflected in recital 4 of the WTD which states: 'The improvement of workers' safety, hygiene and health at work is an objective which should not be subordinated to purely economic considerations.' We see the connection with health and safety clearly in the articulation of Article 31 of the Charter where the first paragraph reads: 'Every worker has the right to working conditions which respect his or her health, safety and dignity.' The next paragraphs further mention rights regarding the limitation of maximum working hours, daily and weekly rest periods and a period of paid annual leave.

The current EU Working Time Directive of 2003 can be seen as a modern piece of legislation laying down the main principles of working time, while offering ample flexibility and considerably simplifying the existing regulatory framework. Still, the WTD can seem rather complicated and is not easy to understand on a first reading, because it entails several precise legal norms. Nowak succeeded in summarising its main material scope as follows:

> The WTD prescribes: minimum daily rest periods of 11 hours; breaks when working days are longer than six hours, the details of which are left to collective agreements; a weekly rest period of 24 uninterrupted hours; weekly working hours of not more than 48 hours; annual leave of at least four weeks; and night work to be no longer than an average of eight hours in a 24 hour period.[24]

However, this framework of substantive norms is considerably complicated by a wide range of derogations and options (set out in WTD, Arts 17–22). For our purposes, it is important to note that the WTD neither defines nor sets limits on *overtime*. The maximum number of working hours, i.e., 48 hours with possible (sectoral) derogations, is supposed to include any possible overtime.

[23] D Ulber, 'Digitalization and Working Time Law: Contemporary Challenges and Solutions' (Labour Law Research Network Conference, Warsaw, June 2023).

[24] T Nowak, 'The Turbulent Life of the Working Time Directive' (2018) 25 *Maastricht Journal of European and Comparative Law* 118, 120.

3.2 Stand-by Time and the Dichotomy Between Working Time and Rest Time

Perhaps more important than the working time limits is the fact that the EU Court of Justice (CJEU or 'the Court') has interpreted the main concepts of the WTD – 'working time' and 'rest time' – as mutually exclusive. That means that workers' time must be qualified either as working time or rest time. There is no intermediate category. This would imply that everything outside the regular working hours of a particular worker is to be qualified as rest time.

However, this dichotomy has been mitigated by the CJEU through its case law on so-called 'stand-by' or 'on-call' shifts.[25] These are periods of time in which the workers are not performing their regular duties – they are not working in the strict sense – but they must be available and at the employer's disposal to resume working (usually) as soon as possible after they receive a call. In the words of Mitrus: 'The nature of stand-by time is that a worker is available (contactable) and ready to undertake duties.'[26] Now, it is obvious that when a worker is called and they resume work, working time starts. But how does the CJEU deal with the 'inactive' or 'waiting' time during such shifts?

Analysing the case law, we see that – broadly speaking – these shifts can be divided in two categories. First are shifts that oblige the worker to be present at a certain place, usually the workplace, during which the worker is not required to perform work, unless called upon. Hospitals and care facilities are good examples of workplaces that have designated areas where workers on stand-by can rest, eg sleep, until they are called to resume their duties. Second are stand-by shifts that do not require the worker to be present at a certain place. The worker can choose where to stay, eg at home, but they need to remain at the employer's disposal to resume the work when called upon.

The first category of shifts will in principle qualify as working time. When the worker is required to be physically present at the place determined by the employer and to remain available to the employer to be able, if necessary, to provide their services immediately, then this time should count as working time according to the landmark rulings *Simap* and *Jaeger*.[27] These judgments have had important consequences for the organisation and regulation of working time across the EU.

Matzak was another landmark judgment where the Court ruled that stand-by shifts from the second category *can* qualify as working time.[28] Since *Matzak*, the Court seems to distinguish between what can be called 'ordinary' stand-by duties

[25] Bazzani (n 1) at 114. Also see N Zekić, 'Setting boundaries: Do we need a right to disconnect when we have a fundamental right to rest?' (2026) 51(2) *European Law Review* 210–227.

[26] L Mitrus, 'Defining Working Time Versus Rest Time: An Analysis of the Recent CJEU Case Law on Stand-By Time' (2023) 14 *European Labour Law Journal* 35, 47.

[27] Case C-303/98 *Simap* ECLI:EU:C:2000:528, [2000] ECR I-07963; Case C-151/02 *Jaeger* ECLI:EU:C:2000:528, [2003] ECR I-08389. See also Case C-14/04 *Dellas and Others* ECLI:EU:C:2005:728, [2005] ECR I-10253.

[28] Case C-518/15 *Matzak* ECLI:EU:C:2005:728, [2018] 2 CMLR 37.

(ie duties during which the worker must 'simply be at his employer's disposal inasmuch as it must be possible to contact him') and stand-by duties that are so onerous that they qualify as working time.[29] *Matzak* involved such an onerous stand-by duty. Matzak was a fireman who could stay at home during his on-call duty, but he had to keep himself available to his employer, so that he could arrive at his workplace within eight minutes of a call. The Court looks solely at the formal obligations that follow from a stand-by duty, i.e. constraints imposed on the worker by the law, a collective agreement or the employer.[30] According to the CJEU, the obligations were such 'as to objectively limit the opportunities which a worker in Mr Matzak's circumstances has to devote himself to his personal and social interests'.[31]

Later, the Court also cited this distinction in *Offenbach* and in *Radiotelevizija Slovenija*.[32] It is for the national court to examine whether a stand-by duty falls into the category of working time or in the category of rest time, given all the circumstances of the case. When a stand-by duty entails obligations of such a nature as to have an 'objective and very significant impact' on the worker's ability to devote himself to his personal and social interests, then the stand-by duty is treated in its entirety as working time. Conversely, when stand-by duties 'do not reach such a level of intensity' and they allow the workers to manage their own time, and to pursue their own interests 'without major constraints', only the time linked to the provision of work actually carried out during that period constitutes working time.[33]

Thus, as Mitrus explains: 'There is no *prima facie* presumption that a stand-by period should be classified either as working time or a rest period.'[34] To determine whether the constraints from a stand-by duty have an objective and significant impact on the worker's ability to devote himself to his personal and social interests one should look at the time period available to the worker to return to his professional activities, starting from the moment at which the employer requests it (in short: response time), coupled with the average frequency of the interventions (or call-outs) that the worker is actually called upon to undertake over the course of that period.[35] Later, the Court added that the predictability of interventions are relevant as well.[36] The response time and the intervention frequency seem to

[29] Case C-518/15 *Matzak* ECLI:EU:C:2018:82, [2018] 2 CMLR 37 para 64.

[30] All kinds of 'organisational difficulties' that a period of stand-by time may generate for the worker, which are not the result of such constraints but are, eg, the consequence of natural factors or of the worker's own free choice, may not be taken into account, see Case C-580/19 *Stadt Offenbach am Main* ECLI:EU:C:2021:183 (CJEU, 9 March 2021) para 41.

[31] Case C-518/15 *Matzak* ECLI:EU:C:2018:82, [2018] 2 CMLR 37 para 63.

[32] Case C-580/19 *Stadt Offenbach am Main* ECLI:EU:C:2021:183 (CJEU, 9 March 2021); Case C-344/19 *Radio Televizija Slovenija* ECLI:EU:C:2021:182 (CJEU, 9 March 2021).

[33] Case C-580/19 ECLI:EU:C:2021:183 *Stadt Offenbach am Main* (CJEU, 9 March 2021) para 39; Case C-344/19 *Radio Televizija Slovenija* ECLI:EU:C:2021:182 (CJEU, 9 March 2021) para 38 and the case law cited.

[34] Mitrus (n 26) at 45.

[35] Case C-580/19 *Stadt Offenbach am Main* ECLI:EU:C:2021:183 (CJEU, 9 March 2021) para 45.

[36] Case C-107/19 *Dopravní* ECLI:EU:C:2021:722, [2022] 2 CMLR 2 para 41.

be the most important aspects to take into consideration, however, in national courts – who are the ones that need to determine this on a case-by-case basis – *all* relevant circumstances can be taken into consideration as long as they refer to obligations that are imposed on the worker by the employer, the applicable collective agreement or by the law.

However, it is important to emphasise that when a stand-by duty is indeed classified as rest time, this does not mean that there are no obligations for the employer at all. In both *Offenbach am Main* and *Radiotelevizija Slovenija*, the CJEU emphasises that the Directive 89/391 (so-called Framework Directive for Occupational Safety and Health) still applies in full.[37] Stand-by shifts – even when they do not qualify as working time – are a part of the working environment in a broad sense. Hence, the employer remains obliged to evaluate and prevent all risks to the safety and health of workers. This includes certain psychosocial risks, such as stress and burnout. 'It follows that employers cannot establish stand-by periods that are so long or so frequent that they constitute a risk to the safety or health of workers, the Court warns, irrespective of those periods being classified as 'rest periods' within the meaning of the Working Time Directive.[38]

3.3 Dichotomy Eroding for Waiting Time?

We have seen above that when workers are not working, but are on-call, this can still count as rest time as long as the obligations are not of such a nature as to have an 'objective and very significant impact' on the workers' ability to devote themselves to their personal and social interests. It is worth noting that 'significant impact' is not enough, it needs to be a 'very significant impact' for the on-call shift to count as working time. When the frequency of the calls is not too high ánd the workers are given ample time to respond, it is safe to say that, according to the CJEU, such time can count as rest time, even though the workers are formally obliged to be available for calls outside their normal working hours. Thus, for daily and weekly rest periods, the Court does seem to accept the presence of employment obligations as long as these are not 'too heavy'. Bazzani, for example, calls this 'a certain degree of compatibility' between work and rest time, which the CJEU allows in case of stand-by time.[39]

The legal dichotomy between working time and rest time has been eroding, following – or, preceding – the blurring boundaries between work and private life many workers have experienced in real life. Now, some scholars hold the opinion that the Court allows for low-intensity obligation during rest time *only* in case of stand-by time. Bazzani, for example, asserts that 'outside the stand-by time cases, compatibility between rest time and working time must be strictly excluded

[37] Case C-344/19 *Radio Televizija Slovenija* ECLI:EU:C:2021:182 (CJEU, 9 March 2021) paras 61–65.
[38] Case C-580/19 *Stadt Offenbach am Main* ECLI:EU:C:2021:183 (CJEU, 9 March 2021) para 60.
[39] Bazzani (n 1) at 116.

in light of EU law'.[40] It is yet to be seen whether the CJEU will follow this line but, even if it does, this remains a very important exception on the dichotomy between working time and rest time to the point that we can ask whether there still indeed is a dichotomy. Many workers are regularly or occasionally on some kind of stand-by time. Think of medical personnel, firefighters and police, lawyers, mechanics. Stand-by time can have great economic value for employers. Without workers who are on stand-by, the employer would have to employ more workers. Moreover, nowhere in its case law does the CJEU define stand-by time. All kinds of on-call arrangements can be made in practice. What should then qualify as stand-by time to fall under this exception?

But the most important take-away for our purposes is that in the test developed by the CJEU to determine whether waiting time should count as working time, the Court only looked at *explicit* obligations following from the employment contract. It is, thus, safe to conclude that when there are no explicit obligations to be available and to respond to calls by resuming one's duties, there is hardly any reason for the CJEU to classify time spent at home being available and waiting for work as working time, even though the worker might be, due to constant connectivity, permanently reachable by and available to the employer and even though that worker might be working regularly outside normal working hours.

I argue that one of the biggest problems in this regard is that in many cases, such employment obligations to remain available after working hours are *implicit*. Many work arrangements nowadays are such that employers do not need to formally oblige the worker to be available. Instead, the obligations to keep connected and take up additional work if needed are very often implicit. It is true that an increasing number of workers is free to organise their working time as they see fit as long as they finish the assigned tasks on time and in a satisfactory manner.[41] However, despite this 'freedom' some of these workers can end up performing excessive hours when the workload is so big that the work cannot be finished within the contracted hours. They may be reluctant to disconnect if this is perceived as a lack of ambition or if it might have negative consequences on their careers. In addition, the more hours the workers work on employer owned devices the more data the employer can gather. The more irregular their working hours are, the richer the data is. However, we will turn to the privacy regulation-framework more in detail below.

Regarding the working time regulation framework, it is important to note that due to technological advances, an increasing number of workers, enjoy the flexibility of working from home, but this flexibility is also often accompanied by an 'always-on culture'. The so-called atypical or flexible workers, such as fixed-term, (involuntary) part-time or temporary agency workers, who have less job security than the so-called permanent workers, can feel the pressure to respond to calls and

[40] ibid 119; 116.

[41] Such workers are sometimes called *autonomous workers*, see, eg S Huybrechts, 'Working Time and Autonomy: Lessons for the New Ways of Working' (2023) 14 *European Labour Law Journal* 570.

keep working well after their working hours. In fact, there is a strong relationship between working time regulation and flexible forms of employment contracts.[42] When dismissal protection is reduced, as is the case with flexible employment contracts, this affects other employment conditions, such as protection against excessive overtime.

3.4 Does the Right to Rest Encompass a Right to Disconnect?

Codifying a right to disconnect has been opposed with the reference to the already existing right to rest from work. The main argument is that the EU Working Time Directive and EU case law already imply a right to disconnect.[43] Even proponents have stated that the right to disconnect, eg as adopted in France and Spain, are not new, but affirm existing rights.[44] While the European Trade Union Confederation (ETUC) supports the European Parliament's request to legislate a right to disconnect, its formal statement has been that there is no need for a right to disconnect to be *introduced*, since such a right already exists; it only needs to be further described and enforced in the form of an EU Directive.[45]

However, in many sectors, such as care work, security, hospitals and other essential public services, stand-by shifts that are not always considered working time are prevalent. Moreover, as is explained above, the case law on stand-by shifts shows that the CJEU accepts employment obligations during daily and weekly rest periods as long as they are of low intensity and they do not put the health and safety of the worker in jeopardy. That means that workers in these sectors are required to remain connected – and, indeed, remain standing-by to resume work – even during their rest time. The CJEU does warn that there should be a minimum rest time in which the workers can freely and without interruption devote themselves to their personal and social interests. But there are still many unanswered questions about this minimum period of rest time.

Moreover, many work arrangements do not require workers to be explicitly available; the obligations are often implicit. Particularly precarious workers, such as temporary (agency) workers, can be reluctant to 'switch off' if the culture within their profession is to always be available for work (communication). Enforcement of working time laws will not suffice when the obligation to stay connected and available is not made explicit by the employer nor does the enforcement of working

[42] J Popma and W Roozendaal, 'Arbeidsomstandigheden en arbeidstijden' in F Pennings and S Peters (eds), *Europees arbeidsrecht* (Deventer, Wolters Kluwer, 2021) 366.

[43] See, eg, Bazzani (n 1) at 118; H Collins, 'Privacy and the Right to (Dis)connect' (2025) 45 *Comparative Labor Law & Policy Journal* 467.

[44] L Lerouge and FT Pons, 'Contribution to the Study on the "Right to Disconnect" from Work. Are France and Spain Examples for Other Countries and EU Law?' (2022) 13 *European Labour Law Journal* 450, 457–58.

[45] 'ETUC Response to the Commission's First-Phase Consultation of the European Social Partners on Possible Action in the Area of Telework and Workers' Right to Disconnect', adopted at the ETUC Executive Committee meeting of 25 June 2024, 2.

time laws protect workers from victimisation. In its Resolution, the European Parliament proposed including in a possible directive the insurance that workers who invoke their right to disconnect are protected from victimisation and other negative repercussions and there are mechanisms in place to deal with complaints or breaches of such a right.[46]

More importantly, the clarity of the 'right to disconnect' is perhaps its biggest advantage. It's easy to comprehend. Even the 'softest' existing proclamations of a right to disconnect aim to make the implicit obligations that might exist outside working hours more explicit and raises awareness on the importance of rest time.[47] Legislation at the EU-level would ensure all EU workers are given the same minimum level of protection. By the end of 2023, the Commissioner for Jobs and Social Rights, Nicolas Schmit, affirmed that the Commission would follow up its commitment to legislate on the right to disconnect; however, to date, no legislative steps have been made.

4 Privacy Regulation

4.1 A Reasonable Expectation of Privacy

As stated, the right to disconnect can be important for protecting both workers' time and their privacy. However, as explained before, the need to codify a right to disconnect is still very much debated in the context of existing regulations. In this section, we turn to the privacy regulation framework to find out whether a right to disconnect can be said to exist based on *this* legal framework. Section 2 described different types of digital monitoring together with the risks they pose to workers' health and privacy. Specifically, so-called 'wearables' and similar types of equipment for monitoring employees and collecting data still seem to be in their infancy.

However, employee surveillance is as old as are the first factories.[48] Since the late 19th century, the so-called 'scientific management' developed by Frederick Taylor became popular in which the work performance of small tasks was carefully timed. The rationale for surveillance of workers has always been that employers need to supervise and monitor the workers to monitor the *work performance*. In that way the supervisors can give instructions, supress any security risks, improve performance, and, ultimately, increase productivity. The employer's power to

[46] European Parliament resolution with recommendations to the Commission on the right to disconnect [2021] OJ C456/161, sub 22.

[47] See, eg the French regulation: France was the first MS to adopt legislation on a right to disconnect, in 2016, and now regulated by the Labour Code, Art L2242-17.

[48] Noorda and Hariharan (n 17); M Molè, *Monitored at Work: The Legitimate Exercise of the Employer's Monitoring Power in the age of Artificial Intelligence and the Internet of Things*, PhD thesis University of Groningen (Groningen, 2025) 19–29.

monitor the workplace and work performance is usually not codified in labour law, but it is derived from employer *authority*, which is a constitutive element of the employment contract.[49]

What is different now is that digital tools make monitoring and collection of data easier, faster, and more precise. In addition, in the past, surveillance needed to be done by a person, but since technology has taken over that task, surveillance can become constant. Moreover, when the worker is using employer-provided devices for personal use or when the work is done remotely, eg in the home, the employer can (easily) gather large amounts of information, or data, on the workers and perhaps even their surroundings. This data goes beyond the work performed and can include all kinds of personal information. Employers can use this data for work-related decisions, but also potentially for other purposes. After all, we are living in the era when data is considered to be 'the new gold'. For workers, besides invading their privacy, the control and monitoring can be more intense, invasive, and stressful.[50]

However, even though digital monitoring can be far reaching, it is not unrestricted.[51] How far the employers can go in monitoring the workers and in gathering and processing their data is of course subject to rules following from the right to privacy. In terms of legal permissibility, the issue of employee monitoring is typically analysed through the lens of data protection legislation, i.e. in the European context, the General Data Protection Regulation (GDPR), and compatibility with the right to 'private and family life, home and correspondence' enshrined in Article 8 of the European Convention on Human Rights (ECHR).[52] Drawing from the European Court of Human Rights' (ECtHR) case law, legal scholars tend to emphasise that 'employees continue to enjoy the right to respect for private life within the workplace itself, as well as a right to be free of employer interference outside of working time'.[53] However, that is to some degree. Indeed, in general 'private life' is considered broad enough to include professional activities.[54] But, as is almost always the case with human rights, the right to privacy is not absolute. Since it is commonly assumed that the employer has a right to monitor the work performance; there is a conflict of interests that need to be balanced against each other. It might be more accurate to say that, according to the case law,

[49] F Hendrickx, 'How Privacy Shapes the Meaning of Work: Developing Freedom and Autonomy in Labour Law' in F Hendrickx and C Hiessl (eds), *The Meaning of Work: A Labour Law Perspective*, Bulletin of Comparative Labour Relations Vol 119 (Alphen aan den Rijn, Kluwer Law International, 2025) 230.

[50] See Ball (n 2).

[51] See chapter 4 in this volume by J Atkinson, 'Managerial Authority and the Boundaries of Legitimate Workplace Monitoring' in H Noorda and J Hariharan (eds), *Digitally Monitored: Freedom, Surveillance and the Law* (London, Bloomsbury Publishing, 2026), for a more elaborate analysis.

[52] J Hariharan and H Noorda, 'Imprisoned at Work: The Impact of Employee Monitoring on Physical Privacy and Individual Liberty' (2025) 88 *Modern Law Review* 333, 334.

[53] PM Collins, *Putting Human Rights to Work: Labour Law, The ECHR, and the Employment Relation* (Oxford, Oxford University Press, 2022) 184.

[54] *Antović and Mirković v Montenegro* App no 70838/13 (ECtHR, 28 November 2017).

employees may retain *a reasonable expectation of privacy* in relation to their online activities.[55]

In determining whether and to what extent employee monitoring is legally permissible, the notions *legitimacy* and *proportionality* play a big role. The legitimacy-test in employment relations is usually not difficult to meet for employers, since eg protection of employer's property or management, planning and organisation of work are easily considered legitimate aims for monitoring of workers.[56] However, the more intrusive digital monitoring becomes, the more pressing the question of legitimacy becomes.[57] Looking at the current case law, however, the legitimacy-test has not often proven to be problematic in terms of legal permissibility.

In fact, very often legal cases on workers' privacy boil down to the proportionality-test. In turn, this means that the courts have ample room to weigh the interests of the parties. It is not uncommon that the courts find that legitimate interest of the employer in monitoring the work performance outweigh the privacy interest of the employee. It has been signalled that court rulings suggest that data protection regulations should not be an impediment to the employer's ability to pursue its goals of productivity and employee monitoring.[58]

Next to legitimacy and proportionality, *transparency* and, relatedly, the questions whether employee was given prior notice or had given consent seem to be very important as well.[59] In the well-known *Bărbulescu*-judgment, the ECtHR established a set of criteria to be met for proportionate and necessary interference with Article 8 of the ECHR, the first of them being 'whether the employee was informed about the possibility of the employer implementing monitoring measures and the implementation of such measures'.[60] In the GDPR as well, informed consent is the first ground for lawfully processing data (Art 6). However, in the framework of data processing, it is acknowledged that consent by the employee cannot be considered to have been freely given.[61] Still the ECtHR and most national courts consider transparency and the requirement of prior notification as key principles

[55] *Bărbulescu v Romania* App no 61496/08 (ECtHR, 5 September 2017) para 80.

[56] See eg, 'controlling company expenses' was considered a legitimate aim for constant GPS-tracking of car movements also when using the company-car for private purposes, see *Florindo De Almeida Vasconcelos Gramaxo v Portugal* App no 26968/16 (ECtHR, 3 April 2023).

[57] See eg, Hendrickx (n 49) at 221–36.

[58] A Todolí-Signes, 'Privacy at Work in Spain' in F Hendrickx, D Mangan and E Gramano (eds), *Privacy@work: A European and Comparative Perspective* (Kluwer Law International, 2023) 504.

[59] The specific rules and notions to be taken into account will differ per country, since national courts approach monitoring and surveillance of workers on a case-by-case-basis. The notions mentioned here are general key-notions. For an elaborated analysis, see Atkinson (n 51). For country-specific insights, see F Hendrickx, D Mangan and E Gramano (eds), *Privacy@work. A European and Comparative Perspective* (Alphen aan den Rijn, Kluwer Law International, 2023).

[60] *Bărbulescu v Romania* App no 61496/08 (ECtHR, 5 September 2017).

[61] The European Data Protection Working Party has explicitly denied consent as a legal basis for data processing in employment relationships. See, eg F Hendrickx, 'Privacy@work: A Systemic Introduction' in F Hendrickx, D Mangan and E Gramano (eds), *Privacy@work: A European and Comparative Perspective* (Alphen aan den Rijn, Kluwer Law International, 2023) 16; S Riso, *Employee Monitoring and Surveillance: The Challenges of Digitalisation* (Luxembourg, Publications Office of the European Union, 2020) 7.

in the framework of privacy in employment relations. In *Florindo de Almeida Vasconcelos Gramaxo v Portugal* the ECtHR found no violation of Art 8 ECHR mainly because the employee was informed that his vehicle was tracked via GPS and he was therefore aware that disciplinary measures could be taken against him.[62] The GPS-tracking of car movements – both for work ánd private use – by the employer was, however, *constant* and lasted several years. The case shows how relying heavily on this requirement risks reducing the right to private life in labour relations to 'procedural justice'.

In addition, many workers use devices provided by the employer for personal use. As Eisenstadt explains, many of them are aware, to some extent, that their employers have access to their personal information, but they still make the choice to allow that incursion in order to make their lives easier and more convenient.[63] The fact that workers at some point might have been informed that the employer has access to their personal data, does not mean that every worker comprehends the possible consequences and is able to act accordingly. Even the employers who use data analytics do not always know what kind of decisions they will be making down the road. There is a serious risk that many of these new tools to monitor workers are beyond scrutiny.[64]

However, it is not even clear whether transparency *is* actually a starting principle for *all* national courts and to what extent they allow for exceptions on this principle. For Spain, for example, Todolí-Signes explains how 'several high courts of justice rulings have upheld the right to search a worker's computer and e-mail without first informing them that such checks are being conducted or the purpose of them'.[65] Video surveillance installed for other purposes, can be used for disciplinary matters, eg, disciplinary dismissal, despite the fact that the employees were not informed of the existence of the cameras and the fact that they could be used as a disciplinary measure.[66] In the context of transparency, the usage of *secret* monitoring is particularly problematic. Even though in general most legal systems provide that secret monitoring is not allowed, national courts often allow for exceptions, certainly in cases of theft or other serious wrongdoings.[67] The ECtHR has as well justified covert video-surveillance when there is a reasonable suspicion of serious misconduct.[68] Courts are thus prone to accept employers having certain *investigative powers* – that usually belong to the police – when they have 'legitimate suspicion' that the employee has committed a serious breach of official duties. For example, the Estonian Supreme Court accepted such an intrusion to employees'

[62] *Florindo De Almeida Vasconcelos Gramaxo v Portugal* App no 26968/16 (ECtHR, 3 April 2023).

[63] Eisenstadt (n 9) at 492.

[64] See, eg M Molè and D Mangan, '"Just More Surveillance": The ECtHR and Workplace Monitoring' (2023) 14 *European Labour Law Journal* 694.

[65] Todolí-Signes (n 58) at 500.

[66] See Spanish Constitutional Court (STC) ruling 39/2016. See also STS rulings of 2 February 2017 (appeal 554/2016) of 21 July 2021 (appeal 4877/2018), STS of 13 October 2021 and the recent STS of 25 January 2022 (appeal 4468/2018).

[67] Hendrickx (n 61) at 35.

[68] *López Ribalda and Others v Spain* (2020) 71 EHRR 7.

privacy when the employer suspected that a member of the company's management board was acting in a disloyal manner towards the company and thereby harming the company's property interests.[69] Furthermore, even when monitoring is found to be unlawful, that does not in itself imply that the evidence of worker wrongdoing obtained from monitoring is unlawful. In Spain, for example, various judgments handed down by the Constitutional Court and by the Spanish Supreme Court permit evidence obtained in this way for a disciplinary dismissal.[70] The same is true, for example, for the Netherlands.[71]

4.2 Does the Right to Privacy Entail a Right to Disconnect?

The brief explanation in the previous paragraph of the main principles of privacy regulation shows that the application of existing privacy rules can lead to very different results in terms of legal permissibility to monitor the workers depending inter alia on the aim of and the need for monitoring, the proportionality of the monitoring measures, and the extent of transparency on the part of the employer (ie, were the employees aware of monitoring being performed? did their representatives like trade unions or works councils give permission for monitoring?). This is especially true if we take account of the application of privacy rules by *national* judges instead of the ECtHR, who seem even more inclined than the ECtHR to believe that monitoring workers is a logical part of the general employer's right to direct and control the workers.[72] Furthermore, case law seems to lag behind the technological developments in surveillance software. There is, for instance, no ECtHR case law on wearables yet. Even though the GDPR has been drafted with the intention of covering technological developments, scholars repeatedly argue that the GDPR is not fully equipped to address the specificities of workplace data governance.[73] These researchers argue that GDPR enforcement in the workplace is fragmented and incomplete. However, a general conclusion can be that both the GDPR and the existing ECtHR's case law on digital surveillance seem to recognise a *procedural* right to privacy only. To use the words of Mangan: 'This approach

[69] Estonian Supreme Court of 3 March 2021 in case no 1-17-2359 paras 52–54; see about the case M Erikson and S Suder, 'Privacy at Work in Estonia' in F Hendrickx, D Mangan and E Gramano (eds), *Privacy@work: A European and Comparative Perspective* (Alphen aan den Rijn, Kluwer Law International, 2023) 197.

[70] Failure to comply with data protection regulation may give rise to a right to compensation for damages in favour of the employee, but it will not invalidate the evidence. See Todolí-Signes (n 58) at 504–05.

[71] N Zekić, 'Privacy at Work in the Netherlands' in F Hendrickx, D Mangan and E Gramano (eds), *Privacy@work: A European and Comparative Perspective* (Alphen aan den Rijn, Kluwer Law International, 2023) 388.

[72] F Hendrickx, 'Privacy@work: A Systemic Introduction' in F Hendrickx, D Mangan and E Gramano (eds), *Privacy@work: A European and Comparative Perspective* (Alphen aan den Rijn, Kluwer Law International, 2023) 39.

[73] G Gaudio and J Nogarede, *Worker Data Rights under the GDPR and Beyond: Enforcement and Legal Mobilisation Across the EU* (Bonn, Friedrich-Ebert-Stiftung e.V., 2025); Riso (n 61) at 8.

cedes the *prima facie* right to privacy at work, replacing it instead with a procedural requirement for employers to notify of surveillance.'[74] In addition, we need to consider if there are exceptions to this notification obligation.

It is highly questionable whether these procedural requirements can protect the workers from risks stemming from modern digital surveillance. Surveillance software promises to enable employers to analyse how employees use their time and identify inefficiencies or unproductive behaviours to optimise productivity. However, it cannot be ruled out that the employers use surveillance in a targeted manner, for example, to discipline (certain) employees or to monitor non-work-related activities. For example, in 2024, Amazon was fined by the French Data Protection Authority (*CNIL*) for using an 'excessively intrusive' surveillance system to track the activities of its workers.[75] In the US, Amazon has been accused of using 'intrusive algorithms' as part of a surveillance program to monitor and deter union organising activities.[76] Amazon is by now an infamous example, but there are many more examples of illegal or at least unethical use of employee monitoring technology.[77]

Even if we assume that incongruent monitoring and misuse of employee data can be adequately addressed through existing legal mechanisms, the enforcement of privacy rights will in most cases happen *after* the invasion of privacy has occurred. Enforcement will, furthermore, require action of both affected employees and public enforcement authorities, such as courts or data protections authorities. That is why the question whether the right to privacy includes a right to disconnect is so relevant. The right to disconnect would give the workers the possibility to evade digital surveillance data gathering in the first place.

We are already accustomed to thinking about the right to disconnect in terms of disconnecting from work *outside* the working hours and the working place. However, an interesting question would be whether the right to disconnect should extend to the work-sphere itself. The deployment of digital technology and artificial intelligence is a growing trend across various industries and, the fact is, that workers are increasingly interacting with 'smart' or 'autonomous' digital technology that influences their everyday working life.[78] Do workers have legal grounds to

[74] D Mangan, 'Privacy and Labour Law Traditions' in F Hendrickx and C Hiessl (eds), *The Meaning of Work: A Labour Law Perspective*, Bulletin of Comparative Labour Relations Vol 119 (Alphen aan den Rijn, Kluwer Law International, 2025) 145.

[75] A Cooban, 'Amazon Tracks its French Warehouse Workers to the Second, Regulator Finds' *CNN* (London, 23 January 2024). Available AT: https://edition.cnn.com/2024/01/23/tech/amazon-france-fine-worker-surveillance/index.html.

[76] M Sainato, '"You Feel Like You're in Prison": Workers Claim Amazon's Surveillance Violates Labor Law' *The Guardian* (London, 21 May 2024). Available at: www.theguardian.com/us-news/article/2024/may/21/amazon-surveillance-lawsuit-union.

[77] Examples include other large employers, such as Ikea, H&M and McDonalds.

[78] S Taes, 'Work as a Code: Humanization of Labour in the Robot Age' in F Hendrickx and C Hiessl (eds), *The Meaning of Work: A Labour Law Perspective*, Bulletin of Comparative Labour Relations Vol 119 (Alphen aan den Rijn, Kluwer Law International, 2025) 207.

successfully oppose working with certain types of technological devices or software? Can they oppose digital monitoring altogether?

If we view digital monitoring simply as technological progress, it may seem radical and perhaps impractical to oppose the digitalisation of monitoring. The alternative would be going back to human surveillance only or no monitoring at all. That is perhaps the reason why courts tend to permit (proportionate) digital monitoring of work and the workplace for legitimate reasons. It should be noted, however, that no concrete cases have been yet brought to court on whether workers can successfully oppose certain types of technological devices or software being implemented at the workplace while invoking the right to privacy. Even the GDPR practice shows that the majority of cases still deal with established technologies, like video surveillance and email.[79] The most far-reaching privacy-right is not to be subject to a decision based solely on automated processing which produces legal effects or similarly significantly affects the worker (GDPR, Art 22) but there is no existing right not to be subject to digital monitoring at all. Thus, invoking the right to privacy – on an individual basis – to oppose digital monitoring would probably prove unsuccessful, except for perhaps wearable technology (especially the 'in body' devices), since they may not be deemed proportionate. It seems that workers would be more successful using their collective bargaining rights or their collective consultation and participation rights to stop the introduction of certain types of technology in the workplace; that is, insofar as they have such rights, since these vary across countries.

It might be different, however, when the worker is working from home. Their home could be considered as their most private physical space and workers have high expectations about the protection of their privacy. Indeed, where certain conduct prevents a person from enjoying the amenities of their home or when children are involved, the ECtHR has determined that the invasion is particularly serious.[80] As Hariharan and Noorda argue, where the monitoring is occurring in a work-from-home setting, particularly where there is scope to capture the movements of other family members such as children, there should always be an acknowledgment that the interference is serious.[81] But is there legal ground to oppose certain use of technology by the employer and make surveillance impossible?

Except for some of the countries that have codified a right to disconnect, most countries do not have specific rules addressing privacy when working from home. Instead, the issue tends to be covered by the general provisions on monitoring in the GDPR, the right to privacy and the proportionality of the employer

[79] Gaudio and Nogarede (n 73) at 5.

[80] *Moreno Gomez v Spain* (2005) 41 EHRR 40 para 53; *Söderman v Sweden* (2014) 58 EHRR 36 para 81.

[81] Hariharan and Noorda (n 52) at 349–50.

prerogative.[82] Most legal scholars will probably agree that *constant* surveillance by way of computer cameras, audio devices, or software monitoring activities, etc, when homeworking is not necessary to control the employee's efficiency in tasks and working time. It can be presumed that employees may not be obliged to be connected to a professional digital tool *outside* of working hours. However, this brings us to the above discussion on workers being on stand-by shifts and shows that, again, exceptions are possible on that rule. Furthermore, it cannot be ruled out that less-intrusive monitoring may pass the proportionality test. Labour law scholars also agree that monitoring employees while working from home can have the same objective business purposes as work performed at the workplace. For example, the purposes of monitoring working time and employee duties remain relevant to the employer's interests. They may even gain more weight, 'as the work performed from home cannot be as immediately observed as work performed at the workplace of the employer'.[83]

We may conclude that digitally monitoring employees for what are considered legitimate reasons while they work from home is in principle allowed, if monitoring is proportionate and workers are made aware they are being monitored. The existing privacy-rules may shield workers from excessive and intrusive digital surveillance *if* the rights are being exercised and enforced. There is, however, no legal basis for individual workers to completely exempt themselves from digital monitoring altogether. A right to disconnect provides us with a concept to think about such possibilities.

5 Conclusions

The use of technology in working relationships as discussed in this chapter can be seen as *enabling*, in the sense that it enables workers to – with consent by their employers – work in a more flexible manner and adjust it better to their preferences. However, by doing that they take their work with them into their personal space. This causes the boundaries between work and personal life to blur, as is already the case for a large number of workers. This is already problematic, even though some workers don't mind the blending of work and personal time as it is often accompanied by increased flexibility and a sense of autonomy. Most employers don't mind it either since they benefit from 'nearly round-the-clock accessibility of workers'.[84]

However, the divide is very important. In the first place to protect them from being permanently available to the employer, because this may have serious

[82] F Hendrickx, D Mangan and E Gramano (eds), *Privacy@work: A European and Comparative Perspective* (Alphen aan den Rijn, Kluwer Law International, 2023).

[83] NV Munkholm, 'Privacy at Work in Denmark' in F Hendrickx, D Mangan and E Gramano (eds), *Privacy@work: A European and Comparative Perspective* (Alphen aan den Rijn, Kluwer Law International, 2023) 182.

[84] Eisenstadt (n 9) at 470.

consequences for their health and safety. Working time regulations aim to protect the health and safety of the workers by providing maximum working hours and minimum rest periods. But we have seen that the boundaries between working time and rest time are blurring in legal protection as well. Thus, to protect their health and safety, workers require a right to disconnect. But that is not the only reason why it's important to legally demarcate between work and non-work time. The divide marks off employees' leisure time, their private time in which they can pursue their own goals. In addition, the divide helps workers to establish a work-life balance with hopefully positive effects on their wellbeing. Just as health and safety, this is a public concern as much as the workers' concern.

When the right to disconnect is being debated – is it necessary to introduce such a right? – this is the first matter that is at stake: health and safety of the working population. A right to disconnect – when it's implemented in such a way as to give individual workers a right to swich off the digital connection to work – can empower workers to take measures to protect their private time and their health, especially when it is backed by the insurance that workers who invoke their right to disconnect are protected from victimisation and other negative repercussions.[85]

In addition to disconnecting to live a healthier life and pursuing and enjoying personal instead of professional interests, workers may want to disconnect to protect their privacy. The same digital technology that enables workers to work from home and increase their autonomy can be deployed by employers for surveillance and monitoring. This has been called 'the technology paradox'.[86] As many have already shown, digital surveillance can intrude even more on workers' private lives when they are being monitored at home. Even though the right to disconnect has been primarily associated with working time regulation and availability outside working hours, it can be incorporated in the privacy discussion as well. In fact, it might mean more for privacy purposes than for recovery from work, since it potentially introduces a more radical approach to thinking about privacy rights. Instead of 'merely' aiming to protect workers from the most excessive forms of digital surveillance, the right to disconnect can be a concept that empowers workers and gives them the possibility to make their own decisions on how far they let technology into their lives.

It is, however, also important to ask who can disconnect. Workers with atypical employment contracts, which can usually be terminated more easily than the traditional open-ended contract, might still feel the pressure to always remain available for their employer. It is expected that, in the future, telework, under different modalities, might well become a standard modality of work for many

[85] As opposed to *only* requiring that workers and employers have conversations and work together on workplace policies on availability outside working hours.
[86] Hendrickx (n 49) at 234.

workers.[87] Not only might it result in fragmentation of the working population and inequality between workers who can benefit from this modality of work and workers who cannot, but there might also be a divide between workers who can disconnect and those who cannot. This is why a right to disconnect, besides being backed by the prohibition of adverse treatment, should be part of a greater project aimed at removing differences in the level of labour law protection for the different types of employment contracts that currently exist in Europe.

[87] S Robin-Olivier, 'The Future of Work' in F Hendrickx and C Hiessl (eds), *The Meaning of Work: A Labour Law Perspective*, Bulletin of Comparative Labour Relations Vol 119 (Alphen aan den Rijn, Kluwer Law International, 2025) 27.

6

Labour is Not a Commodity, Employer Authority Is?

The Consumption of Digital Monitoring at Work and its Regulation

MICHELE MOLÈ

1 Introduction

The employer's monitoring power is open-ended and flexible, enabling the observation and assessment of employees as part of ensuring contractual performance, and overseeing compliance with Occupational Safety and Health (OSH) standards.[1] Economic and legal scholarship, from Coase's *The Nature of the Firm* to Macneil's studies on relational contracts, describes this power as one that has evolved over time to adapt to changing organisational needs, technological developments, and legal constraints.[2]

In the digital era, this adaptability increasingly encompasses digital monitoring, where Artificial Intelligence (AI), the Internet of Things (IoT), and other technologies expand the scope and intensity of monitoring.[3] For instance, the AI-powered *Driveri* camera by Netradyne monitors the behaviour of employees such as truck

[1] M Gruber-Risak and T Dullinger, *The Concept of 'Worker' in EU Law: Status Quo and Potential for Change* (Brussels, European Trade Union Institute, 2018) 35–37; see also: A Cefaliello and N Henry, *The Influence of the Court of Justice on EU Health and Safety Legislation: An Analysis of the Case Law (1989–2022)* (Brussels, European Trade Union Institute, 2025).

[2] RH Coase, 'The Nature of the Firm' (1937) 4 *Economica* 386; IR Macneil, 'Relational Contract: What We Do and Do Not Know' (1985) *Wisconsin Law Review* 483.

[3] M Molè, 'The Internet of Things and Artificial Intelligence as Workplace Supervisors: Explaining and Understanding the New Surveillance to Employees Beyond Art. 8 ECHR' (2022) 15(1) *Italian Labour Law e-Journal* 87.

drivers, alerting management when they deviate from established safety standards.[4] Similarly, Deloitte has developed a suite of nine AI 'agents' that extend monitoring capabilities into white-collar environments. These agents, built on Amazon Web Services (AWS) and available via its marketplace, automate Human Resources (HR) processes such as tracking recruitment activities, monitoring employee performance, and analysing workforce trends.[5] Driveri and Deloitte AI Agents are only two examples from a vast market of specialised companies developing and selling workforce monitoring tools.[6]

A well-established finding in the literature is that such tools are spreading across European workplaces and amplify employers' monitoring powers.[7] This trend makes the International Labour Organization (ILO)'s principle that 'Labour is not a commodity' particularly relevant today, raising questions on how to prevent employees from having their freedoms curtailed in algorithmically managed workplaces, constraining their informational, physical and spatial liberty.[8] Accordingly, current legal research investigates whether European Union (EU) legal frameworks – including the General Data Protection Regulation (GDPR), the Artificial Intelligence Act (AI Act), the Platform Work Directive (PWD), and EU non-discrimination law – can hold employers accountable for the use of these technologies and guide their deployment in ways that respect employees' fundamental rights.[9]

[4] Netradyne and Amazon, 'The Power of Vision'. Available at: www.amazon.com/stores/Netradyne/Netradyne/page/3304DF88-2CA0-4498-96B3-28F7F9F1A57C.

[5] 'Workforce Management and Planning' (*Amazon Web Services Marketplace*). Available at: https//aws.amazon.com/marketplace/pp/prodview-mfqalvk3dp5bc?sr=0-5&ref_=beagle&applicationId=AWSMPContessa.

[6] W Negrón, 'Little Tech Is Coming for Workers: A Framework for Reclaiming and Building Worker Power' (CoWorker.org, 2021).

[7] K Ball, *Electronic Monitoring and Surveillance in the Workplace: Literature Review and Policy Recommendations* (Luxembourg, Publications Office of the European Union, 2021); A Ponce Del Castillo and M Molè, 'Worker Monitoring vs Worker Surveillance: The Need for a Legal Differentiation' in A Ponce Del Castillo (ed), *Artificial Intelligence, Labour and Society* (Brussels, European Trade Union Institute, 2024); S Riso, *Employee Monitoring and Surveillance: The Challenges of Digitalisation* (Luxembourg, Publications Office of the European Union, 2020).

[8] On the values implicated by employee monitoring see J Hariharan and H Noorda, 'Imprisoned at Work: The Impact of Employee Monitoring on Physical Privacy and Individual Liberty' (2025) 88 *MLR* 333; see also: A Supiot, 'Labour Is Not a Commodity: The Content and Meaning of Work in the Twenty-First Century' (2021) 160 *International Labour Review* 1; see also: A Perulli, 'The Meaning of Work Between Labour Law and Philosophy' in F Hendrickx and C Hiessl (eds), *The Meaning of Work: A Labour Law Perspective* (Alphen aan den Rijn, Kluwer Law International, 2025).

[9] Regulation 2016/679 of the European Parliament and of the Council on the protection of natural persons with regard to the processing of personal data and on the free movement of such data, and repealing Directive 95/46/EC (General Data Protection Regulation) [2016] OJ L119/1; H Abraha, 'Regulating Algorithmic Employment Decisions through Data Protection Law' (2023) 14 *European Labour Law Journal* 117; Regulation 2024/1689 of the European Parliament and of the Council laying down harmonised rules on artificial intelligence and amending Regulations (EC) No 300/2008, (EU) No 167/2013, (EU) No 168/2013, (EU) 2018/858, (EU) 2018/1139 and (EU) 2019/2144 and Directives 2014/90/EU, (EU) 2016/797 and (EU) 2020/1828 (Artificial Intelligence Act) [2024] OJ L2024/1689; C Cristofolini, 'Navigating the Impact of AI Systems in the Workplace: Strengths and Loopholes of the EU AI Act from a Labour Perspective' (2024) 17 *Italian Labour Law e-Journal* 75; Directive 2024/2831 of the European Parliament and of the Council on improving working conditions in platform work [2024] OJ L2024/2831; M Guglielmetti, 'Automated Work and Workers' Rights: Platform Work and

In this chapter, I challenge the prevailing assumption that the primary focus should be solely on limiting the excessive powers employers hold today. This framing overlooks a fact: the impact on employees' well-being and rights stems from the tools their employers purchase, what I have elsewhere called 'bosses-as-a-service'.[10] I do not dispute the well-established finding that such tools amplify employer authority in subordinate employment. Rather, I argue that the form and scope of this authority are increasingly shaped by the design and operational choices of external providers, and this can significantly influence workplace hierarchies and the dynamics of subordination. In this chapter, I argue that when employers outsource monitoring functions to third-party providers, they may themselves be subject to asymmetries akin to those experienced by consumers under EU law. From this perspective, I propose a new framework for understanding employers' *authority as a commodity in a consumer society* (*authority-commodity*). This framework draws on Bernard Stiegler's critique of consumer society[11] in which the employer is simultaneously a bearer of authority over employees and a consumer of monitoring services – akin to someone subscribing to Spotify or Disney+, effectively purchasing a boss-as-a-service subscription.[12] I then argue that this new understanding of employer authority within the legal debate should guide a new approach to regulating technologies used for employee monitoring. In particular, I contend that regulation should rather focus on which technologies can be developed and marketed to employers, to prevent the workforce from being treated as commodities under algorithmic managers. This frictionless access to online marketplaces and innovative tools, in fact, conceals information and power asymmetries between employers and providers – gaps in knowledge and control that must not be overlooked by scholars, legislators, and courts.[13]

In section 2, I introduce the *authority-commodity* framework and the EU law notion of consumer. Section 3 confronts authority-commodity with the concept of employer authority embedded in EU labour law and the GDPR's data controller

AI Work Management Systems' in A Ponce Del Castillo (ed), *Artificial Intelligence, Labour and Society* (Brussels, European Trade Union Institute, 2024); eg, Council Directive 2000/43/EC implementing the principle of equal treatment between persons irrespective of racial or ethnic origin [2000] OJ L180/22; Council Directive 2000/78/EC establishing a general framework for equal treatment in employment and occupation [2000] OJ L303/16; and Directive 2006/54/EC of the European Parliament and of the Council on the implementation of the principle of equal opportunities and equal treatment of men and women in matters of employment and occupation (recast) [2006] OJ L204/23; F Palmirotta, 'Disruptive, yet Inclusive AI: Solution and Boundaries from a Labour Law Perspective.' (2025) 18 *Italian Labour Law e-Journal* 83; A Aloisi, 'Regulating Algorithmic Management at Work in the European Union: Data Protection, Non-Discrimination and Collective Rights' (2024) 40 *International Journal of Comparative Labour Law and Industrial Relations* 37.

[10] M Molè, 'Commodified, Outsourced Authority: A Research Agenda for Algorithmic Management at Work' (2024) 17 *Italian Labour Law e-Journal* 169.

[11] B Stiegler, *Symbolic Misery. Volume 1: The Hyper-Industrial Epoch* (English edn, Cambridge, Polity Press, 2014); B Stiegler, *Automatic Society* (Cambridge, Polity Press, 2016).

[12] Molè (n 10) at 175.

[13] On some missed opportunities in the European Court of Human Rights case law: M Molè and D Mangan, '"Just More Surveillance": The ECtHR and Workplace Monitoring' (2023) 14 *European Labour Law Journal* 694.

and data processors definitions. In doing so, it critically examines how these legal categories assume that employers can meaningfully control how such technologies process employee data – a premise that often overlooks the significant role of third-party providers in reshaping employer authority. In section 4, I turn to the AI Act as a more suitable framework for regulating authority-commodity. I focus on the Act's prohibitions for providers (Article 5) and the requirements for high-risk systems (Chapter III), as well as its regulation of providers' and deployers' relationship. Section 5 expands the discussion by arguing that regulating digital monitoring requires more specific and stricter rules on what can be developed and sold by providers to employers or other public and private entities. Section 6 concludes the chapter by outlining the key challenges involved in regulating *authority-commodity* and the implications of its consumption by employers.

2 Authority-Commodity: Employers in a Consumer Society

Consider an employer who purchases the AI-enabled *Driveri* camera, installs it, and activates it. Once deployed, the camera issues auditory signals and instructions to drivers regarding appropriate driving behaviour, while a dashboard displays individual traffic compliance indices.[14] The employer neither intervenes in nor determines the criteria that trigger these alerts; such parameters are established by *Netradyne*, the provider, during the system's development. Similarly, an employer subscribing to *Cogito Dialog* (available on AWS Marketplace for $200,000 per year) enables *CogitoCorp* to access customer care phone calls and provide employees with real-time feedback on how to improve their interactions.[15] In both cases, the employer, as the hierarchical superior, delegates specific monitoring functions to the service provider, subscribing to these tools for benefitting from the insights generated by those services.[16]

One might conclude adopting such technologies constitutes an unremarkable exercise of managerial discretion. However, limiting the analysis to the observation that these tools provide employers more insights about the workforce, and, by extension, their authority over employees, neglects an important aspect. When an employer subscribes to a service such as *Cogito Dialog*, they also enter into an end-user licence agreement (EULA) with the provider *CogitoCorp*.[17] This grants a licence to use the product, even though the system is operated and maintained

[14] Netradyne and Amazon (n 4).

[15] 'Cogito Dialog' (*Amazon Web Services Marketplace*). Available at: aws.amazon.com/marketplace/pp/prodview-tw4sqfpoyopzw.

[16] Molè (n 10) at 174.

[17] M McRoberts, 'Software Licensing in the Cloud Age' (2013) 3 *The International Journal of soft Computing and Software Engineering* 395.

externally as software-as-a-service (SaaS).[18] In such arrangements, monitoring functions are not fully internalised within the organisation but are mediated, sustained and, to some degree, controlled by an external entity, under contractual terms that may influence the scope and nature of the employer's authority.[19]

This contractual structure positions the employer not only as a hierarchical superior but also as a user of service supplied by a third party. That peculiar capacity to monitor and assess employees' voice through *Cogito Dialog*, is acquired only through the purchase of a licensed service from *CogitoCorp* rather than being generated within the employer's organisational apparatus. In this sense, authority over employees becomes intertwined with a commodity form: subscribed to, updated and maintained much like any other SaaS product. This is the premise of the present *authority-commodity* framework, in which the employer is simultaneously the bearer of managerial authority and a customer in the market for surveillance technologies. Recognising this dual position is crucial to understanding not only the expansion of monitoring powers but also the redistribution of informational and decision-making capacities between employers and technology providers.[20]

Stiegler's account on consumption and authority provides a critical lens for situating this transformation. In his analysis, a consumer society is defined by the capture and control by industry of all 'retentional processes' – the means by which memory, knowledge, and behaviour are created and reproduced in a society – including those most intimate to human subjectivity.[21] Under these conditions, memory, knowledge, and behaviour are subsumed into technical and economic systems.[22] When employers consume workplace monitoring technologies, this process can extend to authority itself, as a relational activity, which becomes mediated and shaped by the technological and commercial logics of the providers. The outsourcing of monitoring functions to third-party providers can be read as part of this broader process: the managerial role itself is increasingly 'grammatised' into operational protocols embedded in technological systems, shifting the locus of control from human judgement to automated, externalised processes.[23] As Stiegler observes, this produces a 'becoming-machine' of the managerial worker,

[18] SJJ Gould, 'Measuring Work Is Hard. Subcontracting It Won't Help. Explainable AI Won't Help' in A Ponce Del Castillo (ed), *Artificial intelligence, Labour and Society* (Brussels, European Trade Union Institute, 2024).

[19] Molè (n 10) at 175–76.

[20] Agre observes that algorithmic management tools do more than monitor, they encode 'grammars of action,' formal representations of workplace activities translated into machine-readable units. In subscribing to such systems, employers adopt not just a tool but an embedded model of how work should be structured and evaluated, effectively accepting the technology provider's conception of management. See: PE Agre, 'Surveillance and Capture: Two Models of Privacy' (1994) 10 *The Information Society* 101, 108–09; PE Agre, 'From High Tech to Human Tech: Empowerment, Measurement, and Social Studies of Computing' (1995) 3 *Computer Supported Cooperative Work (CSCW)* 167.

[21] Stiegler defines a consumer society a 'hyper-industrialised' one. In this contribution I use 'consumer society'.

[22] Stiegler, *Symbolic Misery* (n 11) at 62–63.

[23] Agre 'Surveillance and Capture' (n 20) at 108–09.

whose authority is exercised less through direct coordination and more through the consumption of ready-made governance solutions.[24]

In this context, we can start to view employer authority as a social relationship undergoing commodification, transforming into a service that can be exchanged on the market. This shift creates something similar to a consumption dynamic where employers, driven by specific needs or influenced by traditional product marketing, seek out solutions in the market. They then outsource certain authoritative functions (eg performance assessment) to companies like *CogitoCorp* for specialised managerial or supervisory functions. In return, they receive a dashboard with insights, observations and optimisation recommendations.[25]

Outsourcing to seek external expertise (for instance, consulting an external firm for advice on OSH or workflow design) is common for companies as it provides employers with additional information to inform their managerial judgement while leaving the final decision and its rationale within the organisation. By contrast, outsourcing the entire decision-making process – as in the case of *Cogito Dialog*, where performance insights are generated automatically through continuous data collection and algorithmic evaluation – transfers not merely knowledge but the very exercise of employers' assessment which has repercussions on the employment relationship. In this configuration, managerial authority is no longer simply supported by technology but performed through it, effectively relocating the interpretive and normative dimensions of management to the technological infrastructure itself.[26]

This contrasts with the traditional view of the employer as an all-powerful figure, highlighting instead the reality of a non-specialised agent purchasing complex information technology services from companies that design and manage sophisticated forms of data-driven authority. Agents such as consumers that, indeed, have peculiar and different status from the one usually attributed to an employer. The latter might in fact purchase an digital monitoring service of which does not fully grasp the functionalities or potential harms over working conditions.[27] Reducing these harms – that is raising awareness and provide information to consumers purchasing the product – can be done by 'ensuring [that] goods and services are more likely to be in line with realistic consumer expectations based on reliable information'.[28] This implies that if certain services/products prove to be not legally

[24] Stiegler, *Symbolic Misery* (n 11) at 59; Stiegler, *Automatic Society* (n 11) at 18.

[25] Molè (n 10).

[26] ibid.

[27] US Amazon apologised and changed some features of the AI cameras and the work schedule of drivers after trade unions brought to the public press multiple cases of workers peeing in bottles to skip proper toilet breaks due for the subtle pressure coming from all sorts of surveillance from cameras and other tools, even if they were mainly implemented for OSH standards. See 'Amazon Apologises for Wrongly Denying Drivers Need to Urinate in Bottles' *BBC* (London, 4 April 2021) Available at: www.bbc.com/news/world-us-canada-56628745.

[28] G Howells, 'The Potential and Limits of Consumer Empowerment by Information' (2005) 32 *Journal of Law and Society* 349, 355.

compliant (with, for instance, OSH or fundamental labour standards) or to have other ethical issues, consumers might decide not to reward that product by purchasing it.[29]

2.1 Comparing Employers to EU Consumers

When employers purchase and rely on workplace monitoring technologies, they enter into relationships with providers that are not unlike those of consumers engaging with branded goods or services. While EU consumer law formally defines a 'consumer' only a natural person acting outside the scope of their trade, business, craft, or profession (see, eg, Article 2(1) of Directive 2011/83/EU on consumer rights and Article 2(a) of Directive 2005/29/EC on unfair commercial practices), the structural imbalances between employers and technology providers often mirror the asymmetries addressed in the consumer law protection framework.[30] Despite acting squarely within their professional capacity, employers may nonetheless encounter the same informational and power asymmetries that consumer law seeks to address. I draw this parallel between employers and consumers to highlight the need to better understand the contractual and operational dependencies involved.[31]

Unlike ordinary consumers, employers occupy the apex of the organisational hierarchy, with agency and responsibility for shaping the organisation they establish. Both labour laws and the GDPR place on employers a duty to design and implement monitoring tools in a way that complies with applicable legislation (see section 3). Yet this position of authority within the firm might not exempt employers from asymmetries of knowledge and control when dealing with external technology providers. In the following sections I show that these potential asymmetries create a structural tension: the law assumes that employers can shape and control such tools, while in practice their understanding and choices may be constrained by the technological and commercial prerogatives of third-party providers.[32] In this sense, although employers do not neatly fit the category of consumer, that EU law category offers a useful analytical lens. It highlights the informational and power asymmetries between vendors and customers and the protection needs arising from this relationship. I now turn to show how EU

[29] CN Markou, *Consumer Protection, Automated Shopping Platforms and EU Law* (Abingdon, Routledge, 2020) 19–20.

[30] '"Consumer" means any natural person who, in contracts covered by this Directive, is acting for purposes which are outside his trade, business, craft or profession'; '"consumer" means any natural person who, in commercial practices covered by this Directive, is acting for purposes which are outside his trade, business, craft or profession'.

[31] AI Act, art 79(1): 'AI systems presenting a risk shall be understood as a "product presenting a risk" as defined in Regulation (EU) 2019/1020, Article 3, point 19, in so far as they present risks to the health or safety, or to fundamental rights, of persons.'; Molè (n 10) at 183.

[32] M Kalsi, 'Still Losing the Race with Technology? Understanding the Scope of Data Controllers' Responsibility to Implement Data Protection by Design and by Default' (2024) 38 *International Review of Law, Computers & Technology* 346.

labour law and data protection law rarely regulate the employer as a natural/legal person acting outside their trade or profession and in need of empowerment. Instead, they conceive of the employer as an organisational actor presumed to possess a high level of agency and responsibility to shape and control monitoring practices, whether through traditional methods or complex data processing of employees' data.

3 Employer Authority in EU Labour Law and Data Protection Law

What is the notion of employer authority in EU labour law and data protection law? Starting with EU labour law, the EU so far has not issued a framework directive on employment; we thus find directives on aspects of employment (eg working hours, work-life balance, transfer of undertakings).[33] By taking a case law perspective, however, the Court of Justice of the European Union (CJEU) offers useful guidance in defining what is employer authority.[34] One of the essential elements of an employment relationship, the Court has clarified, is 'that for a certain period of time a person performs services for and under the direction of another person'.[35] In *Lawrie-Blum*, for example, the Court confirmed the existence of an employment relationship by noting that the employee (a teacher) was under the direction and monitoring of the school, which oversaw the tasks performed and monitored the start and end of working hours.[36] From this line of CJEU case law, it follows that from a EU labour law perspective employers' authority can be defined as the authority to verify an employee's compliance with instructions and assess work performance.[37] This means that employers, as the apex of the organisational

[33] Directive 2003/88/EC of the European Parliament and of the Council concerning certain aspects of the organisation of working time [2003] OJ L299/9; Directive 2019/1158 of the European Parliament and of the Council of on work–life balance for parents and carers and repealing Council Directive 2010/18/EU [2019] OJ L188/79; Council Directive 2001/23/EC of on the approximation of the laws of the Member States relating to the safeguarding of employees' rights in the event of transfers of undertakings, businesses or parts of undertakings or businesses [2008] OJ L82/16; N Kountouris, 'The Concept of "Worker" in European Labour Law: Fragmentation, Autonomy and Scope' (2018) 47 *Industrial Law Journal* 192.

[34] For a review of the CJEU case law see Risak and Dullinger (n 1).

[35] Case C-66/85 *Deborah Lawrie-Blum v Land Baden-Württemberg* ECLI:EU:C:1986:284, [1986] ECR 02121, para 17; see also in this regard similar findings of the ECJ: Case C-197/86 *Steven Malcolm Brown v The Secretary of State for Scotland* ECLI:EU:C:1988:323, [1988] ECR 03205, para 21; Case C-344/87 *I. Bettray v Staatssecretaris van Justitie* ECLI:EU:C:1989:226, [1989] ECR 01621, para 14; Case C-94/07 *Andrea Raccanelli v Max-Planck-Gesellschaft zur Förderung der Wissenschaften eV* ECLI:EU:C:2008:425, [2008] ECR I-05939, para 34.

[36] Case C-66/85 *Deborah Lawrie-Blum v Land Baden-Württemberg* ECLI:EU:C:1986:284, [1986] ECR 02121, para 18; see further with Case C-256/01 *Debra Allonby v Accrington & Rossendale College and Others* ECLI:EU:C:2004:18, [2004] ECR I-00873, para 72; see also the CJEU case law review from Risak and Dullinger (n 1).

[37] See also in this regard: Case C-270/13 *Iraklis Haralambidis. v Calogero Casilli* ECLI:EU:C:2014:2185, [2014] (CFI 5 June 2014), Opinion of AG Wahl, para 30.

hierarchy, hold both a greater degree of power over employees and a deeper, more continuous understanding of their work and behaviour. Moreover, this authority is open-ended in nature: the intensity, quality, and pace of work can rarely be fully anticipated in contractual terms, and the law thus entrusts the employer with the power to monitor how the organisation and individuals work.[38] Employers, however, must ensure that the exercise of this authority is compliant with existing legislation, whether it concerns OSH requirements, privacy protections, or other relevant regulatory frameworks.[39]

By examining EU data protection law, we can observe that the GDPR frames employer authority in terms that are analogous to those found in EU labour law. When collecting data for organisational, performance assessment or security purposes, the employer acts as a data controller within the meaning of Article 4(7) of the GDPR – that is, a natural or legal person determining the purposes and means of processing employees' personal data.[40] As the hierarchical superior, the controller is presumed capable of ensuring that any data processing, including through external technologies, complies with the GDPR (Articles 24–25).[41] Article 24 makes controllers responsible for implementing technical and organisational measures to ensure and demonstrate compliance, while Article 25 requires data protection by design and by default, integrating safeguards and limiting data collection to what is necessary for specific purposes.[42]

When employers purchase AI or IoT-enabled technologies, the technology provider typically acts as a processor under Article 4(8) of the GDPR, processing data on behalf of the controller and only according to its documented instructions (Article 28(3)(a)). Controllers must choose processors offering 'sufficient guarantees' of compliance with the GDPR (Article 28(1)). When an employer signs an agreement with a processor, the latter must assist with certain obligations – such as handling data subject requests (Article 28(3)(e)) and supporting Data Protection Impact Assessments (Article 28(3)(f)) – yet they are not directly bound by core principles like data protection by design and by default. The GDPR thus assumes that employers, as controllers, have the technical capacity to select GDPR-compliant processors and oversee their compliance during data processing activities.[43] Data

[38] J Carby-Hall, 'The Contractual Nature of Social Law' (2003) 45 *Managerial Law* 23, 34.

[39] A Aloisi and E Gramano, 'Artificial Intelligence Is Watching You at Work. Digital Surveillance, Employee Monitoring, and Regulatory Issues in the EU Context' (2019) 41 *Comparative Labor Law & Policy Journal* 95.

[40] 'Opinion 02/2017 on Data Processing at Work' (23 June 2017). Available at: https//ec.europa.eu/newsroom/article29/items/610169/en; see also: Abraha (n 9).

[41] E Koulierakis, 'The Challenge of Incorporating Legal Rules into Digital Applications: A Theoretical Exploration of Art 25 GDPR' (2022) 18 *Illyrius – International Scientific Review* 35.

[42] European Data Protection Board, 'Guidelines 4/2019 on Article 25: Data Protection by Design and by Default' (20 October 2020). Available at: www.edpb.europa.eu/sites/default/files/files/file1/edpb_guidelines_201904_dataprotection_by_design_and_by_default_v2.0_en.pdf.

[43] GDPR, art 28(1): 'Where processing is to be carried out on behalf of a controller, the controller shall use only processors providing sufficient guarantees to implement appropriate technical and organisational measures in such a manner that processing will meet the requirements of this Regulation and ensure the protection of the rights of the data subject.'

Protection Authorities (DPAs) have reinforced this through enforcement actions – such as the Italian DPA's fine against *Wind Tre* for inadequate processor oversight and the Spanish DPA's fine against *Vodafone* for similar failures.[44] However, if a processor independently determines the purposes and means of processing, it becomes a joint controller under Article 26, sharing full accountability with the employer.[45] CJEU case law confirms that identifying who effectively determines purposes and means is essential for assigning responsibility.[46]

In conclusion, in EU labour law, authority arises from the employer's position at the apex of the organisational hierarchy and consists of the right to direct, monitor, and assess the employees' activities. Similarly, under EU data protection law, the GDPR conceptualises employer authority through the figure of the data controller, who determines the purposes and means of personal data processing. This framing mirrors the managerial authority recognised in labour law, insofar as the controller bears responsibility for ensuring lawful, fair, and proportionate data processing, including when delegating operations to processors. Both frameworks thus construct employer authority as a form of hierarchical power and complete agency, i.e. a capacity to rationally act, decide and comply with the law.

3.1 Employers Consuming Digital Monitoring Tools of Third Parties: Problems of Accountability

I argue that the notion of employer authority outlined by EU labour law and data protection law presents important problems when faced with the phenomenon outlined in section 2 ('Authority-commodity: employers in a consumer society'). Even the notion of joint controllership (GDPR, Article 26) is hardly applicable in employment contexts. As seen in section 2, employers seeking to use *Cogito Dialog*'s services aim to integrate this type of data processing into their operations. They enter into an end-user licence agreement (EULA) for the SaaS product, without owning the software or having any real capacity to alter the processing activities. In this sense, I suggest, employers adopt the means and purposes of processing

[44] 'Ordinanza ingiunzione nei confronti di Wind Tre S.p.A. - 9 luglio 2020 [9435753]' (*Garante Per La Protezione Dei Dati Personali*, 9 July 2020). Available at: www.gpdp.it/web/guest/home/docweb/-/docweb-display/docweb/9435753; 'Procedimiento Nº: PS/00059/2020' (*Agencia Española de Protección de Datos*, 2021). Available at: www.aepd.es/documento/ps-00059-2020.pdf; see also: Kalsi (n 32) at 357.

[45] C Millard and D Kamarinou, 'Article 26 Joint Controllers' in C Kuner et al (eds), *The EU General Data Protection Regulation (GDPR): A Commentary* (New York, Oxford University Press, 2020); see also European Data Protection Board, 'Guidelines 07/2020 on the Concepts of Controller and Processor in the GDPR' (7 July 2020). Available at: www.edpb.europa.eu/our-work-tools/our-documents/guidelines/guidelines-072020-concepts-controller-and-processor-gdpr_en 27–28.

[46] Case C-131/12 *Google Spain SL and Google Inc. v Agencia Española de Protección de Datos (AEPD) and Mario Costeja González* ECLI:EU:C:2014:317, [2014], para 34; Case C-210/16 *Unabhängiges Landeszentrum für Datenschutz Schleswig-Holstein v Wirtschaftsakademie Schleswig-Holstein GmbH* ECLI:EU:C:2018:388, [2018], para 28; Case C-40/17 *Fashion ID GmbH & Co KG v Verbraucherzentrale NRW eV* ECLI:EU:C:2019:629 [2019], para 66.

predefined by *Cogito Dialog* and make them their own, motivated by the interest to monitor their customer service employees. The resulting data is then used by employers in their capacity as data controllers: to manage, monitor, and discipline employees. *Cogito Dialog*, in turn, as the processor, collects and processes the data on behalf of the employer, even though the latter has no control or understanding of how the service works and whether it complies with the GDPR. This places the employer in a position closer to someone acting outside the scope of their trade, business, craft, or profession, using a pre-configured digital service.

Controllers consuming AI and IoT-enabled technologies may lack the expertise to know what information to request processors, especially when complex data processing is involved. This creates an asymmetry, as controllers depend on processors to disclose relevant details, leaving them poorly equipped to assess compliance risks.[47] Kalsi, in this regard, observes that Article 25 of the GDPR (on data protection by design and by default) assumes controllers can influence processors, turning it into a vague catch-all that undermines robust data protection through technology design.[48]

This gap is further illustrated in the Data Protection Impact Assessment (DPIA) under Article 35 of the GDPR. This assessment requires employers, prior to the data processing, to identify, assess, and mitigate risks to individuals' rights and freedoms arising from high-risk personal data-processing activities. Even in this instance, although processors are often better placed to conduct a DPIA, responsibility still remains with the data controller. Processors are obliged to assist in the draft of a DPIA only when 'necessary' and upon explicit request of the data controller (GDPR, Article 28(3)(f), Recital 95), restricting the flow of critical technical information.[49] This reliance on controllers to know what to ask for is especially problematic with opaque or adaptive AI systems. For example, *Cogito Dialog* analyses paralinguistic features of employee prosody in ways that are neither transparent nor stable, making it nearly impossible for an employer to identify what questions to raise or what risks to audit.[50] While Article 28(3)(f) of the GDPR requires processors to make information available and contribute to audits, the provision presupposes that controllers understand the system well enough to target their requests. In practice, this

[47] ibid.

[48] Kalsi (n 32) at 352–53.

[49] M Molè, 'Lost in Translation: Is Data Protection Labour Law Protection?' (2025) 45 *Comparative Labor Law & Policy Journal* 553.

[50] Systems like *Cogito Dialog* rely on prosodic cues – such as intonation, rhythm, stress, and pauses – to draw inferences about an employee's emotional state or engagement. Yet prosody is highly language- and culture-dependent. Speakers using a second language, those with regional accents, or individuals with speech impairments may display prosodic patterns that diverge from the 'norm' embedded in the training data. This creates a risk of discriminatory outcomes, as such employees may be misclassified as disengaged, stressed, or uncooperative, not because of their actual performance or emotional state but because the system encodes majority-language prosodic standards as benchmarks of 'appropriate' communication; see for instance: V Shakuf et al, 'Processing Emotional Prosody in a Foreign Language: The Case of German and Hebrew' (2022) 6 *Journal of Cultural Cognitive Science* 251.

asymmetry of knowledge means that controllers are unable to exercise meaningful oversight, leaving accountability obligations under the GDPR at risk of becoming purely formalistic.[51]

I argue that this demonstrates how processors, by developing and marketing such technologies, can significantly shape the exercise of employer authority. These tools substitute functions that were previously exercised directly by the employer, such as assessing employee performance, verifying compliance or enforcing contractual obligations. In other words, the relational and hierarchical judgement that underpins employer authority is partially outsourced to a machine. While employers may require specialised expertise to manage complex organisational needs, the consumerisation of what is fundamentally a relational and hierarchical function raises risks: it shifts agency away from the human employer, embeds opaque decision-making into workplace practices, and can undermine the enjoyment of employees' fundamental rights.[52]

4 Closing the Accountability Gap: Providers' Duties Under the AI Act

Regulating digital monitoring technologies in a way that restores employers' agency over the tools they deploy is essential for safeguarding employees' rights – just as consumer law seeks to empower individuals to make informed and responsible choices in the marketplace. Because AI and IoT-enabled technologies can substitute functions that were traditionally exercised through human judgement, empowering employers to understand, control, and meaningfully oversee these tools ensures that hierarchical authority remains both responsible and accountable. Notably, the EU appears to move in this direction with the AI Act, whose adoption represents an important first step in bridging the gap between controllers and processors and in regulating the deployment of high-risk monitoring technologies in a way that aligns with fundamental rights.[53]

The Regulation places most obligations on AI providers – such are, for instance, *Netradyne* or *CogitoCorp* – to steer AI systems development before and during their use. According to Article 3(3), a 'provider' is

> a natural or legal person, public authority, agency or other body that develops an AI system or a general-purpose AI model or that has an AI system or a general-purpose

[51] Molè (n 49).
[52] Molè (n 10).
[53] The AI Act is only applicable to AI systems as defined by art 3(1): '"AI system" means a machine-based system that is designed to operate with varying levels of autonomy and that may exhibit adaptiveness after deployment, and that, for explicit or implicit objectives, infers, from the input it receives, how to generate outputs such as predictions, content, recommendations, or decisions that can influence physical or virtual environments'. Recital 12 specifies that AI system's notion 'should not cover systems that are based on the rules defined solely by natural persons to automatically execute operations.'

AI model developed and places it on the market or puts the AI system into service under its own name or trademark, whether for payment or free of charge.

This includes companies that create, sell, or operate AI systems for employee monitoring. Providers must register themselves and their high-risk systems (Article 49) in the EU Commission's database, as outlined in Article 6 and Annex III (Article 71), except for banned systems under Article 5, which cannot be marketed.

Article 3(4), instead, defines 'deployers' a 'natural or legal person, public authority, agency or other body using an AI system under its authority except where the AI system is used in the course of a personal non-professional activity'. Deployers are the primary recipients of protection in the Regulation. Recital 5 highlights the risk to the public interest and fundamental rights under Union law, which may result in physical, psychological, societal or economic harm. This is particularly relevant in workplaces, where AI can negatively affect working conditions and increase the likelihood of disproportionate disciplinary actions.[54] Recitals 28 and 29 highlight how AI can be misused for manipulative, exploitative and socially controlling practices, which violate EU values such as human dignity, freedom, equality and non-discrimination. As stated in Recitals 6, 7 and 8, the Regulation ultimately seeks to strike a balance by fostering innovation and the uptake of AI, while at the same time ensuring that deployers are equipped to prevent these risks. In doing so, the AI Act frames empowerment of deployers not only as a condition for trustworthy AI adoption but also as a necessary safeguard for the fundamental rights of those affected, particularly employees in the workplace.[55]

To ensure AI serves European citizens and workers, the AI Act adopts a risk-based approach in Chapter III. This framework distinguishes between different levels of risk. At the highest level, certain AI practices are prohibited under Article 5, such as manipulative or exploitative techniques that distort human behaviour, social scoring by public authorities, or biometric categorisation using sensitive data. Beneath this category, high-risk AI systems are defined in Articles 6 and 7 and listed in Annex III, which expressly includes AI used for the employee monitoring. These systems must comply with the obligations set out in Articles 8 to 15, including requirements for risk management, data governance, transparency, human oversight and robustness. AI systems considered to present only limited risk are regulated by Article 52, which imposes transparency duties such as informing individuals when they are interacting with AI. Finally, AI systems that are regarded as posing minimal or no risk and, as indicated in Recital 60, may be freely developed and deployed without further regulatory constraints. This approach ensures that the strictest safeguards apply where the risks to fundamental

[54] PT Kim and MT Bodie, 'Artificial Intelligence and the Challenges of Workplace Discrimination and Privacy' (2021) 35 *Journal of Labor and Employment Law* 289.

[55] P Van Eecke and B Regenhardt, 'Article 2 Scope' in CN Pehlivan, N Forgó and V Peggy (eds), *The EU Artificial Intelligence (AI) Act: A Commentary* (Alphen aan den Rijn, Wolters Kluwer, 2024).

rights are most serious, particularly in the context of workplace monitoring, while leaving space for innovation in low-risk applications.[56]

Article 5 of the AI Act prohibits certain AI applications that pose unacceptable risks to EU fundamental rights and values, some of which are highly relevant in the employment context. While many prohibitions target public spaces or criminal justice, four provisions may affect workplace uses of AI. Article 5(1)(b) prohibits systems exploiting vulnerabilities linked to age, disability, or socio-economic dependence, a clause that could encompass the inherent economic vulnerability of employees, though current Commission guidelines remain vague on this point.[57] Article 5(1)(c) bans AI-based social scoring, which may capture workplace practices aggregating personal or behavioural data beyond job-related criteria, but again the guidelines provide little clarity on employment-specific applications.[58] By contrast, Article 5(1)(f) explicitly addresses the workplace, prohibiting AI systems that infer emotions, except for narrow safety or medical purposes, with Recital 44 recognising the power imbalance in employment relationships. Finally, Article 5(1)(g) prohibits biometric categorisation to infer sensitive traits such as race, religion, sexual orientation or trade union membership, thereby directly safeguarding workers from discriminatory monitoring practices. Together, these provisions signal the legislator's awareness of the risk AI systems pose in the employment context.

It is unclear whether and how these prohibitions will be enforceable due to some ambiguities in their formulation.[59] One relevant fact emerges, however: the European legislator begins to determine which technologies (and purposes) can enter the market and which cannot. This is a substantial difference with the GDPR: especially if we consider that employee monitoring, ex Article 6 Annex III, is considered as a 'high risk' implementation of AI systems.[60] AI systems developed for employee monitoring must comply with the requirements of Articles 8–49 before entering the market. A key requirement is the establishment of a comprehensive risk management system, as specified in Article 9. This system must be

[56] P Van Eecke and B Regenhardt, 'Article 1 Subject Matter' in CN Pehlivan, N Forgó and V Peggy (eds), *The EU Artificial Intelligence (AI) Act: A Commentary* (Alphen aan den Rijn, Wolters Kluwer, 2024); Van Eecke and Regenhardt (n 55).

[57] 'Commission Guidelines on Prohibited Artificial Intelligence Practices Established by Regulation (EU) 2024/1689 (AI Act)' (*European Commission*, 29 July 2025). Available at: https//digital-strategy.ec.europa.eu/en/library/commission-publishes-guidelines-prohibited-artificial-intelligence-ai-practices-defined-ai-act 33–50.

[58] ibid 54–55.

[59] S Marassi, 'The Prohibition of AI Emotion Recognition Technologies in the Workplace under the AI Act' (*Global Workplace Law & Policy*, 14 April 2025). Available at: https:// legalblogs.wolterskluwer.com/global-workplace-law-and-policy/the-prohibition-of-ai-emotion-recognition-technologies-in-the-workplace-under-the-ai-act/.

[60] The Regulation acknowledges that rigidly defining AI use cases in law risks becoming outdated given the rapid pace of technological advancement. To address this, arts 7(1) and 97 grant the EU Commission the authority to update Annex III by adding or modifying high-risk AI systems. However, this power is limited by art 7(2), which requires the Commission to consider specific criteria, including the system's purpose, its prevalence in the EU market, the nature and scale of data processed, any harm to fundamental rights and the power imbalances where the system is used, such as in workplaces.

integrated into the AI's lifecycle, involving continuous risk assessment, mitigation measures and real-world testing before commercialisation. In addition, Article 10 mandates data governance practices. Providers must ensure that training, validation, and testing data are managed appropriately, reflecting the AI system's intended use and contextual factors. This includes considering the specific characteristics of the environment in which the AI will operate. Article 11 requires the creation and maintenance of technical documentation that demonstrates compliance with the Regulation. This should include system logs to facilitate monitoring, risk identification and post-market oversight. Furthermore, Articles 13 and 14 provide for transparency and effective human oversight. Providers must design AI systems in a way that allows deployers to interpret and monitor their outputs, with clear instructions on system operation, limitations and maintenance. Deployers must be equipped to oversee and, if necessary, override AI decisions to ensure the system does not compromise fundamental rights or safety.[61]

Without going further into the details of the AI Act, we can already clearly see what underscores this new piece of legislation: the deployer – the employer, in our instance – as that 'weak party' of service contracts with AI providers. This is, moreover, clearly acknowledged later in Article 79(1), which reads as follows:

> AI systems presenting a risk shall be understood as a 'product presenting a risk' as defined in Article 3, point 19 of Regulation (EU) 2019/1020, in so far as they present risks to the health or safety, or to fundamental rights, of persons.[62]

According to that definition, a product presenting a risk is one that may adversely affect health and safety, including in the workplace, beyond what is considered reasonable or acceptable under normal or foreseeable conditions of use. In this light, the AI Act treats the deployer much like a consumer of potentially hazardous products – someone who requires protection, transparency and reliable information to make responsible use of complex technologies.

The AI Act thus fills the informational and accountability gaps left by the GDPR. Whereas the GDPR relies on controllers to 'extract' information from processors, the AI Act shifts responsibility upstream, requiring providers to deliver risk management frameworks, technical documentation, and human oversight mechanisms. This ensures that even if a provider has minimal duties under Article 28 of the GDPR as a processor, it remains accountable as a developer of high-risk AI.[63] As a result, even if

[61] Cristofolini (n 9).

[62] More specifically EU Regulation 2019/1020, Art 3, point 19 defines 'product presenting a risk means a product having the potential to affect adversely health and safety of persons in general, health and safety in the workplace, … protected by the applicable Union harmonisation legislation, to a degree which goes beyond that considered reasonable and acceptable in relation to its intended purpose or under the normal or reasonably foreseeable conditions of use of the product concerned, including the duration of use and, where applicable, its putting into service, installation and maintenance requirements'.

[63] A Aloisi and V De Stefano, 'Between Risk Mitigation and Labour Rights Enforcement: Assessing the Transatlantic Race to Govern AI-Driven Decision-Making through a Comparative Lens' (2023) 14 *European Labour Law Journal* 283.

not framed in explicit terms, employers benefit from a form of consumer protection law, being shielded from the risks of informational disadvantage and over-reliance on potentially hazardous technologies for employees' rights.[64]

5 Consumption of Work Surveillance: Reflections and Future Directions for (Effective) Regulation

While the regulation of digital monitoring at work may be advancing through the lens of consumer law in the AI Act, labour law continues to grapple with a long-standing construct: the employer is the head of the enterprise, responsible for establishing and managing hierarchies, while bearing all associated risks – not only economic, but also compliance with national and supranational labour standards.[65] How does this legal construct align with an employer who, like any ordinary e-commerce customer, purchases services or technologies based on marketing claims, often beyond their full comprehension?

When discussing workplace monitoring regulation, moreover, it is crucial to consider the unique needs and values of labour law, which differ from other fields.[66] 'Labour is not a commodity' underscores a range of economic and social issues that have gained renewed relevance with increasing digitalisation.[67] This principle addresses contractual imbalances, not merely by informing and empowering individuals like consumer protection laws, but by imposing minimum standards to safeguard employees' dignity.[68] These standards cover critical aspects such as working hours, wages, privacy and OSH, ensuring that the protection of employee goes beyond market dynamics.[69] In other words, addressing labour issues solely through technology-focused policies risks overlooking core values essential to labour law protection.[70]

Take the example of the *Driveri* camera: the camera's constant monitoring, which micromanages drivers' actions has created a climate of fear among workers in some companies.[71] This fear has led to extreme behaviours, such as drivers

[64] Molè (n 10) at 183–84.

[65] SJJ Gould, 'Stochastic Machine Witnesses at Work: Today's Critiques of Taylorism Are Inadequate for Workplace Surveillance Epistemologies of the Future' *Proceedings of the CHI Conference on Human Factors in Computing Systems (CHI '24)* (Honolulu, 2024) 1.

[66] G Davidov, *A Purposive Approach to Labour Law* (Oxford, Oxford University Press, 2016) 45–54.

[67] Supiot (n 8).

[68] Davidov (n 66).

[69] L Ratti, 'The Sword and the Shield: The Directive on Adequate Minimum Wages in the EU' (2023) 52 *Industrial Law Journal* 477; Cefaliello and Henry (n 1); A Cefaliello, PV Moore and R Donoghue, 'Making Algorithmic Management Safe and Healthy for Workers: Addressing Psychosocial Risks in New Legal Provisions' (2023) 14 *European Labour Law Journal* 192; H Collins, 'Is the Contract of Employment Illiberal?' in H Collins, G Lester and V Mantouvalou (eds), *Philosophical Foundations of Labour Law* (Oxford, Oxford University Press, 2018).

[70] Molè (n 49).

[71] Netradyne and Amazon (n 4).

urinating in bottles during their routes to avoid being flagged for toilet breaks by the system to their managers.[72] This crude example highlights the significant power and information asymmetries present in work environments, which extend into the social and economic lives of workers. Losing a job, having a family, struggles with debt, create vulnerabilities that make employees more likely to endure degrading conditions.[73] Labour law exists to regulate these imbalances and ensure that the weaker party is protected from having to accept such conditions. European legislation should thus have a uniform and harmonised approach for the regulation of all digital tools at work – legislation that is not just limited to platform work.[74]

An ideal labour law-orientated solution could go beyond the current framework based on technology-specific regulation inspired by consumer law-style protections.[75] As I have shown in section IV of this chapter, the combined application of the GDPR and the AI Act provides safeguards. Yet these instruments only cover a subset of the technologies currently used in workplaces. The AI Act applies solely to 'AI systems' as defined in Article 3(1), leaving outside its scope a wide range of digital monitoring tools that employers routinely deploy. For instance, IoT devices such as radio-frequency identification badges and wearable sensors can be used to track workers' physical movements or productivity rates; HR management systems often include time-logging and keystroke-tracking functions that measure efficiency; these tools are commonly installed on corporate laptops or smartphones, records screenshots, application use, and even GPS locations. These systems can profoundly affect working conditions and employee autonomy without necessarily qualifying as AI systems. The requirements of the AI Act do not extend to non-AI monitoring technologies. Nor can the GDPR alone resolve these concerns, as it leaves unaddressed the structural power imbalances inherent in the employment relationship.[76]

By contrast, the Platform Work Directive (PWD) introduces a labour-law orientated approach in Chapter III ('Algorithmic Management'); however, this applies only to digital labour platforms and individuals performing platform work.[77]

[72] 'Amazon Apologises for Wrongly Denying Drivers Need to Urinate in Bottles' (n 27). On the impact of digital monitoring on the meaning of employees' work see G Jansen et al 'Watched but Not Seen: Electronic Employee Monitoring as Workplace Imprisonment and Its Effect on Social Recognition' (2025) *Sociology*. Available at: https//journals.sagepub.com/doi/10.1177/00380385251359077.

[73] M Niezna, 'Consent to Labour Exploitation' (2024) 53 *Industrial Law Journal* 3; M Niezna and G Davidov, 'Consent in Contracts of Employment' (2023) 86 *MLR* 1134.

[74] Directive 2024/2831 of the European Parliament and of the Council on improving working conditions in platform work [2024].

[75] There are already some proposals for an algorithmic management directive: J Adams-Prassl et al, 'Regulating Algorithmic Management: A Blueprint' (2023) 14 *European Labour Law Journal* 124; N Potocka-Sionek and A Aloisi, 'The Spillover Effect of Algorithmic Management and How (Not) to Tame It' in K Vandale and S Rainone (eds) *The Elgar Companion to Regulating Platform Work. Insights from the Food Delivery Sector* (Cheltenham, Edward Elgar Publishing, 2025).

[76] Molè (n 49).

[77] The PWD applies to certain employers, workers, and employees. According to PWD, art 1(a), its applicability is restricted to employers that qualify as 'digital labour platforms'. Art 1(b) PWD clarifies

Article 7 of the PWD sets out targeted prohibitions against intrusive monitoring, such as processing data about a worker's emotional or psychological state (Article 7(1)(a)), monitoring private communications (Article 7(1)(b)), or predicting the exercise of fundamental rights like union membership (Article 7(1)(d)). Article 7(1)(c) of the PWD further establishes temporal boundaries by prohibiting data collection when a worker is not actively performing tasks, while Article 7(1)(e)–(f) bans the use of sensitive or biometric data. These provisions go beyond what is available in the AI Act, reflecting the specific vulnerabilities of workers working for digital labour platforms. A similar regulatory approach is needed to deal with the widespread 'consumption' of surveillance technologies in the workplace.

In conclusion, while the AI Act represents an important first step in rebalancing the asymmetry between technology providers and employers, its prohibitions and requirements are orientated towards the societal impact of AI as a whole and insufficiently tailored to the employment context. By framing employers under a consumer-like protection, the Act recognises their informational disadvantage vis-à-vis providers, but it leaves open more specific and critical questions on what should be permissible at work. What is needed is a broader EU legislative initiative that, like the AI Act, regulates the provider–employer relationship, but with far greater attention to employment-specific risks.[78] A framework combining the AI Act's market regulation approach with the PWD's labour protections could offer such a model: limiting intrusive monitoring (such as emotion recognition or monitoring of private communications), establishing clear temporal boundaries for data collection, banning predictive analytics that target trade union rights, and imposing transparency, human oversight, and OSH safeguards. Extending this approach beyond platform work to all forms of employment could ensure that digital monitoring tools are regulated both as market products but also and as instruments of managerial power.

6 Conclusion

This research explored how the adoption of digital monitoring tools has transformed the nature of employer authority. When employers deploy tools such as *Deloitte AI Agents*, *Driveri* cameras or *Cogito Dialog*, they do not directly configure or operate these systems; instead, they purchase access to authority-commodity services whose monitoring functions are defined, maintained, and updated by external providers. *Authority-commodity*, therefore, generates *consumption*: managerial power is mediated, standardised and outsourced via technological and contractual arrangements such as end-user licence agreements (EULAs). I argued that this process signals a commodification and consumerisation of employer

that it applies to those workers engaged in 'platform work'. The scope of the PWD is thus limited to platform work as a specific and non-standard form of employment.

[78] Adams-Prassl et al (n 75).

authority, in which managerial judgement is increasingly absorbed into automated systems designed and controlled by technology providers. Employers thus occupy a dual role as hierarchical superiors and as consumers of governance solutions, creating a paradox in which formal authority coexists with dependence on opaque technological infrastructures.

The GDPR places formal responsibility on employers as controllers but relies on them to oversee processors, an expectation often unrealistic in practice. Complex, adaptive AI- and IoT-enabled technologies challenge employers' technical capacity, leaving them dependent on providers for compliance-relevant information. Current GDPR provisions, including Articles 24, 25, 26, 28, and 35, inadequately address this asymmetry, limiting employers' ability to exercise meaningful oversight and increasing the risk of disproportionate impacts on employees' rights.

The AI Act represents, however, an important regulatory development that addresses these gaps by placing primary obligations on providers of high-risk AI systems. By treating high-risk AI as a 'product presenting a risk' under a product-safety paradigm, the AI Act effectively grants employers a form of consumer protection, counterbalancing informational and power asymmetries in the marketplace for surveillance technologies.

However, the consumer law approach in the AI Act does not resolve broader labour law concerns. This approach addresses informational asymmetries between providers and employers but does not engage with the specific vulnerabilities and values at stake in employment contexts. A framework informed solely by technology and consumer-law approaches cannot fully address the specific challenges of workplace surveillance or the broader protections demanded by labour law. The findings indicate the need for a tailored EU framework, combining the AI Act's market-orientated, provider-focused safeguards with labour law protections that explicitly address workplace vulnerabilities. Such a framework should regulate digital monitoring tools not merely as technological products but as instruments of managerial authority, limiting disproportionate monitoring practices violating employees' fundamental rights and ensuring meaningful human oversight.

PART III

Privacy, Initimacy and the Digitally Monitored Self

7

Intimate Digital Monitoring

A Tale of Two Case Studies

TSACHI KEREN-PAZ*

The chapter reflects on digital surveillance in its intersection with intimate privacy based on two case studies: Femtech products and non-consensual intimate images (NCII).[1] These case studies are informed by my long-standing interest in private law responses to gendered harms and on the role of distributive justice and equality in private (mainly tort) law, with a recent focus on privacy.[2] I would like to make three types of claims in this chapter. First, based on distinguishing between narrow and broad understandings of surveillance, Femtech is an instance of surveillance in the narrow sense, while NCII, is in a broader sense. This distinction relates to the boundary between breach of physical (intrusion) and informational privacy. The normative relevance of this distinction is limited, however, since in NCII the surveillance does not serve the interests of the person surveilled, while in Femtech the picture is much more nuanced.

* I would like to thank Hadassa Noorda and Jeevan Hariharan for the invitation to the Digital Monitoring workshop, to the participants and to Jeevan Hariharan and Maria Tzanou for excellent comments on previous drafts of this chapter. The section summarising the Femtech case study draws on a co-authored article in preparation and was principally drafted by Anna Nelson, the PDRA on the Femtech Surveillance project.

[1] M Tzanou and T Keren-Paz, 'FemTech Surveillance: Gendered Digital Harms and Regulatory Approaches'. Available at: https://sheffield.ac.uk/siccl/projects/femtech-surveillance-gendered-digital-harms-and-regulatory-approaches; M Tzanou et al, *Research Report: Femtech Apps and Wearables and GDPR Compliance: An Empirical Study of Femtech's Privacy Policies and Terms of Service under the GDPR* (2025), Available at: https://ssrn.com/abstract=5177016; T Keren-Paz, A Nelson and M Tzanou, 'Femtech Wearables and Embodied Harms: A New Regulatory Approach' (forthcoming); T Keren-Paz, M Tzanou and A Nelson, 'Femtech Wearables and Embodied Harms: Privacy Torts to the Rescue?' (forthcoming); T Keren-Paz, *Egalitarian Digital Privacy: Image-Based Abuse and Beyond* (Bristol, Bristol University Press, 2023); T Keren-Paz, 'Pornographic Deep Fakes: Liability for Breach of Privacy in Cases of Parody?' (2025) *Journal of Tort Law.* Available at: www.degruyterbrill.com/document/doi/10.1515/jtl-2025-0030/html.

[2] T Keren-Paz, *Torts, Egalitarianism and Distributive Justice* (Farnham, Ashgate, 2007); T Keren-Paz, *Sex Trafficking: A Private Law Response* (Abingdon, Routledge, 2013); T Keren-Paz and R Wright, 'Liability for Mass Sexual Abuse' (2019) 56 *American Criminal Law Review* 185.

Secondly, combatting the viewing of NCII raises classic concerns about monitoring of internet users (here I will focus on viewers). 'Poetic justice' demands that those who undermine the privacy of others will be themselves subject to a more aggressive form of surveillance despite the negative effect on their privacy.

Finally, theoretically and normatively, both case studies could be analysed according to two major frameworks: (1) A critical private law lens highlighting the normative relevance of power gaps, of the gendered nature of the harm and of distributive justice to deciding how to regulate the issue; this embeds a critical angle applicable to law in general and to private law in particular while highlighting private law's empowering potential; and (2) the distinction between state surveillance and private surveillance, and within the latter, between not for profit and 'surveillance capitalism'.

I will first introduce the case studies and then classify them on the grid of narrow vs broad understandings of surveillance. I will next argue that NCII raises also a concern of surveillance of viewers but that for reasons of 'poetic justice' such surveillance is justified. Finally, I will glean insights on how to regulate the two monitoring phenomena against the frameworks of critical private law and of non/financially motivated privatisation of surveillance.

1. The Case Studies

1.1 Femtech

Femtech is a term that was coined by Ida Tin, the founder of the digital menstruation application (app) Clue, in 2016.[3] It refers to 'the wide range of digital products designed with women's health in mind', including 'menstrual, sexual and procreative health as well as nursing [breastfeeding] care'.[4] 'Femtech' is a broad umbrella term, and is now used to refer to a wide range of innovations, including (1) tools geared towards those working within the healthcare system (such as applications which improve screening for breast and ovarian cancer), (2) an in-between category which exists at the interface of users and healthcare professionals, such as platforms which connect patients with abortion providers or gynaecologists (known as 'telehealth' platforms), and (3) those intended for use by individuals in the general population.[5]

[3] L Dodgson, 'The Entrepreneur Who Coined the Term "Femtech" Founded a Period Tracking App That's Helping Women Understand and Accept Their Bodies' *Business Insider* (New York, 5 June 2020). Available at: www.insider.com/founder-of-clue-ida-tin-coined-the-term-femtech-2020-6.

[4] LA Balfour, *The Digital Future of Hospitality* (London, Palgrave Macmillan Cham, 2023) 105. I recognise that not all those who use 'Femtech', and who may experience the harms described in this chapter, are women; T Hendl and B Jansky, 'Tales of Self-Empowerment through Digital Health Technologies: A Closer Look at "Femtech"' (2022) 80 *Review of Social Economy* 29, 29.

[5] Vara AI, www.vara.ai; Sorina Mihaila '"New Hope" for Millions Whose Dense Breast Tissue Masks Cancer on Mammograms' *Femtech World* (11 January 2024). Available at: www.femtechworld.co.uk/news/new-hope-for-millions-whose-dense-breast-tissue-masks-cancer-on-mammograms.

My focus is on the latter category which encompasses a broad range of software and hardware aimed at supporting women and gender minorities to track, understand and manage their menstrual, reproductive and sexual health.

'Femtech' apps exist to track not only menstruation, fertility and ovulation, but also menopause symptoms, pregnancy and breast milk production.[6] Alongside these apps sit 'wearables' – these are devices which are worn on the body which use sensors to gather biometric information, such as body temperature, menstrual flow or heart rate. Examples here include smart pelvic floor trainers, smart menstrual cups, smart sports bras, smart underwear, smart breast pumps and basal body temperature sensors.[7] These operate in conjunction with a specific app, which can combine data from the wearable with additional data inputted by the user.[8] Finally, Femtech also includes smart sex toys designed for use by women, such as smart vibrators and smart dildos.[9] Many smart sex toys are able to be remotely controlled by another person, while some – such as the Lioness Smart Vibrator – also collect biometric data (including body temperature and the intensity, frequency and duration of pelvic floor contractions) from the user.[10]

Alongside the empowering potential of Femtech products – by potentially furthering women's reproductive autonomy, whether they would like to get pregnant or avoid it – such products involve several potential harms.[11] One issue is about functionality: such products are not considered a reliable pregnancy avoidance

[6] 'Flo Period & Cycles Tracker' (Version 9.41). Available at: https:// apps.apple.com/nl/app/flo-period-cycles-tracker/id1038369065?l=en-GB; 'Femometer: Fertility Tracker' (Version 5.33.1). Available at: https://apps.apple.com/us/app/femometer-fertility-tracker/id1269972832; 'Natural Cycles – Birth Control' (Version 5.2.9). Available at: https:// play.google.com/store/apps/details?id=com.naturalcycles.cordova&hl=en-US&pli=1; 'Clue Period, Ovulation Tracker' (Version 147.0). Available at: https:// play.google.com/store/apps/details?id=com.clue.android&hl=en-IN; 'Health & Her App' (Version 1.6.6) Available at: https://apps.apple.com/gb/app/health-her-app/id1519199698; 'Pregnancy App: Amila' (Version 1.1.40). Available at: https:// play.google.com/store/apps/details?id=com.easymobs.pregnancy; 'Pump Log – Track Breast Milk' (Version 69). Available at: https:// apps.apple.com/us/app/pump-log-track-breast-milk/id814112299.

[7] Elvie, 'Elvie Trainer Smart Kegel Exerciser'. Available at: www.elvie.com/en-gb/shop/elvie-trainer; Emm, 'All-Day Comfort: Full-Cycle Insights'. Available at: www.emm.co; Myzone, 'Sports Bra' buy.myzone.org/product/?code=MYZONE-BRA-M; ALMA, 'ALMA Smart Underwear'. Available at: https://al-ma.org/Smart-Underwear; Elvie, 'Elvie Pump'. Available at: www.elvie.com/en-gb/shop/elvie-pump; Kyri, 'Kyri Ring – Generation 2'. Available at: https://kyricycles.co/collections/all/products/kyri-ring.

[8] The Elvie smart breast pump is to be used in conjunction with the 'Pump with Elvie' app: Pump with Elvie, (Version 1.32.1). Available at: https:// play.google.com/store/apps/details?id=com.chiaro.elviepump&hl=en-US.

[9] Lioness, 'Lioness Smart Vibrator'. Available at: https://lioness.io/products/the-lioness-vibrator; Lovense, 'Gravity'. Available at: www.lovense.com/thrusting-vibrating-dildo.

[10] M Wynn et al, 'Sexual Intimacy in the Age of Smart Devices: Are We Practicing Safe IoT?' (2017) *Proceedings of the 2017 Workshop on Internet of Things Security and Privacy* 25, 25. For examples of devices which can be remotely controlled by another, see: WeVibe, 'Long Distance Sex Toys'. Available at: www.we-vibe.com/uk/long-distance; Lioness, 'How It Works'. Available at: https:// lioness.io/pages/how-it-works.

[11] For a recent mixed evaluation taking into account empowerment, see D Hoffman, 'FemTech: Empowering Reproductive Rights or FEM-TRAP for Surveillance?' (2024) 32 *Medical Law Review* 468.

technique, and the extent to which they help conceiving has also been doubted.[12] If useful, and when understood as an instance of privatisation of healthcare – ie, as a substitute to state-funded fertility or contraception measures – there is a question of unequal access to such services which might implicate both lay healthcare consciousness (although one can imagine that knowledge about the existence of such products is not limited to the higher echelons in society) and costs: while most apps include free versions some users argue that adequate functionality depends on reverting to paid versions.[13] Beyond issues around functionality and access, Femtech apps may cause harm by reinforcing existing gender inequalities, and by having data gathered used in a manner which results in (gender-based) discrimination.[14] Sextech apps give rise to a 'significant risk' of sexual assault.[15] Femtech undermines users' privacy and puts them under surveillance. Users risk criminalisation for seeking abortion; and Femtech might facilitate or enable intimate partner surveillance and/or violence, and/or reproductive coercion and abuse.[16] Another potential privacy-related harm stems from the intersection of the Femtech industry with the Adtech industry; where the data from the former is shared with or sold to the latter.[17] Indeed, as the Information Commissioner's Office (ICO) has noted, 'over half of people (54 per cent) who use the apps believed they had noticed an increase in baby or fertility-related adverts since signing up.'[18]

[12] C McMillan, 'Rethinking the Regulation of Digital Contraception Under the Medical Devices Regime' (2023) 23 *Medical Law International* 3, 17–22; R Ali, ZB Gürtin and JC Harper, 'Do Fertility Tracking Applications Offer Women Useful Information About Their Fertile Window' (2021) 42 *Reproductive BioMedicine Online* 273 (concluding that 'Unreliable calendar apps remain the most commonly available fertility apps on the market').

[13] Hoffman (n 11); A Zokaityte, 'FemTech Assets' *Feminist Legal Studies* (2025). Available at: doi.org/10.1007/s10691-025-09570-7; access to a device and connectivity involve their own costs, but it is fair to say that these are widely spread in contemporary societies. A 2021 World Bank blog mentioned an International Telecommunication Union estimate that of the 7 billion people on Earth, 6.5 billion have access to a mobile phone. K Farooq and P Kustor, 'How Can Mobile Government (mGov) Work in Developing Countries?' (2 February 2021). Available at: https:// blogs.worldbank.org/en/governance/how-can-mobile-government-mgov-work-developing-countries; this is a finding in a research report on users' reviews which is currently in the final stages of preparation: A Nelson et al, 'Research Report: Analysis of User Reviews of Android Apps for Femtech: Qualitative and Quantitative Analysis' (forthcoming). A common theme was complaint about 'excessive paywalling' which was the second most populated theme in our sample.

[14] ME Gilman, 'Periods for Profit and the Rise of Menstrual Surveillance' (2021) 41 *Columbia Journal of Gender and Law* 100, 108. See also: Hendl and Jansky (n 4) at 40; EA Brown, 'The Femtech Paradox: How Workplace Monitoring Threatens Women's Equity' (2021) 61 *Jurimetrics* 289; J Erickson, JY Yuzon and T Bonaci, 'What You Do Not Expect When You Are Expecting: Privacy Analysis of Femtech' (2022) 3 *IEEE Transactions of Technology and Society* 121, 123.

[15] R Sparrow and L Karas, 'Teledildonics and Rape by Deception' (2020) 12 *Law, Innovation, and Technology* 175, 185.

[16] M Domingo, 'One Nation, Under Dobbs: How Dobbs v. Jackson Women's Health Impacts Data Privacy for All' (2024) 15 *UC Law Science and Technology Journal* 35, 48; Erickson, Yuzon and Bonaci (n 14) at 125; L Tarzia and K Hegarty, 'A Conceptual Re-evaluation of Reproductive Coercion: Centring Intent, Fear and Control' (2021) 18 *Reproductive Health* 1, 1.

[17] See eg, Elvie's privacy policy 13.1. Available at: www.elvie.ae/privacy-policy.

[18] Information Commissioner's Office, 'PACE Project: Fertility & Menstruation Apps – Internal Report' (2024). Available at: https://ico.org.uk/media2/migrated/4030034/in-scope-ic-308094-z0s7-fem-

Sharing information beyond the consent of users arose in relation to the We-Vibe 4 Plus Smart Vibrator – a wearable – where it was revealed that large quantities of users' data (regarding the minute-by-minute temperature of the vibrator, and changes in its intensity) was being shared with the parent company Standard Innovation.[19] In a lawsuit brought in Illinois the two anonymous plaintiffs argued that 'the usage…is extraordinarily intimate and private.'[20] The complaint alleged that the Defendant's 'intrusion upon Plaintiff's … sexual privacy caused … embarrassment, anxiety, and concern regarding the safety of her Usage Information.'[21] Similarly, in a case brought by the Federal Trade Commission against Flo Health, Inc the Federal Trade Commission noted that the unauthorised sharing of the data made users feel '"outraged," "incredibly upset," "disturbed," "appalled," and "very angry." Indeed, they felt "victimized" and "violated" by Respondent's actions.'[22] On 22 May 2025, District Judge James Donato ruled that key claims in a related class action lawsuit against Flo Health must go to trial.[23]

1.2 Non-Consensual Intimate Images (NCII)

NCII – also referred to as intimate image abuse, image based (sexual) abuse or more colloquially 'revenge porn' – is the taking, the making (as in deep fakes) and sharing of intimate images without consent.[24] The NCII spectrum includes taking (creation) of images of an underlying independent sexual abuse (as of filming a rape), the non-consensual taking of an image of a consensual sexual act or of one's nudity (as in voyeurism, 'creepshots', 'up-skirting' and 'down-blousing'), hacking and sharing of intimate images taken by the claimant and the non-authorised dissemination of images shared consensually with the distributor. Unauthorised *taking* of an intimate image (whether or not it is followed by dissemination) and unauthorised *dissemination* of an intimate image (even if the taking of the image is consensual) are independently wrong.[25] The new frontiers of liability (or responsibility) for the phenomenon are the creation and sharing of non-consensual intimate deep fake images, including possibly, of images known to be fake, liability

tech-report_redacted.pdf 28 (Redacted Version Provided to Project Team in Response to Freedom of Information Request).

[19] A Toor, 'Maker of Connected Vibrator Agrees to Destroy Sensitive User Data' *The Verge* (New York, 14 March 2017). Available at: www.theverge.com/2017/3/14/14920510/sex-toy-vibrator-we-vibe-4-lawsuit-settlement-privacy.

[20] *NP and PS v Standard Innovation Corp* (2016) Case No 1:16-cv-8655 (settlement agreement) 3.

[21] ibid (complaint) para 56.

[22] Flo Health, Inc. Complaint, Federal Trade Commission (Docket No C-4747, 22 June 2021) paras 3 and 6. Available at: www.ftc.gov/system/files/documents/cases/192_3133_flo_health_complaint.pdf

[23] A O'Sullivan, 'Flo Health to Face Jury Trial Over Alleged Mishandling of Sensitive Health Data' (*FutureFemHealth*, 3 June 2025). Available at: www.futurefemhealth.com/p/flo-health-to-face-jury-trial-over.

[24] N Henry et al, *Image-based Sexual Abuse: A Study on the Causes and Consequences of Non-consensual Nude or Sexual Imagery* (Abingdon, Routledge, 2020).

[25] Keren-Paz, *Egalitarian Digital Privacy* (n 1).

of hosts and viewers, and the criminalisation of threats to share such images.[26] NCII's eco-system includes dedicate 'revenge porn' websites, images indicated as non-consensual in porn platforms, images which are not so indicated but are nonetheless non-consensual in porn and other platforms (such as Facebook), or which are shared via direct messaging (such as WhatsApp), email or non-digitally either in broad circulation or to targeted individuals (such as the victim's employer, family members and friends).[27] The perpetrators' motivations vary and include 'fun/amusement; financial gain; notoriety; bragging; sexual gratification; control; harassment; blackmail/ extortion'. In a 2017 study 79 per cent of perpetrators self-identified as not intending to hurt the person while 12 per cent did.[28]

NCII has been conceptualised as a serious breach of privacy, a phenomenon on the spectrum of sexual abuse, causing systemic and gendered harm, discriminatory and an instance of hate crime whose harms are severe, multifaceted and largely irreparable and which affects individual women (and members of other marginalised groups) as a group and has profound effects both online and offline including on digital citizenship and political (and other public-facing) participation.[29]

2. Narrow vs Broad Understandings of Surveillance

Having surveyed the two case studies, I turn now to map them against a narrow and broad understanding of surveillance. While Femtech fits more squarely with the narrow definition, I explain why it is useful to think of NCII through the broader monitoring lens. Like many concepts, surveillance or monitoring – I used the terms interchangeably – can have a core or narrow meaning and a broader

[26] C McGlynn and RT Toparlak, 'The New Voyeurism: Criminalising the Creation of "Deepfake Porn"' (2025) 52 *Journal of Law and Society* 204; JCP Goldberg and C Zipursky, 'A Tort for the Digital Age: False Light Invasion of Privacy Reconsidered' (2024) 73 *DePaul Law Review* 461; Keren-Paz, 'Pornographic Deep Fakes' (n 1); Keren-Paz, *Egalitarian Digital Privacy* (n 1); Sexual Offences Act 2003 s 66B–66D.

[27] C Uhl et al, 'An Examination of Nonconsensual Pornography Websites' (2018) 28 *Feminism & Psychology* 50; F Vera-Gray et al, 'Sexual Violence as a Sexual Script in Mainstream Online Pornography' (2021) 61 *The British Journal of Criminology* 1243.

[28] J Davidson et al, *Adult Online Hate, Harassment and Abuse: A Rapid Evidence Assessment* (UK Council for Internet Safety, 2019) 54; AA Eaton, H Jacobs and Y Ruvalcaba, *Nationwide Online Study of Nonconsensual Porn Victimization and Perpetration: A Summary Report* (Cyber Civil Rights Initiative, 2017). Available at: www.cybercivilrights.org/wp-content/uploads/2017/06/CCRI-2017-Research-Report.pdf.

[29] Keren-Paz, *Egalitarian Digital Privacy* (n 1) at 87–89, 90–94, 108–09, 135–39; C McGlynn and E Rackley, 'Image-Based Sexual Abuse' (2017) 37 *OJLS* 534; Davidson et al (n 28) at 54; E Sharratt, *Intimate Image Abuse in Adults and Under 18s* (Exeter, SWGfl et al, 2019) 14–15, 19; K Zaleski, 'The Long Trauma of Revenge Porn' (*OUP Blog*, 22 September 2019) blog.oup.com/2019/09/the-long-trauma-of-revenge-porn; Keren-Paz, 'Pornographic Deep Fakes' (n 1); S Sobieraj, *Credible Threat: Attacks Against Women Online and the Future of Democracy* (New York, Oxford University Press, 2020); 'Online Violence Against Women Parliamentarians Hinders Democracy, and All Parliamentarians Are Responsible for Addressing It' (*Commonwealth Parliamentary Association UK*, 14 June 2021). Available at: www.uk-cpa.org/news-and-views/online-violence-against-women-parliamentarians-hinders-democracy-and-all-parliamentarians-are-responsible-for-addressing-it.

meaning in the penumbra. Building on David Lyon's definition of surveillance as 'a focused attention to personal details aimed at exerting an influence over or managing the objects of the data' I explain how FemTech fits the characteristics of a narrow definition, listed below, and contrast it with a broader understanding of surveillance to which NCII better belongs.[30]

2.1 Monitoring is Purposeful

The activity is pursued by the observer to gather the relevant information on the subject of monitoring, the observed, regardless of whether the motive is benign (baby monitor) or sinister (attendance tracker). In Femtech, the entire point of the exercise is to gather information about the user's fertility; indeed, the scholarly analysis of Femtech clearly recognises Femtech as a clear instance of monitoring and of surveillance capitalism at that.[31] Whether NCII involve any purposeful monitoring could be argued both ways. At some level, the core of NCII is about loss of control over information, rather than merely a physical privacy intrusion; this strengthens the understanding of NCII as monitoring narrowly understood. On the other hand, for all the actors involved, what matters is not the content (the 'instantiation' or 'value') of the information, but rather the fact that the detail is intimate.[32]

2.2 Disciplinary Effect is Purposeful

While clandestine surveillance and monitoring exists (and might produce its own disciplinary effect), monitoring is often done in an overt way to produce a disciplinary effect: speed cameras and police cars are visible to produce speed compliance; timecards are used to avoid skiving off work and so on. In Femtech, the core disciplinary effect is clearly purposeful, and an instance of self-discipline (the user monitors her behaviour to achieve a desired reproductive result). Whether third-party access to the data amounts to purposeful monitoring and, even more so, one involving purposeful disciplinary effect, is less clear. Contrast, for example, (1) producing personalised advice to the user about best date to attempt getting

[30] D Lyon, 'Everyday Surveillance: Personal Data and Social Classifications' (2002) 5 *Information, Communication & Society* 242, 242.

[31] D Lupton, 'Quantified Sex: A Critical Analysis of Sexual and Reproductive Self-Tracking Using Apps' (2014) 17 *Culture, Health & Sexuality* 440; Hoffman (n 11); J Alcantara, 'Monitoring Bodies and Selves: Unveiling Menstrual Tracking Apps Under Foucault's Concepts' in I Amaral, RB de Simões and AMM Flores (eds), *Young Adulthood Across Digital Platforms* (Leeds, Emerald Publishing Limited, 2024); A Ford, G de Togni and L Miller, 'Hormonal Health: Period Tracking Apps, Wellness, and Self-management in the Era of Surveillance Capitalism' (2021) 7(1), *Engaging Science, Technology, and Society,* 48.

[32] See *Douglas v Hello! Ltd & Ors (No 3)* [2003] EWHC 55 (Ch), [2003] 1 All ER 1087, para 105.

pregnant; (2) use of the data to improve the algorithm; (3) target advertising; and (4) law enforcement investigating the user to alleged illegal termination. In NCII, at the individual level, NCII's disciplinary nature is neither straightforward nor consistently present. This is partly because the person sharing an image may not intend for the subject to be aware of its dissemination, and because the motivations for sharing are not always clearly disciplinary. Additionally, some viewers whose actions contribute to the disciplinary effect may not realise that the images have been shared without consent.

2.3 Gathering, Rather Than Disclosure of Information, is at Monitoring's Essence

It is usually the gathering of the information rather than its dissemination that is at the heart of both the monitoring itself and its hopeful disciplinary effect. So, whether a disciplinary effect is sought (as in speed cameras or attendance monitoring) or not (as in baby monitoring) there is usually no need for a public disclosure to achieve the purpose of monitoring. This distinction will be familiar to privacy scholars, although some would not buy the mapping of physical vs informational privacy into gathering vs disclosure. Certainly, in the context of mass state surveillance, both collection and access to the data (which is different from dissemination) are relevant in terms of both privacy and surveillance. Physical privacy intrusions undermine one's negative liberty; the right to be let alone. At times, this right can be violated even if no information is gathered at all; but even when, as is more common, the intrusion involves the gathering of information, the essence of the violation lies in producing (and at times storing) the information, rather than in sharing them with third parties. In contrast, undermining of informational privacy is mainly about the unauthorised sharing of private information with a third party (eg breach of confidentiality) or with the public (eg public disclosure of private facts). Exceptions of course exist, in which shaming (or reputational effects) are essential for disciplining (eg gossip), and arguably for surveillance – indeed this is most relevant to regulating women's sexuality and I will return to this point below. For now, recall that the qualified privilege defence in defamation (and while less established, in privacy as well) is based exactly on the distinction between permissibly disclosing the information to a relevant individual, and unlawfully sharing it with one (or more) who do(es) not have an interest in receiving it. In Femtech, gathering the information is the point of the exercise and the data is disseminated either to enhance the user's interests (although not necessarily with her full consent) or for profit. The *sharing*, however, is not intended to achieve a disciplinary effect, ie, to incentivise or discourage the user from behaving in a particular way. It is the unauthorised *sharing* of the intimate images (or its threat) that makes up much of what makes NCII both wrong and harmful.

2.4 Self-monitoring Included

The idea of self-discipline connects closely to the concept of surveillance – especially when people know they are being (or might be) watched by others. This link was made explicit in Foucault's later work about inscription and technologies of the self.[33] I would suggest that it should be included in the narrow definition of surveillance, although whether self-monitoring could exist without such knowledge is more controversial. So, if I count calories because I know I will be judged by my significant other (or by others) based on my weight, this is an instance of monitoring in the narrow sense; but if my motivation is my long-term health, it is probably 'monitoring' only in a broader sense. Femtech is predominantly an instance of self-monitoring. As this self-monitoring is related to society's expectations about fertility and motherhood it is an instance of a narrow case of monitoring: As Alcantara argued recently 'the technology of menstrual tracking apps acts subtly and uninterruptedly to docilise female bodies and make them useful'.[34] NCII is clearly *not* a case of self-monitoring given the lack of consent, but the core case of monitoring allows, but does not require, self-monitoring.

2.5 Special Relationship?

Surveillance often occurs in the context of a pre-existing relationship between the observer – the monitoring person or on whose behalf the monitoring occurs – and the observed, although, to be sure, some examples, most notably mass surveillance (eg by the police or security at airports), stretch this condition to nearly breaking point. An alternative way to think of this is that the effects of monitoring when a pre-existing relationship exists or when the relationship is significant, are potentially more oppressive both because the monitoring is more consequential and because it adds the insult of lack of trust to the injury from the practice of surveillance itself.[35] In Femtech, with the exception of self-monitoring, usually there is no special relationship between the user and those who act on the information. An interesting exception are apps – some having to do with smart vibrators and others with menstrual trackers – that allow the user to share information with their partner.[36] Certainly, this option is a core (and potentially problematic) case of monitoring, in that it enables the user's partner to monitor their (usually his) partner's sexuality and fertility. Given that a refusal to enable sharing might be costly to the user, the technological availability

[33] I Manokha, 'Surveillance, Panoptism and Self-Discipline in the Digital Age' (2018) 16 *Surveillance & Society* 219.

[34] For a similar observation see Lupton (n 31) (the devices 'working to tame the sexual and reproductive body by rendering it amenable to monitoring').

[35] This tracks an (in my opinion, a bit under-recognised) observation in privacy law that the interest in privacy is much more prominent with respect to people who already know, or are likely to know the claimant, compared with other people. See Keren-Paz, *Egalitarian Digital Privacy* (n 1) at 130, 155, 213.

[36] See Yuzon and Bonaci (n 14) at 125; Tarzia and Hegarty (n 16) at 1.

of sharing both casts doubt as to whether the user's consent to the sharing is voluntary and produces a significant and troubling disciplinary effect. Indeed, the use of Femtech, specifically this feature, has been associated with the risk of furthering domestic violence.[37] In NCII, those initially distributing the images will not always have a special relationship with its subject, although they often would (eg ex partners, students in the same institution and so on). When we shift the focus away from the person distributing the image to those hosting or viewing it, there will rarely be any meaningful pre-existing relationship between them and the victim, although the harm from viewing is mainly from those who know or might recognise the victim.[38]

2.6 Power?

The next point is likewise controversial: usually, it is the powerful who monitor the less powerful, rather than the other way around. Power and its relationship with knowledge, not only features prominently in a Foucauldian analysis of surveillance, but is also a popular theme throughout the surveillance literature.[39] This is also relevant to the relationship between monitoring and privacy: the observation erases the information asymmetry under which prior to the observation the observed knew more about themselves (or at least not less) than the observer. As a result of monitoring, the observer knows as much as or more than the observed knows about themselves. The interest in informational privacy could be understood as being about maintaining this information asymmetry, thus avoiding the redistribution of power (and often wealth) from the observed to the observer.[40] Now, it might be that the powerful just have more effective means to monitor others and to avoid others' monitoring of them. It might also be that the powerful have more means to discipline the disempowered based on the information gathered by monitoring than the other way around. However, the powerful are also monitored by the less powerful, who might resort to different disciplinary methods such as gossip and humour. For example, throughout history, spouses of either gender monitored the sexual fidelity of their partners notwithstanding that men were (and still are) more powerful than women and despite the fact that the consequences of infidelity were much more serious for women; a mere attempt by women to monitor their husband's fidelity was sometimes met with a setback to the observer wife, at times being subject to physical violence by the observed husband.

[37] ibid.

[38] Keren-Paz, *Egalitarian Digital Privacy* (n 1) at 89, 131, 211–13.

[39] eg, H Parfitt, 'Think with Google: Foucauldian Challenges to Zuboff's Surveillance Capitalism' (2021) 18 *Jura gentium* 160; eg, J Hariharan and H Noorda, 'Imprisoned at Work: The Impact of Employee Monitoring on Physical Privacy and Individual Liberty' (2025) 88 *MLR* 333.

[40] T Keren-Paz, 'Privacy Preserving Lies' in S Santatzoglou, M Wasik and A Wrigley (eds) *Dishonesty, Liability and the Law: Exploring the Moral Importance of Context* (Abingdon, Routledge, 2025) 166, 187; RA Woodcock, 'Personalized Pricing as Monopolization' (2019) 51 *Connecticut Law Review* 311, 321–26; A Porat and O Yadlin, 'A Welfarist Perspective on Lies' (2016) 91 *Indiana Law Journal* 617, 634–38.

The clear gendered aspect of reproduction/its governance makes Femtech a clear case in which the observer is more powerful than the observed; this observation pulls Femtech into the narrow definition of monitoring. It should be noted, for the sake of nuance, that the following observations push back against the understanding of Femtech monitoring as belonging to the 'men oppressing women' category. First, Femtech is mainly an instance of self-monitoring; second, the monitoring or the gaze are carried out by corporations and by society in general; third, as with many issues having to do with reproduction, fertility and sexuality, lots of the discipline is extracted by other women, rather than by men.[41] In terms of power relationships in NCII, at the individual level, the multiplicity of relationships (and the fact there are many viewers) makes generalisations difficult; however, (1) NCII is a gendered phenomenon and, as such, both contributes to and is constituted by existing power imbalances between women and men; (2) NCII is on the continuum of sexual abuse, which is to a large extent about power; and (3) perpetration in the context of heterosexual intimate relationships (of creating or disseminating NCII) is a reflection of power relationships at the individual level.[42]

The discussion above demonstrated that it is easier to fit Femtech into the narrow definition of monitoring than it is NCII, mainly since in Femtech, but not in NCII, the monitoring itself and its disciplinary effects are more clearly purposeful and are more focused on gathering the information rather than on disseminating it. It is my claim, however, that on a broader understanding of monitoring, NCII should be understood as an instance of digital monitoring. Regardless, the harms ensuing from NCII are similar in nature to the harms from monitoring, therefore, those who are rightly concerned about the harms from monitoring should be concerned about the harms from NCII. In fact, it seems that the harm from unauthorised dissemination of the claimant's intimate image is much more significant than that from unauthorised retaining or sharing of information about the claimant's fertility, a fact that is reflected in the recent consensus about the criminalisation of the former, while the regulatory response to the latter is quite limited.[43] This suggests that – assuming that I am right that Femtech is closer to the core of monitoring than NCII – there is only limited overlap between the interests in privacy and in not being monitored. Moreover, the following three distinctions seem to be more important for the difference in how the two phenomena are regulated than the extent to which they present a core or penumbral case of monitoring: (1) in NCII

[41] But as I suggested elsewhere, this does not undermine the conclusion that the phenomenon or harm are gendered: Keren-Paz, *Egalitarian Digital Privacy* (n 1) at 104–05; C Bohannon, *Eve: How the Female Body Drove 200 Million Years of Human Evolution* (London, Penguin Random House, 2023) 400–01. Within my distributive-egalitarian framework this means that monitoring involves not only inter-group justice/distribution but also intra-groups. Keren-Paz, *Torts, Egalitarianism and Distributive Justice* (n 2) at chs 4, 6.

[42] Keren-Paz, *Egalitarian Digital Privacy* (n 1) at 93.

[43] See in the UK the criminalisation of NCII in the Sexual Offences Act 2003, ss 66B–66H and the Information Commissioner's Office (n 18) at 35 concluding that, despite having identified data compliance issues around consent and transparency, it did not consider it 'appropriate to take formal investigative action'.

the monitoring is non-consensual, while in Femtech it largely is (although the quality of consent could be questioned); (2) the extent of the harm matters and in NCII the harm seems much more significant; (3) the dissemination of the information is less extensive in Femtech, and partially involves the data subject's anonymity; in general, it risks less the sharing of embarrassing information with people who know the claimant thus reducing embarrassment and reputational risk.[44]

The following features of NCII justify viewing it as a broad case of monitoring or as justifying a robust response given the similarities between breach of privacy and monitoring: (a) at a collective level (of women as a group) its effect and often its purpose are to control women's sexuality; (b) so in this sense it works as an *ex ante* form of monitoring; (c) it can often lead to follow up forms of abuse which in turn could be understood as an instance of monitoring; and (d) a typical harm reported by victims is a fear they will be recognised in the future; this could arguably be understood as a monitoring concern.[45] The overlap between the interests in privacy and in freedom from being monitored is clear.

3. Monitoring of NCII Viewers – Poetic Justice?

Interestingly, it is the legal response against both uploaders and viewers of NCII which arguably implicates monitoring concerns in the narrow sense. First, in the European Union (EU), hosts' liability to victims of NCII still depends on a failure to remove the offending content expeditiously after notice and is still wedded to a prohibition on general monitoring, although what counts as general monitoring is contested; for example a notice and stay down regime is not incompatible with such prohibition.[46] Secondly, at the regulatory level, both at the EU (Digital Services Act) and United Kingdom (UK) (Online Safety Act) levels, due diligence and risk assessment obligations on (certain) platforms are an instance in which monitoring is encouraged and indeed expected.[47] More generally, voluntary content monitoring is an obvious area of monitoring. Third, in the adjacent area of child sexual exploitation and abuse, there is an extensive monitoring activity supported by vigilante groups.[48] Lastly, my own approach goes further in calling for both hosts and viewers to be held strictly liable for hosting and viewing NCII and to impose a duty on hosts to upload-filter intimate images uploaded without

[44] Tzanou et al, *Research Report: Femtech Apps and Wearables and GDPR Compliance* (n 1) at 75–76; Information Commissioner's Office (n 18).

[45] See McGlynn and Rackley (n 29) and accompanying text; Keren-Paz, *Egalitarian Digital Privacy* (n 1) at 63–66, 87–88, 93–94, 155.

[46] Case C-18/18 *Eva Glawischnig-Piesczek v Facebook Ireland Limited* ECLI:EU:C:2019:821, [2019] 1 CMLR 33.

[47] C Rigotti, C McGlynn and F Benning, 'Image-Based Sexual Abuse and EU Law: A Critical Analysis' (2024) 25 *German Law Journal* 1472; Ofcom, 'Quick Guide to Illegal Content Risk Assessments' (9 April 2025). Available at: www.ofcom.org.uk/online-safety/illegal-and-harmful-content/quick-guide-to-online-safety-risk-assessments.

[48] Crown Prosecution Service, 'Online Child Abuse Activist Groups on the Internet' (4 July 2024). Available at: www.cps.gov.uk/legal-guidance/online-child-abuse-activist-groups-internet.

a proof of consent from those depicted in them.[49] In *Egalitarian Digital Privacy* (*EDP*) I explain why such monitoring duty is justified and why chilling effects and loss of spontaneity concerns are unconvincing.[50]

In *EDP*, I also call for (strict) liability to be imposed on viewers of NCII. My approach is based on the realisation that each unauthorised viewing is intrusive, that misuse of private information is an intentional tort imposing strict liability for deliberate acts and that private information should not be protected to a lesser degree than personal property.[51] I will focus here on one objection to such a solution which is undermining the privacy of internet users. Specifically, I deal with the concern that allowing the claimant to obtain from hosts the identity of viewers who viewed the claimant's images – via an order which in the UK is called a Norwich Pharmacal Order (NPO) – unduly undermines the privacy interests of users. In essence, this is a concern about monitoring in the narrow sense. Indeed, a counter argument in this context to my approach is internet users' interest in privacy and in the avoidance of surveillance. Before responding to this concern, we need to reflect on the relationship between monitoring, discipline and deterrence. It is hard to distinguish between monitoring with its disciplinary effect and deterrence as a potential (if disputed) goal of either criminal or tort law. Wherever the point of monitoring is to cause the observed to behave in a way which is contrary to their wishes but rather aligns with the observer's, monitoring (be it of speed, skiving off work, weight or sexual behaviour) with the threat of negative reinforcement has a deterrent effect (and purpose). Relatedly, as detecting a breach of the relevant norm usually requires observation, monitoring produces deterrence. At the same time, the detection of breaches of legal duties (which necessarily produce deterrence) might be justified or motivated by other considerations or purposes, such as attaining retribution in criminal law, or corrective justice in private law. On the latter understanding, the deterrence/disciplinary effect/negative reinforcement is a by-product of the detection whose purpose or motivation is not necessarily to change the future behaviours of the person caught (specific deterrence) or of others (general deterrence) but rather to obtain justice. Finally, as will be explored in the final section, the purpose of the norm (be it legal or cultural) with its **concomitant** monitoring might be to cause its addressees to internalise the norm rather than only to obey it on pain of negative consequences if one does not.

Against this backdrop I argue, that for reasons having to do with reciprocity and 'poetic justice', viewers' interest in privacy/not being monitored should be discounted due to the serious invasion of privacy they inflict on NCII victims. As the main balancing exercise for NPO is between the claimant's interests and the user's privacy and data protection interests, there is much to be said that when the alleged wrongdoing is manifested in a serious undermining of the claimant's privacy, relatively little weight should be given to the user's privacy interest

[49] Keren-Paz, *Egalitarian Digital Privacy* (n 1).

[50] ibid ch 7, especially pp 118–21.

[51] *Douglas v Hello! Ltd & Ors* (n 32) at para 105; *Lloyd v Google LLC* [2021] UKSC 50, [2022] AC 1217, para 133; Keren-Paz, *Egalitarian Digital Privacy* (n 1) at 135–39, 175–76, 178–84.

militating against disclosing his identity. This 'poetic justice' logic is behind claims such as victims of sex trafficking should be allowed to sue innocent clients in conversion since the latter treated the former as property, that restitution of proceeds from a conscious wrongdoer (so not allowing deduction for costs in producing the net profit) is consistent with corrective justice since it denies the defendant a protected interest in his own property, a right he denied the claimant and that society should be intolerant towards the intolerant.[52] More generally, this logic is behind the role of reciprocity in tort theory and in justifying qualified privilege (to protect a defendant's legitimate interest) as a defence to defamation and breach of privacy claims.[53] Some UK and European Court of Human Rights authorities go in a similar direction, emphasising the sexual privacy interests of victims as reason for rejecting privacy-based claims of suspects in the context of gathering evidence against them. *In Sutherland v HM Advocate*, in the context of 'paedophile hunters' the Supreme Court concluded that article 8(1) was not engaged by the decoy divulging the evidence to the police based, inter alia on that:

> The actions of the appellant were aimed at the destruction or limitation of the rights and freedoms of a child under article 8 which are the subject of positive obligations owed to children by the state under that provision, in a context in which those positive obligations outweighed any legitimate interest the appellant could have under article 8(1) to protection for his actions.[54]

The court relied on *KU v Finland* in which the domestic failure to force, based on domestic privacy laws, an Internet Service Provider to identify a user who placed as advert suggesting that the 12-year-old applicant was looking for an intimate relationship, amounted to violation of the applicant's right to respect for his private life.[55] While *Sutherland* emphasises the rights of children and the fact the prohibited behaviour is criminalised – points which distinguish the liability of viewers of NCII from that in *Sutherland* – the court also emphasises that the reason that Article 8 was not engaged was because the evidence was gathered by a private citizen, rather than by the state. This, and the European Court of Human Rights authority that the state might be in breach of its positive obligation to victims in not affording an effective criminal response to serious violations of sexual autonomy, even though a civil remedy is available, suggests that the state might have a positive obligation to enable an effective civil response against viewers of NCII,

[52] Keren-Paz, *Sex Trafficking* (n 2) at ch 5; EJ Weinrib, 'Restitutionary Damages as Corrective Justice' (2000) 1 *Theoretical Enquiries in Law* 1; Y Nehushtan, 'The Limits of Tolerance: A Substantive- Liberal Perspective' (2007) 20 *Ratio Juris* 230.

[53] GP Fletcher, 'Fairness and Utility in Tort Theory' (1972) 85 *Harvard Law Review* 537; *Watt v Longsdon* [1930] 1 KB 130, 147; *CC v AB* [2006] EWHC 3083 (QB); *Mosley v News Group Newspapers Ltd (No 3)* [2008] EWHC 1777 (QB); Keren-Paz (n 40).

[54] *Sutherland v Her Majesty's Advocate* [2020] UKSC 32, para 43.

[55] [2009] 48 EHRR 52. But see Case 62357/14 *Benedik v Slovenia* ECLI:CE:ECHR:2018:-0424JUD006235714, [2018] in which there was an interference with the right of respect for private life in relation to a police investigation into the downloading and copying of child pornography by the applicant via the internet.

at least if viewing is considered as an actionable wrong, and at least against intentional viewers, so that an NPO is likely to be given to reveal viewers' identity.[56] More broadly, for the reasons explained before, one can doubt whether detecting the identity of those breaking the law for purposes of enforcing a legal right (and possibly punishment) is monitoring in the narrow sense. Arguably, the point of detection is not to change the observed behaviour (deterrence) but rather to compensate the claimant (or to punish the accused) for a past wrong.

4. A Normative Framework for Regulating Gendered Harms in Digital Surveillance Cases

Both Femtech and NCII could be analysed from a tripartite normative framework which should improve the way both phenomena are regulated. First, they have a clear gendered aspect. As such, a critical approach alive to the relevance of power structures in society and to gender justice is needed. Second, private law has an important complementary role in keeping excessive and illegitimate monitoring in check. Indeed, like much of my previous writing, these two points reinforce each other so the discussion to follow will treat them together: a critical private law lens is empowering – given the control over the process marginalised people have – in a way the public (including criminal) law responses are not.[57] Finally, in both case studies, the monitoring is largely conducted by private actors, not by the state. While in Femtech the monitoring is financially motivated and, to some extent consensual, in NCII it is (largely) neither.

4.1 The Critical Private Law Lens

That the harms (or more broadly the phenomena producing the harms) are gendered is normatively relevant to the way these phenomena should be regulated. Private law has/should have a role in such regulation and a critical approach in private law is also relevant: a distributive justice, egalitarian, feminist and otherwise critical understanding of these phenomena and the harm as gendered ought to feature in the way private law responds to the issue. A critical approach to surveillance studies is probably mainstream, thanks to Foucault's influence on the field. In data protection, where the General Data Protection Regulation is surprisingly gender blind, an egalitarian lens is on the rise; egalitarian and feminist approaches to privacy (and defamation) are common and are probably on the

[56] Case 8978/80 *X and Y v The Netherlands* ECLI:CE:ECHR:1985:0326JUD000897880, [1986] EHRR 235 para 27; for further analysis of why NPOs should and are likely to be awarded against viewers viewing the claimant's NCII see Keren-Paz, *Egalitarian Digital Privacy* (n 1) at 215–21.

[57] See, eg, Keren-Paz, *Torts, Egalitarianism and Distributive Justice* (n 2); Keren-Paz, *Sex Trafficking* (n 2); Keren-Paz, *Egalitarian Digital Privacy* (n 1).

rise as well.[58] Such analysis highlights the collective or group aspect of gender-based harms, insists that the progressive redistribution of the relevant goods is a(n inconclusive) reason in itself to support a rule leading to such a result, and the fact that the rights' infringements are likely to be suffered by the marginalised make them both more likely to occur and less acceptable.[59] In terms of the two case studies, non-consensual intimate images (including deep fakes) are clearly recognised as instances of gendered harms and amenable to a feminist, critical egalitarian analysis; Femtech, too, is understood through a gender lens.[60] In NCII, the gender aspect of perpetration and victimhood is more conspicuous than in Femtech but elsewhere I have extended the normative ramifications of this fact to the hosting of such images despite the fact that the gender aspect there is less conspicuous.[61] Both contexts involve embodied harm and the relationship between embodied and gendered harms is highlighted.[62] Finally, and close to the subject of this collection, the disciplinary aspects of NCII as a way to control women, to entrench (and not merely build upon) double standards about sexuality and to curtail women's equal participation in public life, especially in politics, have featured with respect to both authentic and fake NCII.[63]

On the point of a private law angle, my argument is based on researching gendered harms in the contexts of sex trafficking, NCII and Femtech. From the perspectives of both policy and theory – mainly jurisprudence and private law

[58] See Lupton (n 31); Hoffman (n 11); J Alcantara (n 31); A Ford, G de Togni and L Miller (n 31); Parfitt (n 39); A Siapka, M Tzanou and A Nelson, 'Re-imagining Data Protection: Femtech and Gendered Risks in the GDPR' in RÁ Costello and M Leiser (eds), *Critical Reflections on the EU's Data Protection Regime: GDPR in the Machine (Oxford,* Hart Publishing, 2024) 101–02; G Malgieri and GG Fuster, 'The Vulnerable Data Subject: A Gendered Data Subject?' (2022) 13 *European Journal of Law and Technology* 1; JT Theilen et al, 'Feminist Data Protection: An Introduction' (2021) 10(4) *Internet Policy Review* 1; M Tzanou, 'The Future of EU Data Privacy Law: Towards a More Egalitarian Data Privacy' (2020) 7 *Journal of International and Comparative Law* 449; J Lake, *The Face That Launched a Thousand Lawsuits* (New Haven and London, Yale University Press, 2017); S Skinner-Thompson, *Privacy at the Margins* (Cambridge, Cambridge University Press, 2020); Keren-Paz, *Egalitarian Digital Privacy* (n 1); M Gray, *Suing For Silence: Sexual Violence and Defamation Law* (Vancouver, UBC Press, 2024); R Moosavian and P Coe, '"The Personal is Political": Sexual Misconduct Allegations, Defamation and Gender Politics' (2025) *Journal of Media Law. Available at: www.tandfonline.com/doi/full/10.1080/17577632.2025.2509997*; Keren-Paz (n 40) at 184–85 (referencing the work of A Allen, K Bridges, D Citron, T Keren-Paz, J Richardson, SS Thompson, L Strahilevitz and A Waldman; and presenting/applying an egalitarian framework to the contours of a right to lie to preserve privacy).

[59] Keren-Paz, *Torts, Egalitarianism and Distributive Justic* (n 2); Keren-Paz, *Egalitarian Digital Privacy* (n 1); S Skinner-Thompson, 'Privacy's Double Standards' (2018) 93 *Washington Law Review* 2051.

[60] Henry et al (n 24); Keren-Paz, *Egalitarian Digital Privacy* (n 1); McGlynn and Toparlak (n 26); Keren-Paz, 'Pornographic Deep Fakes' (n 1); BA Corbin, 'Digital Micro-Aggressions and Discrimination: FemTech and the "Othering" of Women' (2020) 44 *Nova Law Review* 337; Ford, de Togni and Miller (n 31); Gilman (n 14), Siapka, Tzanou and Nelson (n 58).

[61] Keren-Paz, *Egalitarian Digital Privacy* (n 1) at 104–05.

[62] N Henry and A Powell, 'Embodied Harms, Gender, Shame & Technology Facilitated Sexual Violence' (2015) 21 *Violence Against Women* 758; Siapka, Tzanou and Nelson (n 58).

[63] Keren-Paz, *Egalitarian Digital Privacy* (n 1) at 87–89, 90–94, 108–09, 135–39; McGlynn and Rackley (n 29); Davidson et al (n 28) at 54; Sharratt (n 29) at 14–15, 19; Zaleski (n 29); Keren-Paz, 'Pornographic Deep Fakes' (n 1); S Sobieraj (n 29); 'Online Violence Against Women Parliamentarians Hinders Democracy, and All Parliamentarians Are Responsible for Addressing It' (n 29).

theory – I defend the approach that private law is an appropriate regulatory tool to problems most often thought of only or mainly through a criminal law prism; that it has an empowering potential – it allows claimants to decide whether they view themselves as victims, and if so, who is responsible for the right-violation and under what theory (in other words, private law is instrumental in the naming, blaming and claiming process); that it expands the potential pool of those who could and should be responsible for the relevant right-violations (in NCII also platforms and viewers, not only uploaders and distributors); and that it could be used either alongside criminal responsibility (or other regulatory responses) or in lieu of such responsibility.[64] So, for example, even though, following the recent Law Commission's recommendation not to criminalise possession of NCII thus far possession of NCII has not been criminalised, there is still room to impose (strict) civil liability for viewing or possessing these images; hosts of NCII should be strictly liable to persons whose NCII appears on the platform; porn platforms that host NCII should be liable even if liability for breach of privacy should be fault-based; deep fakes should be deemed as a breach of privacy (regardless of whether liability should inhere also in defamation) even if the image comes across as (or is accompanied by a disclaimer that it is) inauthentic; and uninformed consent in the context of Femtech should lead to liability under misuse of private information, and in cases of wearables also for undermining bodily integrity and physical privacy under misuse of private information and possibly negligence or battery.[65]

4.2 (Financially Motivated) Privatisation of Surveillance

In her recent bestseller book *Eve,* Cat Bohannon argues that surveillance of women's reproduction and sexuality was evolutionary adaptive given the unique difficulties of giving birth to a human baby and hence the need to control pregnancies and birth.[66] On this account, surveillance is cultural (and in this sense collective) and predated state's surveillance. Historically (and to a large extent still

[64] Keren-Paz, *Egalitarian Digital Privacy* (n 1) at 215, 226.

[65] Law Commission, *Intimate Image Abuse: A Final Report* (HC 326, 2022) 171; Keren-Paz, *Egalitarian Digital Privacy* (n 1) at 54–71, 77–80, 96–109, 125–31, 135–39, 161–71, 175–84; see eg, A George, 'Defamation in the Time of Deepfakes' (2024) 45 *Columbia Journal of Gender and Law* 122; Keren-Paz, 'Pornographic Deep Fakes' (n 1); Tzanou et al, '*Research Report: Femtech Apps and Wearables and GDPR Compliance*' (n 1) at 75–76; Information Commissioners Office (n 18); Keren-Paz, Nelson and Tzanou, 'Femtech Wearables and Embodied Harms' (n 1). At the same time, liability for non-material damage under the data protection regime ought to compensate for these harms; this could be achieved by taking lessons from the tests for informed consent developed in the medical context. *cf* J Hariharan, 'Physical Privacy and Bodily Integrity' in F Bettini et al (eds), *New Directions in Private Law Theory* (London, UCL Press, 2023) 227.

[66] Bohannon (n 41) at 400-01 ('sexism is one of the ways our ancestors solved our hardest problem ... that we categorically suck at making babies'. The core of sexism is 'a massive set of rules that work to control reproduction').

today) the state supplemented cultural and social norms of monitoring women's reproduction and sexuality by criminal, regulatory and social law. Monitoring a woman's reproduction and sexuality has for long involved the woman herself, her father and then husband (in mostly patriarchal cultures), other members of society, both family members and peers – Bohannon highlights in her book that other women are just as, if not more, sexist than men about other women's sexuality – and the state.[67] In what follows, I focus on Femtech's monitoring, although I weave into the analysis observations about relevant differences from NCII.

On one reading, Femtech is a form of privatisation of state monitoring: at a time that, at least in Western societies, state's monitoring wanes and cultural norms decrease the extent of monitoring – or at least its overt nature, or the level of opprobrium for non-compliance – Femtech products fill the gap and do some of the monitoring previously done by the state (and by more explicit societal norms). This privatisation has three dimensions.[68] First, to some extent, Femtech is privatisation of the health care system's responsibility to assist women not to/conceive and (to a lesser extent) to monitor the normal development of the pregnancy and (arguably) the baby and the adequacy of lactation.[69] Secondly, Femtech, inadvertently or otherwise, serves a disciplinary function of reinforcing societal expectations about normal, if not proper, sexual and reproductive norms. Indeed, as Corbin argues, some of the harms Femtech produces is anxiety about not conforming to these standards.[70] So, Femtech owners supplement or supplant cultural or societal norms. This aspect (but not the previous) is even more pronounced in NCII in which often the motivation behind the unauthorised sharing of the intimate images, but in any event its effect is 'to put women in their place' and to reinforce the gendered double standard about sexuality.[71] Thirdly, to the extent that Femtech products are used as contraceptives, they serve both as a substitute to abortion whose regulation is still a major manifestation of state's lingering monitoring of reproduction and, given the portability of data, a potential tool to evidence a termination hence supporting state's monitoring.[72] At the same time, Hoffman argues that Femtech companies serve a limited gatekeeping function by protecting users from attempts by the state to access their data.[73] So Femtech products enhance both the self-monitoring of each woman who chooses to use it and societal monitoring in which the product owner could be understood to be either an independent actor monitoring directly or a conduit for monitoring by society and at times, the state.

[67] ibid.

[68] See C Kennedy's discussion of the relationship between state and non-state modes of governance of deceptions inducing marriage and sex in *Inducing Intimacy: Deception, Consent and the Law* (Cambridge, Cambridge University Press, 2024) 22. In Kennedy's account, there are three senses of public and private: non/state, collective/individual interests and criminal/civil responses.

[69] Hoffman (n 11) at 482–83.

[70] Corbin (n 60) at 20.

[71] Keren-Paz, *Egalitarian Digital Privacy* (n 1) at 93–94.

[72] Domingo (n 16).

[73] Hoffman (n 11) at 483–84.

Femtech monitoring is privatised in the following ways. First, as already mentioned, the products partially shift responsibility from the healthcare system to the user, especially regarding the responsibility to conceive. This is especially the case where the use of Femtech is recommended by healthcare professionals, but it is likely broader than that. Secondly, to the extent that some of the disciplining that was hitherto carried out by the state is now done by the Femtech industry, this is an instance of privatisation.[74] Again, this holds true for NCII: in conservative societies, women's promiscuous or 'immodest' behaviour can lead to criminal (and other state-imposed) sanctions alongside a strong societal response. In more liberal societies, state's sanctions wane and women are subject to conflicting norms; they can also pay a price for being too 'prudish' or not sufficiently sexy/sexual.[75] This suggests that, with the help of the technological ease with which NCII can be created and shared, there might be a greater role for private enforcement of 'slut shaming' as a substitute to the decline of state monitoring. An important caveat, however, is that, increasingly, the creation and dissemination of NCII is considered illegal, indeed criminal. The criminalisation of private monitoring is incompatible with a classic understanding of privatisation: the handing over of functions which were traditionally carried out by the state to private actors.

The third mode of monitoring is not, strictly speaking, a form of privatisation but might be understood as such on a more relaxed understanding of the term: the disciplinary effects of whatever norms that were hitherto enforced by social norms that now might be expressed less directly. For example, a pro-natalist approach is reflected by 'informing [a user] in welcoming letters and a positive tone that she is seven days late for her period' ignoring the fact that not all pregnancies are welcome.[76] Similarly, 'Many apps use pink color schemes and graphics, such as flowers and hearts, that reinforce feminine notions of gender performativity … these apps also make stereotypical, gendered assumptions about users and their goals in adopting Femtech'.[77] The extent to which this mode is relevant to NCII could be doubted: text ridiculing the subject of the image (either accompanying the original dissemination of the image or as part of follow-up abuse) is part and parcel of the disciplinary effect which is the heart of the dissemination of the unauthorised image. So is the appeal (to some viewers) from knowing that the intimate image is non-consensual.[78]

That Femtech is a manifestation of surveillance capitalism is well understood.[79] In Zuboff's account, human experience becomes free raw material for

[74] A Nelson, M Tzanou and T Keren-Paz, 'Recommending Privately Developed FemTech in Healthcare Part 1: Promises and Pitfalls' (*BMJ Sexual & Reproductive Health Blog*, September 16 2024). Available at: https://blogs.bmj.com/bmjsrh/2024/09/16/femtech-part-1/; A Nelson, M Tzanou and T Keren-Paz, 'Recommending Privately Developed FemTech in Healthcare Part 2: Understanding Healthcare Professionals' Responsibilities' (*BMJ Sexual and Reproductive Health Blog*, October 3 2024). Available at: https://blogs.bmj.com/bmjsrh/2024/10/03/recommending-femtech-part-2/.

[75] C Lunde and M Joleby, 'Being Under Pressure to Sext: Adolescents' Experiences, Reactions, and Counter-Strategies' (2022) 33 *Journal of Research on Adolescence* 188.

[76] Corbin (n 60) at 13.

[77] Gilman (n 14) at 107.

[78] Keren-Paz, *Egalitarian Digital Privacy* (n 1) at 157–61.

[79] Lupton (n 31); Hoffman (n 11); Alcantara (n 31); Ford, de Togni and Miller (n 31).

hidden commercial practices of extraction, prediction and sales whose focus is behavioural modification. This risks the unprecedented concentration of knowledge wealth and power, threatening human nature, thwarting democracy and overthrowing people's sovereignty by imposing new collective order based on total certainty.[80] For current purposes, the fact that the non-state surveillance is financially motivated is important. Similar to other contexts, concerns about financial and gender-based exploitation are interwoven: on one axis is the data subject vs surveillance capitalists; on another, women vs men (or societal structures which are either heterogenous by reflecting the individual of interests of men, women and other genders or themselves a proxy of men's interests despite seemingly being gender-neutral).[81] The first axis transfers value from data subjects to companies, value which is based on data (or labour) which is embodied, intimate and gendered.[82] The second axis is based on gendered monitoring in a way which hampers the individual and collective interests of women.

NCII, by and large, is not a financially motivated phenomenon. While porn and, more generally, salacious and unlawful content have helped the internet to grow and internet intermediaries to flourish – indeed, in *EDP* I defended a claim for hosts' strict liability towards victims of NCII based also on some type of enterprise liability/fairness/business model approach – most uploaders of such content do not receive payment and most viewers do not pay to access such content.[83] As such, surveillance capitalism is less applicable. From a platform's perspective, at least at face value, the uploading of such data is prohibited so there in no explicit intent to transfer value from data subjects to companies. The caveat is that a logic of collusion might exist in which platforms might have an incentive to turn a blind eye to unlawful user-generated content which brings traffic and hence profit.[84] Certainly there are claims that major porn platforms do not enforce their terms and conditions which facially prohibit NCII.[85] Clearly, the second axis of gendered monitoring (facilitated by technology giants) exists to an even greater extent in NCII. In unpacking the normative relevance of the private nature of the monitoring conducted by Femtech actors the following points seem important.

[80] S Zuboff, *The Age of Surveillance Capitalism: The Fight for a Human Future at the New Frontier of Power* (London, Profile Books, 2019).

[81] Keren-Paz, *Egalitarian Digital Privacy* (n 1) at 104–05; Keren-Paz, *Torts, Egalitarianism and Distributive Justice* (n 2). Two contexts which clearly combine the two concerns are prostitution (including some forms of sex trafficking) and pornography. Eco-feminists and some ethical vegans have long pointed out that animal farming is mostly based on commercial exploitation of female reproductive systems.

[82] Siapka, Tzanou and Nelson (n 58).

[83] L Gilmore, 'Porn Pioneers: How Adult Entertainment Boosts Technology' (*The Next Web*, 30 August 2016). Available at: https://thenextweb.com/news/porn-pioneers-adult-entertainment-boosts-technology; Keren-Paz, *Egalitarian Digital Privacy* (n 1) at 38–44, 60–63, 68–70, 125–31, 190–91.

[84] Keren-Paz, *Egalitarian Digital Privacy* (n 1) at 43, 69.

[85] ibid 164–69.

4.2.1 Economic Exploitation, Big Data and Monetisation of Personal Data

First, on the economic axis, Femtech is just one manifestation of the bigger problem of surveillance capitalism – the monetisation of personal data as part of big data. Whether personal data should be the subject of property right and, if so, to whom the right should be allocated, is a big (and rather well-rehearsed) debate, with theories invoking property (including intellectual), labour and unjust enrichment rights being offered or applicable.[86] The fact that the relevant data is gendered, intimate and embodied is also normatively relevant, although similar to debates in contexts of slavery, trafficking and body parts there are arguments in both directions.[87] I belong to the camp that views the fact a profit was made from violation of human rights and from commodifying what should not have been commodified as strengthening the claim for restitution (and that restitution should accumulate with compensation for the harm from the violation). However, others view commodification as a reason against restitution of profits or recognising quasi/property right in the commodified entitlement, in this case personal data.[88] Four points would suffice here:

1. It has been argued that under EU law, personal data is de facto owned and sold by the controller subject to the data subject right enshrined in the General Data Protection Regulation.[89]
2. Whether the claim for the misappropriation of value is based on property, labour, unjust enrichment or indeed another theory, consent is an obstacle for recovery, so the quality of consent in terms of how free and informed it is, is an issue. The information and power gaps which are relevant for assessing the lawfulness of the monitoring thus are relevant also for any theory of recovery of the gains made at the expense of the data subject. In the NCII context, when consent is absent, a property framework is useful in that it allows strict liability towards third parties (like viewers) who inadvertently undermined the right: one's dominion over one's intimate images ought not be less than over one's car.[90]

[86] Some of the debate is summarised in Keren-Paz, *Egalitarian Digital Privacy* (n 1) at ch 4. For some recent contributions see J Harper, 'Personal Information is Property' (2024) 73 *Kansas Law Review* 113; B Custers and G Malgieri, 'Priceless Data: Why the EU Fundamental Right to Data Protection Is at Odds with Trade in Personal Data' (2022) 45 *Computer Law & Security Review*. Available at: www.sciencedirect.com/science/article/pii/S0267364922000309; A Siapka and E Biasin, 'Bleeding Data: The Case of Fertility and Menstruation Tracking Apps' (2021) 10(4) *Internet Policy Review* policyreview.info/articles/analysis/bleeding-data-case-fertility-and-menstruation-tracking-apps; B Chao, 'Unjust Enrichment: Standing Up for Privacy Rights' (2022) 108 *Iowa Law Review Online* 49.

[87] Siapka, Tzanou and Nelson (n 58).

[88] Keren-Paz, *Sex Trafficking* (n 2) at ch 3; Keren-Paz, *Egalitarian Digital Privacy* (n 1) at ch 5; see, in the context of slavery, AL Sebok, 'Reparations, Unjust Enrichment and the Importance of Knowing the Difference Between the Two' (2003) 58 *NYU Annual Survey of American Law* 651; Custers and Malgieri (n 86).

[89] N Duch-Brown, B Martens and F Mueller-Langer, *JRC Digital Economy Working Paper 2017-01: The Economies of Ownership, Access and Trade in Digital Data* (Seville, European Commission, 2017).

[90] Keren-Paz, *Egalitarian Digital Privacy* (n 1) at 79.

3. The data produced serves multiple interests: the data subject's, the Femtech owner and commercially related third parties and arguably women as a group by producing generalisable knowledge relevant to the group of potential/users. This means that Femtech (and, so it seems, other health and wellness tech apps) serves a function similar to clinical research. In future research I would like to examine the normative ramifications of such observation, including whether the regulation of these apps should more closely resemble that of clinical research, including the quality of consent, ethical oversight and how gains from research consent to which was not fully informed should be treated. The data produced from unauthorised creation of intimate images, or from the unauthorised dissemination of intimate images whose creation was consensual does not serve the subject's image interests, has (almost always) no, or very low social value and is harmful to women as a group.[91]
4. Even if Femtech exploitation is more serious than other forms of surveillance capitalism exploitation, given the gendered, intimate and embodied nature of the data, the extent and wrongfulness of such exploitation is much less extreme than in the context of trafficking and unauthorised use of human tissue for two reasons: both consent and protected interests (such as bodily integrity, privacy and autonomy) are undermined to a lesser degree than in the other examples; indeed, as we have seen in the NCII case study: NCII's monitoring is non-consensual and its disciplinary effect is much more harmful since the data subject is typically not anonymised, the circulation is broader, the subject matter is more humiliating, the medium is an image and reputational harm and follow-up abuse is more likely.[92]

4.2.2. Self-Monitoring, Consent and Internalised Values and Expectations

The private nature of Femtech monitoring is normatively relevant in a second sense, which is related to the claim advanced by the industry that Femtech is empowering to its users, where some of the monitoring is done by users themselves and to further their own interests.[93] Monitoring – both in general and in its surveillance capitalism version – often works by convincing the observed to adopt the values and hence produce the behaviour the observer would like; this point is mostly associated with Foucault's technologies of the self, but also, in legal and jurisprudential circles, it parallels Hart's internal view of the law.[94] While Zuboff stresses that a major point (and a source of danger) of surveillance capitalism technique is modifying (and not just predicting) the data subject behaviour to increase profits and sales, the part of the monitoring which corresponds with and indeed enhances the user's preferences (eg, a woman who would like to get pregnant getting a message from the app about a fertility window) is hardly problematic; at the very least, more work is needed to explain what makes it problematic. Is it a

[91] ibid 60–63.
[92] See text to n 43.
[93] Hoffman (n 11).
[94] Parfitt (n 39); HLA Hart, *The Concept of Law* (Oxford, Clarendon Press, 1961).

claim about false consciousness (a claim that is considered problematic by many as it undermines the subject's agency and authenticity), or, relatedly, on conflicts between current, best and ideal versions of autonomy?[95] Is it a tension between material and symbolic effects of the product (or the monitoring it produces)? Is it an issue of externalisation in which the individual interests of the user are enhanced at the expense of a (symbolic?) cost the group or other members of the group?[96] NCII, as non-consensual, is much less plausibly prima facie empowering, notwithstanding (a) sex-positive feminists' critiques of governance feminism, (b) conflicting messages conveyed in liberal societies to women about their sexuality, and (c) responses by some NCII victims – such as Emma Holten – to the non-consensual dissemination of their intimate images manifested in disseminating consensual intimate images of themselves.[97]

4.2.3 *Whose Interests Are Served?*

In further unpacking the normative relevance of the private nature of monitoring it might be useful to distinguish between monitoring whose effect advances the user's interests versus those that are at odds with these interests. Within the former category, one can further distinguish between advancing the user's interests according to her wishes or in an unsolicited way. NCII is a site in which monitoring is clearly at odds with the data subject's interests. In Femtech, a user who would like to get pregnant and receives pushes and advice on how to increase the chances of conception gets what she wants and presumably what she consented to. A user who gets pregnant and receives targeted advertisements might buy the products; and in this sense her interests are served even if she would have preferred not to be solicited. So, while nudging or other sources of soft manipulation are problematic from an autonomy perspective, they are not hugely problematic.[98] Using the data to discipline women (or those who help them) for having an illegal termination is the monitoring's effect which is most at odds with the user's interests. But from the Femtech owner's perspective this is an unintended consequence of monitoring.[99] More generally, the use of Femtech has the potential to harm the users (= bringing about effects

[95] J Coggon, 'Varied and Principled Understandings of Autonomy in English Law: Justifiable Inconsistency or Blinkered Moralism?' (2007) 15 *Health Care Analysis* 235.

[96] *cf*, Keren-Paz, *Torts, Egalitarianism and Distributive Justice* (n 2) at chs 4, 6.

[97] For a critique of NCII exceptionalism see L Karanian, 'Stripped of Dignity? Humiliation, Privacy and the Punishment of Revenge Porn' (LSA Annual Conference, Toronto, 31 May 2019); see Lunde and Joleby (n 75); Keren-Paz, *Egalitarian Digital Privacy* (n 1) at 158.

[98] This resembles the distinction I developed in the context of informed consent between types 1 and 2 of injury to autonomy. T Keren-Paz, 'Compensating Injury to Autonomy: A Conceptual and Normative Analysis' in Barker, Fairweather and Grantham (eds), *Private Law in the Twenty-First Century* (Oxford and Portland, Hart, 2017) 411. Being solicited to purchase a product you need is similar to a type 1 (the less serious) injury, at least if you end up buying the product.

[99] See Tzanou et al, *Research Report: Femtech Apps and Wearables and GDPR Compliance* (n 1) at 37–39 (information provided to law enforcement only under subpoena).

contrary to the user's interests) from discrimination in labour and insurance markets to furthering intimate partner abuse.[100] In these cases, but also in the more mundane and common case of targeted advertising, Femtech products facilitate the monitoring activities of third parties: employers, insurers, partners and advertisers. The case of advertisers is clearly a feature, while the other examples are less clearly so.

Other effects are harder to define. Two examples in the literature are the pain caused to women who have miscarried or had a stillbirth who keep getting pregnancy or baby ads or women who get congratulatory messages for likely pregnancies which are, in fact, unwanted.[101] Some of the problem is clearly functionality related, ie, users' cannot update the status of a pregnancy on the app. Beyond this, there are several points worth noting. It is somewhat ironic that the gist of this critique revolves around the lack of granularity of the app's messaging – namely the heteronormative, natalist bias of the app so the failure to appreciate that different users have different preferences and life plans – while at the same time the major critique of surveillance capitalism is the constant personalisation of marketing techniques with their concomitant privacy loss. In other words, beyond functionality failures, given the plurality of users' preferences, the only way to avoid a uniform message (which is bound to cater to the preferences of some but will be at odds with the preferences of others, and is likely to be majoritarian) is to seek more information at the registration stage of the user's purpose in using the app. Even then, life plans can change as do the circumstances in which the user conceives (or not). So, while an individual message might not match the user's present preferences, it is not evident that this category should be properly classified as a type of monitoring which is at odds with the user's preferences. One cannot (coherently) complain that too much data is requested while, at the same time, complaining that messages are not sufficiently personalised.

The usefulness of conflict of interests as an analytical lens could be demonstrated by contrasting Femtech with employment monitoring such as Teleperformance Observer which scans for worker infractions like 'missing from desk', 'unauthorised mobile phone usage' and 'detecting an idle user'.[102] While in both contexts the observed consents to the practice, the core monitoring in the employment context serves the interests of the employer and is clearly disciplinary in nature; the core monitoring in Femtech (eg, knowing where you are in your cycle and how fertile you are) is self-monitoring so serves the user's interests; even the main unintended effect of Femtech monitoring – targeted pregnancy and baby products ads

[100] See text to nn 14–16.

[101] G Brockwell, 'Dear Tech Companies, I Don't Want to See Pregnancy Ads After My Child Was Stillborn' *The Washington Post* (Washington DC, 12 Dec 2018). Available at: www.washingtonpost.com/lifestyle/2018/12/12/dear-tech-companies-i-dont-want-see-pregnancy-ads-after-my-child-was-stillborn/; L Purdon, *Unfinished Business: Incorporating a Gender Perspective into Digital Advertising Reform in the UK and EU* (Mozilla Foundation, 2023).

[102] Hariharan and Noorda (n 39) at 5.

are not clearly at odds with the user's interests.[103] Moreover, employment scrutiny is more intensive, consequential and arguably intrusive than that done in Femtech. More intensive, since most employees spend the majority of their waking time at work, more consequential, since work infractions detected via monitoring might ultimately cost the employee their livelihood – indeed, this combination of the intensity and its ramifications have caused some commentators to liken employers' power to that of the state – and intrusive, since its effects are to modify behaviour which is both fundamental and with clear implications for human dignity (eg, when to drink and have toilet breaks).[104] Although Femtech monitoring pertains to the intimate sphere, it involves fewer constraints on user choices. Decisions when to attempt conceiving are unconstrained, and receiving unsolicited ads is less intrusive and raises fewer dignitarian concerns.

4.2.4 Interference: In/Direct; Bug or Feature?

The last point on the normative relevance of monitoring being private is this: the more sinister aspects of Femtech monitoring – notably the threat to access to abortions and of intimate partner's abuse – as well as other potential risks (such as discrimination) are directly done by third actors, either private or the state. With reference to the distinction above – economic vs gender exploitation – these risks inhabit a place closer to the gender pole on the continuum but really reflect both. For example, intimate partner monitoring of women's reproduction and sexuality (termed 'mate guarding' by evolutionary biologists) obviously predated the digital revolution. But to the extent that Femtech technology (1) expands the opportunities for such monitoring; (2) normalises it thus further entrenching the norm; and (3) builds the feature enabling partner monitoring based on a business model recognising that feature's monetary value, the two types of exploitation work in tandem. State monitoring of abortion is different both because it is a bug, not a feature and because its likely effect is detrimental to Femtech business model (to the extent that some potential users abstain from using Femtech out of a fear of being detected should they ever have a termination). Discrimination seems to be a feature, since the information is made available to employers and insurers. In NCII, the monitoring is harmful: both the immediate dignitary loss and the consequential reputational losses (affecting for example employability and social relationships and in extreme cases exposing the victim to abuse, at times physical). The heart of the exploitation is along the gender axis, not the economic; those who directly monitor are the uploader and viewers and the economic benefit to companies is indirect and facially unintended.

[103] The quality of consent and whether it encompasses the details of the monitoring are in doubt, but this is an issue separate to the one discussed in the text.
[104] E Anderson, *Private Government: How Employers Rule Our Lives (and Why We Don't Talk about It)* (Princeton, Princeton University Press, 2017).

5. Conclusion

One can distinguish between good and bad types of monitoring – where good monitoring enhances and bad undermines the observed's interests. NCII is clearly and unequivocally bad as it is non-consensual and neither purports to nor does it advance the monitored person's interests but rather clearly harms them and curtails the autonomy of relevant group members. As regards Femtech, one can ask, whether, similar to bad vs good cholesterol, it increases bad monitoring and whether the proportion between good and bad monitoring improves under Femtech. Clearly, good monitoring increases in that Femtech seems to improve women's understanding of their hormonal health and might help them achieve their reproductive goals and improve their reproductive health. But this comes at a cost which could be conceptualised as bad monitoring. Whether the extent of bad monitoring increases under Femtech is a matter of debate. Broadly speaking, state monitoring of women's reproduction and sexuality decreased in the last century, although monitoring reproductive *health* (as distinct from reproductive *choice*) might have increased (whether the increase in monitoring reproductive health is a bad thing is at least debatable).[105] Societal modes of monitoring reproduction and sexuality have changed; it might be that overall (and certainly in Western societies) less monitoring is taking place, options which hitherto were deemed unacceptable have become more so and the sanctions for deviating from accepted norms are more attenuated. But societal monitoring of reproduction and sexuality has certainly not disappeared and is hardly on the wane. Femtech's monitoring, then, might be part of both a decreased overall level of bad monitoring and a broader trend substituting state surveillance with private (societal) monitoring and one which is partially profit seeking. Potentially, it reflects a trade off in which good monitoring increases and bad monitoring is manifested more in economic exploitation and less in gender-based oppression.

Despite the clear differences between these two sites of gendered monitoring, an integrated look yields analytical and normative payoffs. These include the distinctions between broad and narrow understandings of monitoring, between bad, good and mixed instances of monitoring (this distinction in turn is tied with both the existence of consent and the interests being served), between economic and gendered axes of distribution, between individual and group or societal effects, between state and private modes of monitoring and between non/financially motivation for monitoring. The two case studies also demonstrate the relationship between monitoring, physical and informational privacy and the relevance of a critical and egalitarian private law response to instances of unjustified or excessive monitoring. Ultimately, the suggested analytical framework

[105] I acknowledge that the distinction between health and choice is somewhat blurred. The policing of pregnancy with respect to lifestyle choices is also done by healthcare professionals.

demonstrates that despite the better fit of Femtech with a narrow definition of monitoring, NCII is the more problematic phenomena, both because it serves less the interest of those monitored and because it is likely to cause more serious harm. On the gendered harm versus corporate greed axis, NCII falls more closely to the gendered harm side, while Femtech on the corporate greed; this predominantly reflects the greater consensual and hence lawful nature of monitoring in the latter context. Having said that, a better appreciation of a critical-feminist analysis of Femtech, regarding eg the embodied commodification of reproductive data, might contribute to better remedying the harms caused by Femtech, by both questioning the validity of the consent manufactured in the Femtech space and providing stronger justifications for remunerating data subjects for the value extracted from their data.

8

The Privacy of (Not) Being Seen

A Right for the Digital Age

MARTHE GOUDSMIT SAMARITTER

While laws around the world are increasingly changed to accommodate the privacy concerns of the digital age, what counts as a privacy infringement is not always clear-cut. As a result, conduct that might intuitively seem quite obviously privacy-infringing may fall outside privacy protections, and vice versa. One such example can be found in Germany in October 2025, when a case of non-consensual filming in a sauna was dropped because it was not considered a criminal privacy violation.[1] German law either requires that body parts are covered, or that a space is not accessible to the public or is protected against public viewing.[2] This stands in contrast to the approach taken by the European Court of Human Rights (ECtHR), which has found that the following can violate privacy:

- filming in semi-public spaces;
- disclosure of images filmed in public;
- attempting to film someone in their home; and
- actually filming someone in their home without their consent.[3]

The ECtHR understands the right to privacy as encompassing a right to physical and informational integrity and generally as a realm in which to develop one's

[1] H Suliak, 'Heimliches Filmen in der Sauna nicht strafbar?' (*Legal Tribune Online*, 6 October 2025). Available at: www.lto.de/recht/hintergruende/h/unbefugte-nackt-aufnahmen-sauna-strafbarkeit-schutzluecke-upskirting.

[2] German Criminal Code, §184k and §201a.

[3] *Antović and Mirković v Montenegro* App no 70838/13 (ECtHR, 28 November 2017); *Peck v the United Kingdom* (2003) 36 EHRR 41; *Söderman v Sweden* (2013) 58 EHRR 36; *Khadija Ismayilova v Azerbaijan* App nos 65286/13 and 57270/14 (ECtHR, 10 January 2019).

identity.[4] The right to privacy, understood thus, is not so much about being left alone (whether physically or informationally), but about having authority over when to be left alone and when to be seen by whom. 'Being seen' may be as private as 'not being seen', under the right conditions. However, 'being seen' can also be a violation of privacy. Being seen sexually by a partner, for instance, may be a welcome and private expression of intimacy; being seen sexually by a random person, being recorded or having intimate images circulated without consent, as in image-based sexual abuse (IBSA), would be a privacy violation. Being noticed in public by strangers may be quite normal and privacy neutral; being continuously monitored by CCTV (closed-circuit television) or facial recognition software transforms that visibility into surveillance and into a privacy infringement. Being observed by a supervisor while working may be unremarkable; being digitally tracked through keystroke logging or proctoring software can steer behaviour and extensively infringe privacy. These practices in the realm of digital monitoring are widely described in privacy terms in law and policy. Yet the precise nature of the privacy wrong they constitute – especially when they occur in public or semi-public settings, or with some awareness and permission – is not necessarily self-evident.

Digital monitoring practices raise distinctive visibility-related privacy concerns. This chapter examines three such practices: IBSA, public surveillance and digital proctoring. These forms of digital monitoring are analysed using a functional account of privacy – that is, by asking 'what is privacy for?'. Applied to some of the privacy issues typical of the digital age, the chapter offers a partial theoretical foundation for the ECtHR's application of the right to privacy. It suggests that privacy is the realm in which to give rise to, develop and maintain the defining characteristics of our personhood. The chapter presents a relational interpretation of privacy on which engaging with others is a fundamental aspect of the right.[5] On this account, being seen by others is not necessarily a threat to privacy, it can also be privacy enhancing. In the context of digital monitoring this means that the conduct that *can* be a privacy infringement, might equally be a protection of a private realm. This chapter sets out the circumstances under which 'being seen' can be private, and the circumstances under which 'being seen' can be privacy infringing.

While being seen is essential to the development and expression of identity, it can also be privacy infringing, particularly when it is imposed, decontextualised, or otherwise occurs without the seen person's normative authority. The relational understanding of privacy can be contrasted with one that is atomistic, which more

[4] 'Guide on Article 8 of the European Convention on Human Rights: Right to Respect for Private Life, Home and Correspondence' (*Council of Europe and European Court of Human Rights*, 31 August 2020). Available at: https://ks.echr.coe.int/documents/d/echr-ks/guide_art_8_eng.

[5] I hold that persons are increasingly understood as relational beings, as opposed to atomistic beings, and that this can be recognised in the laws of constitutional democracies around the world, as well as in other academic disciplines, see M Goudsmit Samaritter, *The Wrongfulness of Image-Based Sexual Abuse: Relational Personhood as a Theoretical Foundation for Justified Criminalisation* (Oxford University Press, forthcoming 2026). See for some examples J Herring, 'Relational and Emotional Wrongs: Departing from the Soldier Model of Harm in the Criminal Law' (2024) 8 *Direito Penal* 59.

readily maps on to traditional definitions of privacy as a geographical 'right to be left alone', and even the right to informational privacy which captures the right not to be interfered with by others in a less geographically defined way.[6] Moving towards privacy as a realm for developing the defining characteristics of personhood presents a challenge for drawing a conceptual boundary around privacy. However, it also has advantages.

Conceptually, it expands the scope of privacy to include the right to be seen – on one's own terms – alongside the right not to be seen. Practically, it shifts what should be at the focus of legal interventions: from focusing on preventing intrusion into defined spaces or information to ensuring that visibility is subject to a person's normative authority and to protect as privacy infringing both those situations in which a person is seen and not seen without or against their normative authority.[7] This means that visibility should be subject to the person's autonomy, not that all seeing, surveilling, or monitoring (wanted or unwanted) is unjustified. It means that any decision to remove or limit normative authority over visibility must be properly justified.

If privacy is to meet the challenges – such as hypervisibility – of the digital age, it must be understood as more than a defensive shield around the individually conceived person. It must be seen as the protection of a shared space in which persons can appear to one another in ways that affirm their subjectivity. This perspective also rejects the notion that privacy can be completely preserved simply through withdrawal from public or digital life. Avoiding surveillance often entails avoiding participation altogether – at the cost of access to employment, education, services, or social spaces. Similarly, advising victims of digital privacy violations to stay offline is not a sustainable solution; it deprives them of the opportunities for engagement that are essential to personhood.[8]

Notably, this chapter focuses on privacy as it relates to persons, rather than the broader, systemic privacy issues associated with large-scale datafication. That is: the chapter does not address the significant concerns raised by the mass collection and analysis of behavioural data from large groups of (largely anonymised) individuals. Instead, it examines privacy infringements in which the individual is directly and recognisably linked to the exposed information, image or interaction. While these types of privacy concerns may overlap, they can be considered separately. Two different types of privacy threats associated with smartphone use can illustrate this distinction. The first type are abstract privacy concerns about where one's metadata – such as app usage or browsing behaviour – is sent, stored, and processed as part of massive datasets. These may be concerning but can feel distant and/or anonymous to the persons whose privacy is concerned. The second type

[6] SD Warren and LD Brandeis, 'The Right to Privacy' (1890) 4 *Harvard Law Review* 193.

[7] C Mackenzie and N Stoljar, *Relational Autonomy: Feminist Perspectives on Autonomy, Agency, and the Social Self* (Oxford University Press, 2000); this latter point is not part of the core of discussions presented in this chapter but flows from some of its considerations. It feeds into a right not to be lonely, see also K Brownlee, *Being Sure of Each Other: An Essay on Social Rights and Freedoms* (Oxford University Press, 2020).

[8] DK Citron, *Hate Crimes in Cyberspace* (Cambridge MA, Harvard University Press, 2014).

are immediate interpersonal concerns: for instance, your colleague glancing at your screen and reading a message to your partner. In this second case, the person is closely and recognisably connected to the content, and the potential harm is more personal, relational, and identity relevant. A person may feel comfortable using apps that are widely known to harvest personal data yet still install a privacy screen to prevent others from reading over their shoulder. This suggests that the privacy of being seen – and of being recognised as the subject of the information – raises distinct concerns that are not reducible to data governance. These concerns arise not from large-scale data analytics, but from interpersonal forms of unwanted access that disrupt the person *qua* person more tangibly than data collection does. It is this more immediate, relational form of privacy, concerned with how one appears to others and how that appearance is controlled, that this chapter addresses.

Within the limits set out here, the chapter shows how different conceptions of privacy – atomistic and relational – are grounded in different conceptions of personhood. Both accounts can link privacy to identity, but they differ in how that identity is thought to develop. I argue that many contemporary wrongs are best understood through a relational framework. Acts like IBSA, public surveillance, and digital proctoring do not necessarily infringe privacy in the traditional spatial sense (although some subtypes can). Rather, they undermine the conditions under which persons manage how they are seen – by whom, in what way and with what degree of normative authority. All these examples involve acts that can be privacy infringing but which, under different circumstances, could be privacy enhancing. Privacy does not just entail a right *not* to be seen when one does not want to be – it can be equally private to be *seen*. This chapter argues that the relevant distinction is normative authority over visibility: where it is wanted, it can be private; where it is unwanted, it can be privacy infringing. Being seen is a necessary condition of relational personhood; as I will argue below, privacy is the realm in which our personhood can take shape.

1. Privacy as the Realm for Developing Personhood

In this chapter, I understand privacy as the realm in which the defining characteristics of personhood can develop.[9] This functional approach to privacy builds on a substantial body of work that asks not what privacy *is* descriptively, but what privacy is *for*. Cohen, for instance, argues that privacy provides 'breathing room' for the development of selfhood and for resistance to power, whilst Roessler

[9] See on this more extensively JE Cohen, 'What Privacy Is For' (2013) 126 *Harvard Law Review* 1904. Much more has been said about privacy definitions that is beyond the scope of this chapter, see for a typology of privacy BJ Koops et al, 'A Typology of Privacy' (2017) 38 *University of Pennsylvania Journal of International Law* 483; for distinctions of types of privacy and associated protected values NA Moreham, 'Beyond Information: Physical Privacy in English Law ' (2014) 73 *The Cambridge Law Journal* 350; for the scope and theory of privacy AL Allen, *Unpopular Privacy: What Must We Hide?* (Oxford, Oxford University Press, 2011).

identifies decisional, informational, and local dimensions of privacy – each serving to protect personal autonomy.[10] The functional approach recognises that privacy's value lies in enabling human flourishing, though theorists differ on precisely what conditions privacy must protect to achieve this. Here, I consider privacy's function as enabling the development of our personhood.

Section 2 explores personhood theories in more detail, but I note here that different conceptions of personhood require different conditions for their development. As noted, privacy is understood here as the space that enables that development. On an atomistic account of personhood, a person is defined by a particular level of mental capacities.[11] Developing those capacities is something that is traditionally thought of as an individual pursuit: achieved by locking oneself in one's study, free from outside interference, free to do with oneself as one wishes, etc. The development of personhood, on this account, requires 'non-interference' which 'protected isolation' can bring. In that case, the privacy needed for personhood is closely aligned with the traditional framing of privacy as a right to be left alone, free from external interference in the development of one's own mental capacities.[12]

But on a relational account of personhood, isolation is not enough. On that definition, persons are formed through relationships requiring interaction, recognition and distinction from others.[13] Privacy, then, must protect not only seclusion but also the ability to engage with others on one's own terms. It includes both the right not be seen as well as the right to be seen. The relationally grounded functional definition of privacy provides a theoretical foundation for the ECtHR's interpretation of Article 8 of the European Convention on Human Rights, which the ECtHR understands to protect not only geographical isolation, but also dignity, identity development, and relational life – even in public.[14] On this view, privacy is the ability to exercise authority over one's visibility and engagement with others and to shape the terms of one's appearance.

This understanding shares some common ground with control-based accounts of privacy. Such accounts move away from purely spatial conceptions that define privacy by geographical seclusion. Instead, control-based accounts of privacy understand privacy as the exercise of control over information about oneself,

[10] Cohen ibid at 1906; B Rössler, *The Value of Privacy*, RDV Glasgow tr (Cambridge, Polity Press, 2005).

[11] D Wasserman et al, 'Cognitive Disability and Moral Status' in EN Zalta (ed), *Stanford Encyclopaedia of Philosophy*, Fall edn (Redwood City, Stanford University Press, 2017).

[12] Warren and Brandeis (n 6).

[13] C Foster and J Herring, *Identity, Personhood and the Law*, SpringerBriefs in Law (Cham, Springer, 2017); M Kyselo, 'The Body Social: An Enactive Approach to the Self' (2014) 5 *Frontiers in Psychology* 1; eg if one goes to Bali for a year to 'find' oneself, that is not necessarily an indication that atomistic personhood had it right, but can also be seen as the particular person's exercise of distinguishing from others within the range of the relationally defined self between engagement with- and distinction from others.

[14] 'Guide on Article 8 of the European Convention on Human Rights: Right to Respect for Private Life, Home and Correspondence' (n 4; *Von Hannover v Germany* (2012) 55 EHRR 15; *Peck v the United Kingdom* (2003) 36 EHRR 41.

access to oneself, or one's presentation to others.[15] Control-based accounts are a substantial part of contemporary privacy scholarship. On this notion, privacy can be understood as 'the claim of individuals, groups, or institutions to determine for themselves when, how and to what extent information about them is communicated to others'.[16] DeCew holds that privacy encompasses control over information, physical and mental access, and important lifestyle decisions.[17] My understanding of privacy shares some characteristics with control-based conceptions of privacy. Notably, I agree with control-based accounts of privacy that it is a person's own business to decide what to share of themselves with whom. However, on a control-based account of privacy, this may be understood as an individual, one-sided act that is more atomistic than can be reconciled with recognising the importance of relationships for developing personhood and identity. There are more relationally informed control-based accounts, that are more in line with what I propose here: Fried, Bannerman, Cohen and Marwick have all explored how privacy operates within networks of social relationships rather than as purely individual control.[18] Nissenbaum's theory of contextual integrity similarly recognises that privacy norms are context dependent and relational.[19] The understanding of exercising privacy advanced here may be placed within this increasing body of work on privacy and the relational self that recognises the socially constituted nature of personhood and the role of relationships in shaping privacy and privacy concerns. Control-based accounts of privacy can accommodate privacy interests for a relational definition of personhood advanced in this chapter. At the same time, control-based accounts of privacy reflect atomistic personhood foundations when they emphasise individualism and self-determination. As I argue below, self-determination – in the sense of a self that determines itself independently of others – is theoretically impossible.[20]

[15] See, eg AF Westin, *Privacy and Freedom* (London, The Bodley Head, 1970); WA Parent, 'Privacy, Morality, and the Law' (1983) 12 *Philosophy & Public Affairs* 269; JC Inness, *Privacy, Intimacy, and Isolation* (New York, Oxford University Press, 1996).

[16] Westin ibid. See also C Fried, 'Privacy' (1968) 77 *The Yale Law Journal* 475.

[17] See, eg JW DeCew, *In Pursuit of Privacy: Law, Ethics, and the Rise of Technology* (Ithaca, Cornell University Press, 1997).

[18] Fried (n 16); S Bannerman, 'Relational Privacy and the Networked Governance of the Self' (2019) 22 *Information, Communication & Society* 2187; JE Cohen, *Configuring the Networked Self: Law, Code, and the Play of Everyday Practice* (New Haven CT, Yale University Press, 2012); AE Marwick and d boyd, 'Networked Privacy: How Teenagers Negotiate Context in Social Media' (2014) 16 *New Media & Society* 1051.

[19] See H Nissenbaum, 'Privacy as Contextual Integrity' (2004) 79 *Washington Law Review* 119.

[20] Defining privacy in terms of control creates practical difficulties: those who lack capacity to exercise control (such as children or people with severe cognitive disabilities) would seem to lack privacy rights under such accounts. Yet lacking capacity does not mean one lacks rights – rather, it means those rights are exercised differently (eg, through best-interest assessments). Atomistic control-based accounts equate control with self-determination rather than shared decision making, making it difficult to defend privacy rights for those lacking mental capacity. In contrast, normative authority can be exercised through caring best-interest assessments that take a person's own ideas into account without requiring them to control outcomes. See J Herring, *Vulnerable Adults and the Law* (Oxford, Oxford University Press, 2016) 91.

A main distinction between typical control-based accounts of privacy and the understanding of privacy considered in this chapter is that this chapter defines privacy functionally rather than in terms of control. Furthermore, on the account advanced here, having privacy *can* involve an exercise of control, but it need not necessarily. Having normative authority over oneself, even if, in the end, another person makes the final decision on one's behalf (for instance, when a person lacks capacity) could be a genuine exercise of privacy and respect for that privacy, but it might not be an exercise of control.[21] On this account, having normative authority over oneself – including over one's information and visibility – is part of what it means for privacy to be exercised and for this realm to be respected, but that control is not framed, on this approach, as the definition of privacy itself. The relational, functional account of privacy recognises that control over oneself and one's information, in a full sense, is often impossible (because we are constituted through others and we cannot control, fully, what others do even if it affects our privacy).[22] What matters is not total control but normative authority – for the examples discussed in section 4: normative authority over one's visibility.

This functional relational framing helps explain why certain visibility-related practices characteristic of the digital age constitute privacy wrongs even if they are consented to and/or (partially) taking place in public. The crucial distinction is between control and normative authority. Control may refer to a factual ability to grant or deny access – a binary yes/no decision. Normative authority, by contrast, refers to the recognised standing to shape the terms of one's visibility within relationships. This approach does not rely on a binary yes/no for recognising privacy and privacy concerns. When conduct undermines the relational conditions through which identity develops and through which persons manage their visibility across different relational contexts it can be privacy-violating even if executed under the 'control' of the person who is concerned – for instance, if a person gives permission to being monitored but has no genuine alternatives. Exercising binary yes/no control over visibility without having normative authority over that visibility is not a genuine exercise of the right to privacy on the understanding advanced in this chapter.

Personhood itself can be understood as constituted through relationships. Privacy must then protect not just atomistic control, but the relational conditions under which identity develops – the authority over one's visibility across different relational contexts. This chapter invites a re-consideration of the realm of privacy as inquiring whether conduct interferes with a person's development qua person. As I consider in section 4, this can be particularly impactful in recognising novel privacy concerns that arise in the digital age *as* privacy concerns, and which are the topic of this volume. This is because the privacy concerns of the digital age do not always map on neatly to traditional definitions of privacy. A relationally

[21] It is beyond the scope of this chapter to consider the safeguards against abuse in, eg best-interest assessments, which must be taken seriously when decisions are to be made on behalf of someone else in a manner that respects rather than violates their rights.

[22] A Marmor, 'What Is the Right to Privacy?' (2015) 43 *Philosophy & Public Affairs* 3.

grounded functional model, when applied to a relational definition of personhood, helps explain why acts such as covert surveillance, IBSA, or performance-tracking software can constitute privacy violations – even when, for instance, they occur outside the home, or with (partial) consent. These acts interfere not with spatial boundaries, but with the relational conditions that allow people to form, maintain, and engage in their relationships and identity.

2. Personhood and Privacy

Grounding privacy in personhood reveals variations in the scope and interpretation of privacy rights, dependent upon differing conceptions of personhood. How a person is defined can have significant implications for the scope and interpretations of that person's rights: if I am defined by my mental capacities and fully embodied, then everything that is not part of my body or my mental capacities is not part of what defines my personhood. On such an account, it is hard to see how images can be used to infringe the depicted person *as a person*. At most, they could be a separated privacy interest, not unlike the way in which one has an interest in keeping bank statements private. However, if I am defined not through my embodied brain, but through my bodily mediated relationships, then everything that represents me to others is part of my person. On such an understanding, acts that interfere with my relationships – even if they do not interfere with my physical integrity or mental capacities – could be recognised as wronging me.[23]

Questions of what defines personhood are rarely made explicit in legal doctrine, yet they typically underlie judgments about whether a privacy interest is at stake. How we define personhood shapes what privacy protects. It influences whether conduct can be recognised as wrongful and thus captured by the law. A legal subject imagined as self-contained and independent generates very different privacy claims than one conceived as socially constituted and relationally embedded. Acts such as IBSA are increasingly recognised as very seriously privacy-infringing, in addition to violating other human rights, suggesting an increased relational understanding of persons underpinning the interpretation of rights.[24]

2.1 Atomistic Personhood and the Privacy of Visibility

In the liberal legal tradition, personhood is typically understood atomistically: the person is imagined as an embodied, rational, autonomous individual, capable of directing their own life.[25] This view treats persons as fundamentally individual,

[23] Kyselo (n 13); J Herring, *Law and the Relational Self* (Cambridge, Cambridge University Press, 2019).

[24] Goudsmit Samaritter (n 5); Herring (n 5).

[25] Wasserman et al (n 11).

separate units (hence: 'atomistic'), whose value derives from their mental capacities – self-awareness, practical reason, and the ability to make independent choices.[26] The self is conceived as existing separately from a person's relationships with others, and the development of identity is framed primarily as an inward, introspective process that relies on the development of intellectual abilities. Because personhood is defined in terms of independence and rational self-determination, solitude and freedom from interference can be understood to enable the development of the characteristics and flourishing of personhood. Rights, on this view, operate as protective boundaries that allow individuals to be left alone to think, choose, and act without external constraint or interference.[27] Privacy, on the functional model applied to atomistic personhood, protects the mental and spatial conditions in which one can think, choose, and act without interference. Being observed by others, in itself, does not typically threaten this form of personhood, because 'being visible' is not relevant to personhood. So long as one's mind and body remain uninvaded, public observation is generally a matter of exposure, which cannot be privacy on this account. Privacy on this account is a shield for seclusion and mental independence, not a mechanism for managing social presence.

Within the atomistic framework, privacy is thus understood as a shield from intrusion: a realm – whether spatial (the home), bodily (physical integrity), or informational (letters, diaries, or data) – into which others may not penetrate. Violations of privacy are typically seen as breaches of these defined boundaries. Atomistic privacy protects a person against unwanted access, in a binary sense: a space or information is either private, or it is not. Being hidden from the view of others (whether physically or informationally) is a primary characteristic of that understanding of privacy. Visibility, by contrast, is not considered constitutive of personhood on this account and so, 'being seen' is not an inherent part of privacy. Being seen in public can thus not readily be understood as privacy infringing, unless it involves entry into a protected private space.[28] Observation, filming, or sharing information about persons who are in geographically public spaces is not typically framed as a potentially severe infringement of rights.[29] This atomistic conception underpins much of traditional privacy law, particularly its focus on spatial and informational thresholds. It has proved powerful in protecting certain areas of life from state interference (sometimes perhaps too much so).[30] Yet, it is less well-equipped to capture wrongs that occur in public or that arise not from intrusion, but from forms of coerced or

[26] J Locke, *An Essay Concerning Human Understanding* (Oxford, Clarendon Press, 1894), book 2, ch 27.

[27] Atomistic personhood relies heavily on negative liberty, i.e. 'freedom from interference by others', I Berlin, *Two Concepts of Liberty* (Oxford, Oxford University Press, 1958). Relational personhood makes more requirements of both negatvie and positive liberty (eg freedom to act as wanted).

[28] See on privacy interests in public, *in casu* in a public phone booth, the case of *Katz v United States* 389 US 347 (1967).

[29] There are exceptions, but these are not necessarily rule based and could be more readily explained when adopting a relational definition of personhood and privacy.

[30] R Gavison, 'Feminism and the Public/Private Distinction' (1992) 45 *Stanford Law Review* 1; S Choudhry and J Herring, 'Righting Domestic Violence' (2006) 20 *International Journal of Law, Policy and the Family* 95.

distorted visibility. Where law has considered the privacy infringing nature of being seen in public, it has sometimes moved towards a definition of privacy more in line with a relational understanding of personhood.[31]

2.2 Relational Personhood and the Privacy of Visibility

Relational personhood defines personhood through caring relationships.[32] We are inherently relational beings and a relational definition of persons is thus more phenomenologically accurate than atomistic personhood: our identities, sense of selves, even our mental capacities, are not developed in isolation but rather through relationships with others.[33] I know myself as 'Marthe' because my parents have named me that and I have come to understand myself as such.[34] My identity developed through navigating relationships with others, through engaging with others and distinguishing myself from them.[35] Even if I had rejected the name and taken another, that would have been the development of my sense of self in relation to others and the world around me. Although I hold that we are defined through our relationships with the world around us, I do not say that all relationships are equally valuable or constitutive of personhood, or that we always need to engage with others. Distinguishing and separating the self from (engagement with) others is part of the development of the relational self. Abusive, neglectful or exploitative ties do not ground personhood protections.[36] Instead, it is caring relations that ground the protections of personhood, and the disruption of such relationships that can undermine the core of who we are.[37] To infringe or end caring relations in a non-caring way – by neglecting them, misrepresenting them, or making them impossible to sustain – touches on the core of who we are as persons.[38]

On a relational account, being perceived by others is an essential part of developing one's personhood. To participate in a relationship, a person must be present

[31] 'Guide on Article 8 of the European Convention on Human Rights: Right to Respect for Private Life, Home and Correspondence' (n 4); Herring (n 5).

[32] Herring (n 23).

[33] KJ Gergen, *Relational Being: Beyond Self and Community* (Oxford University Press, 2015).

[34] See also AC Baier, 'Cartesian Persons' (1981) 10 *Philosophia* 169.

[35] Kyselo (n 13).

[36] Caring relations are marked by respect, responsibility, and the meeting of needs, in J Herring, *Caring and the Law* (Oxford, Hart Publishing, 2013) 14; see also J Herring, 'The Caring Subject' in SH Vauchez and R Rubio-Marín (eds), *The Cambridge Companion to Gender and the Law*, Cambridge Companions to Law (Cambridge, Cambridge University Press, 2023); Caracciolo di Torella and Masselot place them in constant ongoing responsibilities; absence of choice; financial, physical and emotional costs; and emotionally sensitive personal connection, in E Caracciolo Di Torella and A Masselot, *Caring Responsibilities in European Law and Policy: Who Cares?* (Abingdon, Routledge, 2020) 7–8.

[37] For instance, where there are severe breaches of trust, a person can be severely impaired in their ability to engage in and maintain other relationships, SD Boon and JG Holmes, 'The Dynamics of Interpersonal Trust: Resolving Uncertainty in the Face of Risk' in RA Hinde and J Groebel (eds), *Cooperation and Prosocial Behaviour* (Cambridge, Cambridge University Press, 1991).

[38] Arguably one cannot live without care, see, eg E Feder Kittay, *Love's Labor: Essays on Women, Equality and Dependency* (New York, Routledge, 1999).

to others in some way – seen, heard, or otherwise recognised.[39] Visibility, broadly understood, is thus a constitutive part of becoming and being a person. It enables persons to engage in the relationships that define our personhood. Visibility is therefore not inherently at odds with privacy. In fact, on the functional definition of privacy applied to relational personhood, many exercises of privacy will involve being visible to others. Here, privacy operates as an exercise of autonomy, understood as the normative authority to shape and regulate visibility: to decide when, how, and to whom one appears.[40]

Misplaced or coerced visibility – being seen in the wrong way, by the wrong audience, or stripped of context – can be deeply harmful and can constitute a privacy infringement on the relational account. There are many ways in which visibility welcomed in one context can become unwelcome in another. For example, being naked in a sauna is not typically understood as privacy infringing, but if someone secretly films the sauna and uploads the video to a pornography website, that visibility is taken out of the control of the seen person, and transformed into non-consensual sexual exposure. In this example, there are at least three layers of privacy infringement: the act of filming; the act of publication; and the sexualising context in which the footage is displayed. While visibility is essential to the relationally defined person, it could also detract from one's ability to engage in and maintain relationships. Different relationships call for different visibilities: a partner may see you in a sexual context that you could find entirely inappropriate for colleagues or strangers. Misplaced or coerced visibility – being seen in the wrong way, at the wrong time, or by the wrong audience – can harm the relationships that help constitute personhood. What supports and affirms identity in one context may undermine it in another.

When relational personhood is used to ground the functional definition of privacy, the importance both of being seen and of not being seen is unveiled – to be a person is, at least in part, to be recognised by others, and part of what helps sustain one's caring relations. But being seen in the wrong way (in a wrongful way) can undermine such relations. This helps explain in part why visibility can be private: it is not inherently a threat to the self, it can be private if the perceived person has had normative authority over their visibility.

3. Normative Authority Over Visibility

The distinction between privacy enhancing or privacy neutral, and privacy-infringing visibility lies in whether the person retains normative authority over the terms of their visibility.[41] When visibility is wanted or voluntary and aligned with the

[39] 'Being perceived' includes being seen, heard, read, or recognised through an avatar or other mediated presence.

[40] N Stoljar, 'Feminist Perspectives on Autonomy' in EN Zalta and U Nodelman (eds), *The Stanford Encyclopedia of Philosophy*, Winter edn (Redwood City, Stanford University Press, 2018).

[41] ibid.

roles and relationships that constitute personhood, it is private. When normative authority over visibility is denied, that visibility can become a privacy infringement – regardless of whether it occurs in geographically private or public spaces.

On a relational account of personhood, privacy is not simply the absence of access or observation by others. It is the ability to determine the terms of one's visibility – when, how, and by whom one is perceived. This is 'having normative authority over visibility'. It reframes privacy not as a fixed state of seclusion, but as an ongoing capacity to govern the presentation of the self in ways that sustain caring relationships. On an atomistic account, autonomy is understood as self-determination: the capacity to decide independently and free from external interference. That understanding is not possible on a relational account, because the self is never wholly separate from others; it is constituted through relationships. Complete self-determination would, in effect, require determining aspects of other people who are part of one's person, relationally defined, which makes the concept theoretically impossible on a relational framework. Autonomy in this context must therefore be reconceived. Instead of 'self-determination', I understand it as 'having normative authority over oneself'.[42] Autonomy, on a relational definition, means to have the authority to be involved in decision-making on matters concerning and/or affecting the relational self – including the authority to decide the terms on which one is perceived. It is different from a capacity for self-determination. For instance, people who lack capacity would nevertheless have normative authority over themselves, meaning that if it can be helped, they should not be forced to submit to unwanted conduct, even if, because they lack capacity in a legal sense, their decision may not be the final deciding factor. Autonomy in the sense of normative authority is essential for the development and maintenance of personhood because, on relational personhood, identity is shaped differently across contexts: you are different and would usually want to be seen differently, as a colleague, friend, partner, parent, teacher, and so on. These variations reflect the plural, situated ways in which the self takes shape through relationships. Normative authority over visibility enables a person to navigate the plurality of their identities: to be seen when recognition is affirming, and to withhold their visibility when that is better for the relationships that define that person. All aspects of this can be part of the right to privacy, functionally defined and relationally grounded.

When normative authority is exercised, visibility should be privacy enhancing or privacy neutral. It allows for selective engagement, supports differentiated roles, and resists the collapse of contexts that can occur when visibility escapes its intended boundaries. Without it, visibility becomes a form of capture – something done *to* the person rather than *by* them. This is why coerced, decontextualised or misappropriated visibility is experienced not merely as unwanted exposure but can also be a deep infringement of privacy and personhood.[43] Notably, I am not arguing that the

[42] Goudsmit Samaritter (n 5).

[43] See, eg C McGlynn et al, '"It's Torture for the Soul": The Harms of Image-Based Sexual Abuse' (2021) 30 *Social & Legal Studies* 541.

infringement of privacy can never be justified. For example, there may be a genuine public interest in the private lives of politicians that would justify an infringement into their privacy, for instance where disclosed private information contradicts that politician's expressed political views and so could affect voters' decision making.[44]

Additionally, on a relational account, abusive or otherwise non-caring relationships do not fall within personhood's protective scope; interference in abusive or otherwise non-caring relationships, even if contrary to a stated preference, may even enhance privacy and autonomy by restoring the conditions for engaging in caring relations.[45] Similarly, visibility that entrenches oppression or stems from internalised harmful norms may not reflect genuine normative authority if it lacks both the conditions of positive liberty (genuine options for engagement) and strong normative evaluation (the capacity to critically assess the norms shaping one's choices).[46] Normative authority over visibility is therefore the constitutive core of privacy in a relational framework. It marks the difference between visibility as recognition and visibility as subjugation. Protecting this authority helps ensure that being seen and not being seen remain means of sustaining personhood, rather than tools for undermining it.

4. Digital Age Infringements of Privacy: Some Examples

The preceding sections have set out a relational framework for understanding privacy in terms of normative authority over visibility. On this account, privacy is not the absence of observation but the capacity to govern the terms on which one is seen. This section applies that framework to concrete contexts where visibility is central – examining how certain practices can either enhance privacy by affirming personhood or infringe it by stripping away normative authority. Digital monitoring, through automated recording, algorithmic analysis and persistent tracking, transforms the nature of visibility itself, creating new challenges for privacy law. The examples discussed in the following – namely IBSA, public surveillance, and digital proctoring – are particularly relevant to the digital age, where being seen and being recorded are easier than ever, thus increasing both the scope of privacy, as well as of privacy concerns.

4.1 Image-Based Sexual Abuse

IBSA is any kind of non-consensual taking, making, accessing, and/or sharing of intimate images. It includes not only the sharing of sexual images taken with consent but also recording voyeuristic practices such as secretly filming in a

[44] JW Devine, 'The Political Privacy Dilemma: Private Lives and Public Office' (2024) 41 *Journal of Applied Philosophy* 391.

[45] Choudhry and Herring (n 30).

[46] J Raz, *The Morality of Freedom* (Oxford, Oxford University Press, 1986); Berlin (n 27); Mackenzie and Stoljar (n 7).

dressing room, upskirting and downblousing, as well as the creation of deepfake sexual imagery. It illustrates with particular clarity how visibility can move from privacy enhancing to privacy infringing when normative authority is removed: it often occurs in contexts – intimate relationships, public spaces – where some form of visibility is expected and wanted. The privacy violation lies not in visibility itself, but in the transformation of that visibility: in its decontextualisation, its permanence through recording, and the loss of control over oneself. The wrong does not lie simply in the fact that others view the material, but in the collapse of the relational boundaries within which that visibility was originally situated.[47]

Images or recordings that are private in one context – often intimate or sexual – may be taken with the depicted person's consent and could be an exercise of the depicted person's and their partner's privacy. For example, when an image that was taken with consent, is shared without consent, that is an infringement of the depicted person's privacy: they have been denied normative authority over their visibility, and can suddenly be seen in, for example, a sexual way by many people who they never would have wanted to see them depicted in that way. If a sexual image is taken without consent then the privacy infringement consists of the act of being recorded without consent – even if the person taking the image had the depicted persons permission to *see* them sexually, if they did not have their consent for recording them in that moment this is a privacy infringement because of the objectification that takes place when a person is recorded.[48] Objectification is discussed further in section 5. If the image that was taken without consent is disclosed, then there is an additional layer to the privacy infringement. These cases of IBSA may be recognised as privacy infringing even on a spatial definition of privacy.

IBSA that is taken in public would more readily fall outside the scope of privacy protections, particularly if they are 'mere' recordings of what would have been visible anyway (for example if a person looks up when walking up a flight of stairs, and the person in front of them is wearing a skirt, they might be able to look up their skirt).[49] Acts such as 'upskirting' (taking photos or videos up someone's skirt); 'downblousing' (taking photos or videos down someone's blouse); or recording someone publicly engaged in sexual or 'sexualisable' acts may be more readily recognised on a relationally informed functional definition of privacy.

[47] Goudsmit Samaritter (n 5).

[48] The law in England and Wales was changed so that it could count as voyeurism to film without permission even if one had permission to be in the room, E Saner, 'Emily Hunt: Why She Fought to Make Sure No Woman Is Filmed Naked Without Consent' *The Guardian* (London, 21 July 2021). Available at: www.theguardian.com/society/2021/jul/21/emily-hunt-why-she-fought-to-make-sure-no-woman-is-filmed-naked-without-consent.

[49] M Hall, J Hearn and R Lewis, '"Upskirting," Homosociality, and Craftmanship: A Thematic Analysis of Perpetrator and Viewer Interactions' (2022) 28 *Violence Against Women* 532. See also 'objectification' in section 5.

Despite sometimes elaborate efforts to record voyeuristic acts, it has in the past proven challenging to understand their privacy-infringing nature.[50] In Georgia, United States, for instance, a Court of Appeal ruled that upskirting did not violate privacy laws due to what it described as a 'gap' in the law. The court reasoned that because the filming occurred in public spaces and none of the activities of the victim were occurring in a private place and out of public view, the act fell outside the realm of criminalised privacy infringements.[51] The implication was that by appearing in public, the victim could not rely on privacy protections, and had no authority over whether they would be filmed, even if by a hidden cameras in deliberate violations of social norms and boundaries. This reasoning reflects the limitations of a geographically bound, atomistic conception of privacy. In that account, privacy is tied to spatial seclusion: one has privacy in the home or changing room, but not on the street or in a shop.[52] The law's focus on location rather than the nature and context of the visibility itself meant it could not capture this particular wrongdoing.

Yet, victims of upskirting may have accepted being visible in public in ordinary ways, but they had no opportunity to consent to being recorded, objectified, and potentially shared in sexualised contexts. Indeed, elaborate efforts to capture private images are not unique. For example, a man convicted of upskirting over 250 women in England and Wales had modified a pair of shoes by placing a camera in the tip of the toes, and multiple cases of modified shoes have surfaced over the past decade or so, enabling the person who is filming to obtain angles that they would certainly not have been able to catch without attracting a lot of attention.[53]

On a relational understanding of privacy, it is quite straightforward that acts such as upskirting are privacy violations: the depicted person may have consented or submitted to being seen in a particular way, but they have not had normative

[50] Upskirting has, in the past, proven difficult to recognise as a privacy infringement. In Georgia, USA, for instance, due to a 'gap' in the law: A Sims, 'Secretly filming up a woman's skirt ruled legal by Court of Appeal in Georgia' *The Independent* (London, 22 July 2016). Available at: www.independent.co.uk/news/world/americas/secretly-filming-up-women-s-skirts-ruled-legal-by-court-of-appeal-in-georgia-a7151001.html.

[51] *Gary v State* (Court of Appeals of Georgia, 15 July 2016) A16A0666.

[52] While this means, in theory, that the law can offer more protections against non-consensually filming in a private space, the technology needed for 'spycams' is so small that such cameras may be completely hidden. In South Korea the use of hidden cameras became so prevalent that women formed a habit of covering pinhole sized holes in public restrooms, calling it 'part of daily life', J McCurry and N Kim, "A Part of Daily Life': South Korea Confronts Its Voyeurism Epidemic' *The Guardian* (3 July 2018). In December 2018, 110000 people attended a feminist demonstration calling for better protection against spycams, J Hae-myoung, 'Largest Anti-Gender Discrimination Rally Held' *The Korea Times* (Seoul, 24 December 2018). Available at: www.koreatimes.co.kr/southkorea/law-crime/20181224/largest-anti-gender-discrimination-rally-held.

[53] 'Man Sentenced for Upskirting Offences' (*West Mercia Police*, 20 April 2021). Available at: www.westmercia.police.uk/news/west-mercia/news/2021/april/man-sentenced-for-upskirting-offences/; eg 'Man Secretly Filmed Female Shoppers With Shoe-Mounted Camera' *BBC* (London, 12 June 2013). Available at: www.bbc.com/news/uk-northern-ireland-22880367; 'Wisconsin Man Injured After Upskirting Shoe Camera Explodes' *BBC* (London, 29 June 2018). Available at; www.bbc.com/news/world-us-canada-44655263; 'Spy Cameras in Shoes Add to Rapid Rise of Upskirting in Japan' *The Times* (London, 28 September 2021). Available at: www.thetimes.com/world/asia/article/spy-cameras-add-to-rapid-rise-of-upskirting-in-japan-dfcdckj9x?region=global%2Cglobal.

authority over being recorded, and that should therefore be understood as a privacy infringement. For example: a woman wearing a blouse may accept that if she bends over, someone sitting across from her could have a brief opportunity to look down her blouse. That is a very different thing to accept than to be recorded in that moment, and enabling the person recording to rewatch at will, and potentially share the recording, without consent. In the case of such non-consensual recordings, the depicted person is turned into a tool that can be used against themselves – a substantially different situation than being seen in a fleeting manner. Even being seen can be a violation however: most women wearing skirts in public will not thereby mean to invite people to look up their skirts; they may find it uncomfortable if this happens. It affects women's sense of safety in public spaces both in that moment (between the voyeur and the victim) and in general. Harassment generally causes women who have *not* been subjected to it to feel more unsafe in public.[54] Knowing that others have been harassed is already harming the place of women in the world. When voyeurism is being filmed, that is not the *beginning* of abuse – rather, it is an added layer. Filming up skirts and down blouses is a type of objectification that enables the continued abuse of the filmed person (see section 5).

Some of the privacy wrongs of IBSA arise where images are taken without consent. In such cases, there is no opportunity to determine the terms of visibility in the first place. The subject's relational self is made present to an audience without any grounding in a (caring) relationship, in ways that can damage existing relationships and make it harder to enter into caring relationships in the future.[55] Even if the initial capture was authorised, sharing the image beyond the intended audience transforms the act from one of selective engagement into one of exposure. The visibility is no longer anchored in the relationships that gave it meaning, and the audience, format, or framing may change in ways that infringe the depicted person's (ability to engage in) relationships. A private sexual image between partners may be uploaded to a pornography site, turning the depicted person into a pornographic tool.[56] Or, briefly seeing down someone's blouse may be tolerable to the wearer (even if unwanted), but filming down her blouse and placing that footage on a pornography site is an entirely different set of actions to accept. Such recontextualisation violates the subject's intended boundaries and can undermine or damage the relationships that form part of their personhood.[57] The wrong is not reducible to a loss of spatial seclusion or to the disclosure of information; it lies in the denial of normative authority over how, when and to whom one appears.

[54] 'The Lasting Impact of Violence Against Women and Girls' (*Office for National Statistics*, 24 November 2021). Available at: www.ons.gov.uk/peoplepopulationandcommunity/crimeandjustice/articles/thelastingimpactofviolenceagainstwomenandgirls/2021-11-24.

[55] NM St Vil, T Carter and S Johnson, 'Betrayal Trauma and Barriers to Forming New Intimate Relationships Among Survivors of Intimate Partner Violence' (2021) 36 *Journal of Interpersonal Violence* NP3495.

[56] The argument that pornography is a particular form of violence adds to the wrong done to a person who is turned into pornography without her consent, see, eg A Dworkin, *Pornography: Men Possessing Women* (New York, Plume, 1991).

[57] Victims report difficulties engaging in relations after abuse, see ibid; McGlynn et al (n 43).

4.2 Public Surveillance

Public surveillance shows how visibility in shared spaces can shift from ordinary social presence to privacy-infringing control when normative authority is removed. The wrong lies not simply in being observed, but in the replacement of context-specific recognition with persistent, decontextualised monitoring. Being seen by strangers while walking down the street may be unremarkable, even expected; the visibility is fleeting, can be reciprocal and is usually without record. However, when that same walk is captured by CCTV, logged by facial recognition systems, or analysed by behaviour-tracking software, the terms of visibility change. The idea of such surveillance is that it is in the public interest or to protect property, etc. Indeed, there may be advantages to having surveillance and its used could be justified. But when surveillance becomes all-encompassing, it is questionable whether its positive aspects can ever outweigh the breadth of the intrusion. For instance, Clearview AI made headlines in 2020 for creating an advanced facial recognition tool that scraped social media images to connect faces to names. Any law enforcement agency using it could identify a person from nothing more than a photograph taken on a public street. One example offered in its defence presents what might be its most compelling justification, even if the method is still highly invasive: the software was used to identify 'a person accused of sexually abusing a child whose face appeared in the mirror of someone else's gym photo'.[58] The face of someone appearing in child sexual abuse materials, popped up in *another* person's Instagram photo. As a result, the child abuser could be tracked down. If the same technology were used to track climate protestors, or dissenters opposing an increasingly illegitimate regime, the justification becomes more problematic.[59] It creates, at the very least, a high risk of interference with positive aspects of personal development. The question is whether the justifying aspects are worth that trade off, especially if the justifying qualities may be achieved by different, less invasive means. If a depicted person no longer controls how they are seen or how long that visibility lasts, there is no real normative authority over that visibility. Images and data can be stored indefinitely, combined with other datasets, and repurposed for uses never consented to – from targeted advertising to law-enforcement profiling.

Some surveillance systems remove normative authority entirely. Continuous monitoring can collapse the distinction between different relational roles and contexts, replacing the selective, situational appearances that sustain personhood with a single, all-encompassing profile. The person becomes an object of observation rather than a participant in a shared environment in which they might

[58] K Hill, 'The Secretive Company That Might End Privacy as We Know It' *The New York Times* (New York, 18 January 2020). Available at: www.nytimes.com/2020/01/18/technology/clearview-privacy-facial-recognition.html.

[59] See also the dismissal of the 'nothing to hide' argument as a reason to neglect privacy protections, DJ Solove, *Nothing to Hide: The False Tradeoff between Privacy and Security* (New Haven, Yale University Press, 2011) 23.

exercise normative authority over themselves and reinforce their relational selves. Even where awareness or nominal consent exists – such as entering a building with visible security cameras – the lack of meaningful choice means that consent may be illusory. In many public or semi-public contexts, avoiding surveillance requires avoiding participation altogether, which may restrict access to employment, services or social spaces, which could be very harmful to the relational self.

The wrong of public surveillance, on a relational account, cannot be reduced to the fact of being seen in public. It lies in the loss of control over the scope, duration and audience of that visibility, and in the potential for the resulting record to be used in ways that distort or undermine the relationships through which personhood develops. Surveillance operates not merely by observing but by shaping behaviour through anticipation: when people know they are being watched, they tend to self-censor.[60] Again, there can be positive aspects to this: one of the harmful aspects of the Internet is that people who are anonymous tend to not worry as much about the consequences of their words and are less inhibited, which can sometimes be used in negative ways (for example 'trolling').[61] But the pressure to conform, to behave in ways that appear 'normal' or acceptable to the monitoring entity, can have profound effects on how individuals develop their identities. (Continuous) surveillance can transform mere visibility into a privacy-infringing mechanism, especially where people with minoritised identities, such as members of the LGBTQI+ community, cannot fully develop themselves as they would like as a result of the fear of (and stemming from) being under surveillance. As noted, the fact that surveillance is a privacy wrong does not mean it cannot be justified. That surveillance is prima facie wrong merely means that there need to be good reasons to employ it; if these reasons do not exist, surveillance should not be used.

4.3 Digital Proctoring

Digital monitoring, which is at the heart of this volume, comes in many forms. Digital proctoring software is a particular subset. It is software that is designed to track, for instance, students during the course of an exam, or employees working from home, by tracking things ranging from mouse movement to eyeball movement and flagging it as 'cheating' if the tracked person rests their eyes or goes to use the restroom. Digital proctoring software is thus a type of surveillance technology that can monitor students taking online exams, typically through webcam recording, screen monitoring and automated behaviour analysis. During the COVID-19 pandemic, its use on students taking exams from home and on employees working from home drew attention to the use of proctoring software. The idea is that the software functions as the equivalent of persons proctoring an exam hall,

[60] DK Citron, 'The Surveilled Student' (2024) 76 *Stanford Law Review* 1439.

[61] L Nitschinsk, SJ Tobin and EJ Vanman, 'The Disinhibiting Effects of Anonymity Increase Online Trolling' (2022) 25 *Cyberpsychology, Behavior, and Social Networking* 377.

or supervisors keeping an eye on employees during the workday. However, the proctoring software keeps a much closer eye on each individual member of the group of examinees or employees, and it does so in potentially privacy-infringing ways. Again, the wrong does not consist of being observed during an examination or work task as such, but of the conditions under which that observation takes place: constant, behaviour steering, and without the perceived person's normative authority over determining how they are perceived.[62]

In a traditional in-person examination, an invigilator's observation is bounded. It is limited to the duration of the exam, takes place within a defined space, and is conducted by someone physically present who can respond to the candidate as a person. In such settings, the candidate retains some normative authority: they can anticipate the scope of the observation, understand the interpretive framework applied to their conduct, and, if challenged, offer an explanation.

Remote proctoring software alters these conditions. It often records the student's face, posture, surroundings, and on-screen activity, while using automated systems to flag behaviour that deviates from a prescribed norm. This can include looking away from the screen for more than a few seconds, moving out of frame, or adjusting one's seating position. Such constraints require highly unnatural behaviour and remove the freedom to behave and present oneself in ordinary, context-appropriate ways. For example, a student thinking through an exam question might naturally glance out of the window; under some systems, this could be treated as evidence of misconduct. Another example is that students taking an examination in-person could, for instance, be permitted to use the restroom as long as it can be ascertained that they do not bring their phone nor any books nor have any other way to cheat. The home-examination proctoring software cannot facilitate this; as a result, students may be required to sit at their desk for the duration of the exam, even if that means not using the restroom when they might need to.

The implications can be even more severe for students with darker skin tones, who face discrimination through proctoring software not 'recognising' them as human at all. This is a type of engineered dehumanisation that is the result of training facial recognition software on a poor dataset of only, or overwhelmingly, white people. Black students have reported having to sit in intense lighting just to be recognised by the system.[63] While the racial discrimination inherent in such design raises questions beyond the scope of this chapter, it also engages privacy on a relational account: to deny recognition in this way is to deny the person subject to such software the space in which to develop and express personhood. The message conveyed is not simply that the individual is under suspicion, but that they do not conform to the coded

[62] E Shioji et al, '"It's Been Lovely Watching You": Institutional Decision-Making on Online Proctoring Software' in M Blanton, W Enck and C Nita-Rotaru (eds), *Proceedings: IEEE Symposium on Security and Privacy: SP 2025* (Los Alamitos, Conference Pulishing Services, 2025); H Beetham et al, 'Surveillance Practices, Risks and Responses in the Post Pandemic University' (2022) 14 *Digital Culture and Education* 16.

[63] T Feathers, 'Proctorio Is Using Racist Algorithms to Detect Faces' *Vice* (New York, 8 April 2021). Available at: www.vice.com/en/article/proctorio-is-using-racist-algorithms-to-detect-faces.

expectations of humanness embedded in the technology. It is not far from suggesting that the person who is not recognised by the software is not a person at all.

If there are no genuine alternatives the consent for the use of such software does not respect normative authority. Where refusal entails the loss of an academic or professional opportunity, the choice to be monitored cannot be said to reflect a genuinely autonomous choice.[64] The individual cannot determine when, how, or by whom they are seen; cannot manage the context of their appearance; and cannot adjust their self-presentation to suit the relationships at hand. Workplace surveillance that tracks keystrokes or records screens may extend far beyond what is necessary for legitimate oversight, instead shaping behaviour through constant visibility and undermining trust between colleagues. The role of 'student' or 'worker' is reframed through the lens of suspicion and risk management, while the person is made visible in a manner that is neither negotiated nor responsive to their normative authority. Digital proctoring can make a person visible without voice, undermining the conditions necessary for privacy to protect and sustain personhood.

5. Objectification as a Privacy Infringement

The examples in section 4 show that privacy infringements on a relational account often involve more than unauthorised access to information or the breaching of a spatial boundary. They also involve a change in how the person is *seen*: from a participant in a relationship to an object of observation, analysis, or consumption. This shift is at the core of what I call objectification as a privacy infringement.

Objectification, in the sense relevant here, refers to a subject–object relationship in the grammatical sense: the subject performs an action to which the object is subjected. To *subject a person to treatment* is to make them the grammatical object of the action. This does not automatically mean that the person's subjectivity is denied. A person can be objectified in this grammatical sense while still being recognised as a subject. For example, when a patient visits a doctor and agrees that the doctor will examine their knee, the patient is subjected to the doctor's action, but the patient's perspective, consent, and autonomy are respected. The examination takes place within a caring relationship, and the patient's subjectivity is respected.

Objectification becomes privacy infringing on a relational account when it entails the denial of subjectivity. This happens when the person is treated not as a participant in a relationship, but as an object to be used, monitored or displayed without regard for their autonomy. If a denial of subjectivity were to be complete, then a person would not be treated *as a person* at all. That is not typically the case in the examples discussed above: in some regards a student subjected to proctoring

[64] Genuine options are needed to be able to speak of liberty, and autonomy, in any real sense, see Raz (n 46).

software may be treated as a person by the person(s) using the proctoring software 'on' them, but the use of the software itself could be a way to deny subjectivity in that instance and is thus a form of objectification. Denial of subjectivity, in this way, is to remove the person from the role of subject and to fail to acknowledge that they ought to have normative authority over themselves.

From a relational privacy perspective, the wrong lies not simply in being seen, but in being seen without recognition, from being turned into an image-object: without reciprocity, context, and possibility for engagement that caring relations require. In IBSA, the depicted person is rendered into an image for consumption, detached from the relationships in which their (sexual) visibility might have been affirming. In public surveillance, the person becomes a traceable data point, monitored continuously and outside the ebb and flow of reciprocal public encounters. In digital proctoring, the student is rendered into a stream of behavioural outputs to be assessed against a pre-coded norm, with no scope to explain, contest, or adjust how they are perceived. In very extreme cases, being seen without normative authority goes far beyond 'mere' exposure but can be an all-encompassing infringement of a person's caring relationships and abilities to engage in them.

On a relational account, privacy protects the possibility to present oneself in different capacities in different contexts, on their own terms. To be treated as an object only, without recognition for one's personhood, is to be deprived of the space to enact one's personhood when that personhood is relationally defined. A descriptive privacy definition or atomistic functional privacy definition would not capture objectification as a privacy concern. On the former because objectification does not add anything to crossed geographical boundaries; on the latter because objectification does not interfere with a person's mental capacity and autonomy.[65] However, relational personhood requires persons to navigate between roles, to sustain caring relationships and to be seen in ways that affirm rather than erode identity. Privacy must therefore protect against objectification; being filmed, photographed or otherwise depicted is an essential aspect of objectification with which privacy must be concerned.

Protecting privacy in the relationally informed functional sense is not about protecting invisibility. It is about ensuring that visibility is subject to a person's autonomy. Where visibility is not subject to normative authority, it becomes a privacy infringement not necessarily because something is seen, but because of *how* and *on whose terms* it is seen.

[65] On atomistic personhood, the person is demarcated by their body so an objectification of their image is not regarded as a direct objectification of the person. The privacy wrong is thus only the act of recording, objectification of the subsequent images is only a derivative wrong against the person, not a direct infringement of them. However, in practical terms, if the creation of the image is a wrongful act, the law of constitutional democracies would often have treated the subsequent image as wrongful too.

6. Conclusion

This chapter has argued that privacy is not exhausted by the idea of withdrawal into seclusion, nor by the prevention of access to information. On a relational account of personhood, privacy is concerned with sustaining the conditions under which persons can appear as subjects in the relationships that constitute their personhood status. Visibility, in this framework, is not inherently a threat to privacy. It can affirm and sustain personhood when it is under the person's normative authority; it can undermine and erode personhood when it goes against that autonomy.

Across the examples discussed – image-based sexual abuse, public surveillance, and digital proctoring – the privacy wrong does not lie in the bare fact of being seen, but in the collapse of the contextual boundaries that make visibility meaningful and affirming. In each case, visibility was taken out of the person's hands and repurposed in ways that denied or diminished their subjectivity. The relational account helps explain why such practices are privacy infringing even when they occur in public spaces, with partial consent or without physical intrusion. It also illuminates an additional layer of privacy harm: objectification as denial of subjectivity.

The functional model of privacy, when grounded in a relational conception of personhood, offers a principled way to identify and address these harms. It asks not simply whether someone has been observed, but whether the terms of that observation have been set in ways that allow the person to engage in and maintain their caring relationships and present themselves in ways that affirm their identities. In this sense, normative authority over visibility is not an optional enhancement to privacy but its constitutive core in the relational framework. This account challenges traditional privacy frameworks that focus on spatial seclusion and geographical boundaries. It shifts the focus of legal interventions from preventing intrusion into defined spaces or information to ensuring that visibility remains subject to a person's normative authority. Both unwanted visibility and unwanted invisibility can constitute privacy infringements when they occur without or against that authority.

Returning to the German sauna case, the relational framework helps explain why such filming should be recognised as privacy infringing despite occurring in a semi-public space: the wrong lies not in breaching a spatial boundary but in denying the filmed persons normative authority over their visibility. Being seen by one person is not the same as being seen by everyone: being naked at home is not consent for being naked in a sauna; being naked in a sauna is not consent for being naked on the street; and no kind of nudity is consent for being filmed. Being seen can be private if it is subject to the seen person's normative authority. The same 'visible state' may thus be privacy enhancing if normative authority is respected, and privacy infringing where it is not. A relational understanding of privacy calls not for retreat but for the transformation of shared spaces into environments where visibility is safe, respectful, and enabling of recognition. On this account, protecting privacy means protecting the conditions for recognition. It means safeguarding the realm in which persons can engage, maintain their relationships and identities and develop the defining characteristics of their personhood.

9

Legal Protection as the Protection of the Incomputable Self

MIREILLE HILDEBRANDT

1 Introduction

Digital monitoring is a specific type of surveillance. In this chapter, I will discuss digital monitoring in terms of surveillance to situate it as part and parcel of the constitution of modern states and in terms of the computational assumptions of digital surveillance. This will enable me to uncover the way that specific types of digital monitoring, notably those involving advanced artificial intelligence (AI) systems, may deny, ignore and violate the incomputable self that law in constitutional democracies aims to protect.[1]

Surveillance is key to the modern state.[2] The scope of the jurisdiction of modern states is vast, bringing together a multitude of individual persons under the same rules.[3] Those who share jurisdiction are attributed legal rights and obligations, both towards each other and towards the state that subjects them, offering protection while demanding their adherence to the law of the land rather than that of family (as in non-state societies) or status (as in medieval privilege).[4] To ensure

[1] Note that I avoid the concept of 'liberal democracy' that prevails in Anglo-American discourse, as the vanishing point of legal and moral philosophy. Instead, I deliberately speak of 'constitutional democracy', pinpointing both the Rule of Law (Rechtsstaat) and democracy as the normative and institutional backbone of the law. See other work on the relationship between democracy and the Rule of Law: M Hildebrandt, 'Radbruch's Rechtsstaat and Schmitt's Legal Order: Legalism, Legality, and the Institution of Law' (2015) 2 *Critical Analysis of Law* 42.

[2] The link between the welfare state and surveillance has been discussed by many, eg JC Scott, *Seeing Like a State: How Certain Schemes to Improve the Human Condition Have Failed* (New Haven CT, Yale University Press, 1998).

[3] On the rise of modern positive law as a consequence of the rise of the modern state, see H Berman, *Law and Revolution: The Formation of the Western Legal Tradition* (Cambridge MA, Harvard University Press, 1983).

[4] On the legal order as a network of horizontal and vertical legal relationships N Achterberg, *Die Rechtsordnung als Rechtsverhältnisordnung: Grundlegung der Rechtsverhältnistheorie* (Berlin, Duncker & Humblot, 1982).

this protection, the state must see to it that its subjects can be sure that the law that applies to them applies to all and is sufficiently and equivalently enforced. This has been qualified as distributive justice, which means treating equal cases equally and unequal cases unequally to the extent of their inequality.[5] Though the answer to the question of what cases are equal in what respect is not given (the last word on this is with the courts), freedom depends on the legal certainty offered by the reasonable foreseeability of the consequences of one's actions. Modern positive law affords such foreseeability, by – for instance – making contracts enforceable, imposing private law liability for torts and criminal law liability for criminal offences. Surveillance allows states to become aware of violations of legal norms, especially where the initiative to respond is with the state, notably in the case of the violation of administrative and criminal law norms.

On top of this, modern states have developed an appetite for deciding who falls within their jurisdiction, claiming the sovereign right to prevent subjects of other states from entering their territory, without requiring a justification (unless relevant international law makes an exception, eg when the principle of non-refoulement applies).[6] Monitoring of border-crossings and detecting unlawful immigration are directly connected with the issue of internal and external sovereignty, but also with democracy and the rule of law.[7] For democracy to 'work' it is important to know who is part of the demos (who decide on the rules to live by) and the same goes for the rule of law (to whom does the law apply and who can contest its application).[8] Surveillance thus also contributes to making the difference between those to whom a state has legal duties as they are its subjects and those to whom a state has no or far less legal duties as they are the subjects of another state (or no state).[9]

Surveillance or the monitoring of human behaviour by states, therefore, is not new. What is new is the deployment of a whole range of computational tools to detect violations, transforming the scope, the scale and the speed of human

[5] On distributive justice and legal certainty, see G Radbruch, *The Legal Philosophies of Lask, Radbruch, and Dabin*, Twentieth Century Legal Philosophy, reprint 2014 (Cambridge MA, Harvard University Press, 2014).

[6] R Perruchoud, 'State Sovereignty and Freedom of Movement' in B Opeskin, J Redpath-Cross and R Perruchoud (eds), *Foundations of International Migration Law* (Cambridge, Cambridge University Press, 2012).

[7] V Mantouvalou, 'Electronic Monitoring of Migrants' in H Noorda and J Hariharan (eds), *Digitally Monitored: Freedom, Surveillance and the Law* (London, Bloomsbury Publishing, 2026).

[8] This is also relevant for the competitive transnational normativities arising from the 'borderless' internet, see JR Reidenberg, 'Yahoo and Democracy on the Internet' (2001) 42 *Jurimetrics* 261 and M Hildebrandt, 'Text-Driven Jurisdiction in Cyberspace' in Micheál Ó Floinn et al (eds), *Transformations in Criminal Jurisdiction: Extraterritoriality and Enforcement* (Oxford, Hart Publishing, 2023).

[9] The relationship between sovereign states, the demos and the right to decide on membership is complex and contested, see, eg B Leijssenaar, 'The Demos as a Plural Subject' (2017) 46 *Netherlands Journal of Legal Philosophy* 37. The problems of stateless subjects demonstrates one of the most pressing issues of the modern system of sovereign states, as Hannah Arendt highlighted, see S DeGooyer et al, *The Right to Have Rights*, reprint edn (London, Verso Books, 2020).

monitoring.[10] Automation of monitoring by way of facial recognition technologies, behavioural biometrics, the tracking of location and mobility patterns and a wide range of other sensor technologies (from sound to temperature to movement) allow not only a fine grained picture of individual human behaviour but also a wide range of inferences about their status and future behaviour based on aggregated data of others' behaviour.[11] Such inferences may concern, for instance, an inclination to violence, to tax fraud, to illegal immigration or they may 'predict' that a person is telling lies about their nationality, background or whereabouts. The proliferation of these computational tools has been accompanied with exorbitant claims as to the reliability of their output that is often difficult to corroborate due to the proprietary nature of the software. On top of that, detailed criticism has been provided as to the racial or other bias they may engender and as to the societal, moral and legal implications of depending on these tools when making decisions that have legal or similarly significant effect on the life of individuals.[12] In this chapter, I build on previous work, notably my call for a philosophy of technology for computational law, highlighting the need for lawyers to better understand the affordances of the text-based technologies that constitute modern positive law and the affordances of novel technologies that may disable the kind of legal protection offered by modern positive law.[13]

[10] M Hildebrandt, *Law for Computer Scientists and Other Folk* (Oxford, Oxford University Press, 2020), ch 6.

[11] On the inferences and their discontents M Oswald et al, 'Algorithmic Risk Assessment Policing Models: Lessons from the Durham HART Model and "Experimental" Proportionality' (2018) 27 *Information & Communications Technology Law* 223.

[12] M Díaz et al, 'CrowdWorkSheets: Accounting for Individual and Collective Identities Underlying Crowdsourced Dataset Annotation' in *FAccT '22: Proceedings of the 2022 ACM Conference on Fairness, Accountability, and Transparency* (New York, Association for Computing Machinery, 2022); eg M Hildebrandt and S Gutwirth, *Profiling the European Citizen: Cross-Disciplinary Perspectives* (Berlin, Springer, 2008); E Bayamlioğlu et al (eds), *BEING PROFILED: COGITAS ERGO SUM: 10 Years of Profiling the European Citizen* (Amsterdam, Amsterdam University Press, 2018); M Hildebrandt, 'The Issue of Bias: The Framing Powers of Machine Learning' in M Pelillo and T Scantamburlo (eds), *Machines We Trust: Perspectives on Dependable AI* (Cambridge MA, The MIT Press, 2021); M Hildebrandt, 'The Issue of Proxies and Choice Architectures: Why EU Law Matters for Recommender Systems' (2022) 5 *Frontiers in Artificial Intelligence*. Available at: www.frontiersin.org/article/10.3389/frai.2022.789076; M Hildebrandt, 'Ground-Truthing in the European Health Data Space', in F Cabitza, A Fred and H Gamboa (eds), *Proceedings of the 16th International Joint Conference on Biomedical Engineering Systems and Technologies: Volume 5: HEALTHINF* (Setúbal, Scitepress, 2023); JE Cohen, *Configuring the Networked Self: Law, Code, and the Play of Everyday Practice* (New Haven, Yale University Press, 2012); F Pasquale, *The Black Box Society: The Secret Algorithms That Control Money and Information*, 1st edn (Cambridge MA, Harvard University Press, 2015); M Hildebrandt, *Smart Technologies and the End(s) of Law: Novel Entanglements of Law and Technology* (Cheltenham, Edward Elgar Publishing, 2015); C O'Neil, *Weapons of Math Destruction: How Big Data Increases Inequality and Threatens Democracy* (New York, Crown, 2016); V Eubanks, *Automating Inequality: How High-Tech Tools Profile, Police, and Punish the Poor* (New York, St Matrin's Press, 2018); S Zuboff, *The Age of Surveillance Capitalism: The Fight for a Human Future at the New Frontier of Power*, 1st edn (London, Profile Books Ltd, 2019).

[13] M Hildebrandt, 'A Philosophy of Technology for Computational "Law"' in D Mangan, A Daly and G van Dijck (eds), *Philosophical Foundations of IT Law* (Oxford, Oxford University Press, forthcoming).

In the next section of this chapter, I discuss the limitations of computational systems without ignoring their promise, inviting the reader to follow me in an in-depth investigation of what computing systems can and cannot do. I will highlight that computing systems require proxies to represent, search and predict human behaviour and argue that the decision on proxies is one of qualification that necessarily precedes any quantification. I will also argue that the choice of proxies is not given, as whatever the proxy stands for can be interpreted in different ways. Once a proxy is chosen, the implied interpretation will define who is targeted how and this will inevitably restrict the space for interpretation of both the facts and the law.

Having explained the key role played by proxies in the design of computational systems, I will turn to the nature of human agency and spell out how it differs from that of computing systems. Following the work of philosophers such as Ricoeur and Mead, I highlight the ambiguity of human agency and cognition that grounds the freedom to *act in*, to *think* and *imagine* the world while interacting with our fellows. The scope for this freedom, however, depends on how we organise society, how we institutionalise economic and political power relationships and how we protect the positive freedom to act and the negative freedom from unreasonable constraints on individual and joint liberties. This brings me to the notion of legal subjectivity under the heading of 'Legal subjectivity: the mask that enables and shields'. Here I will argue that legal subjectivity is core to modern positive law and to the protection of both the positive and the negative freedom that defines constitutional democracy. This protection concerns the incomputable nature of the self, including the capability to resist and contest computational targeting. To emphasise the role of positive law, I will briefly discuss how the Charter of Fundamental Rights of the European Union (CFREU), the General Data Protection Regulation (GDPR) and the Artificial Intelligence Act (AI Act) contribute to legal protection as the protection of the incomputable self.

Whether the European Union (EU) legal framework will actually protect us depends on the extent to which big players can instrumentalise the law to serve their own interests, noting that Big Tech can afford to hire Big Law to frustrate the 'practical and effective' protection of fundamental rights. In the semi-final section 'Economic power, democracy and the Rule of Law' I offer a short critique of rogue, global capitalism, demonstrating how it aligns with the assumptions of computability that informs the quest for artificial general intelligence (AGI).

Finally, I will end with conclusions, calling for lawyers and civil society to better grasp what digital surveillance can and cannot achieve, while highlighting the importance of legal subjectivity for natural persons as foundational for protection against digital surveillance that *overdetermines* individual persons. Based on the philosophical analysis provided in this chapter, I conclude that in the era of data-driven surveillance, fundamental rights should be understood as 'practical and effective' protection of the incomputable self, thus also resisting economic theories that reduce human society to computable models, while propagating a type of economic determinism that necessarily overrules human rights as 'nonsense on stilts'.[14]

2 Digital Surveillance: Monitoring and Computational Targeting

2.1 The Constitutive Rules of Computational Systems

2.1.1 The Gatekeepers of Computational Systems

In this section I will dig into the computational assumptions that make monitoring digital. Instead of taking digital monitoring for granted as a practice, I will look at the technological affordances of the computational systems that enable it. This connects with the need for a philosophy of technology in the context of legal philosophy, as argued elsewhere.[15]

Computational systems do not 'have' constitutions.[16] They do not hold an assembly to decide on the rules to live by. Nevertheless, they are bound by a set of rules that form the gateway of their computational abilities (and they have no other abilities). These rules do not *regulate* their behaviour (as they have no choice but to 'abide' by them) but *constitute* their behaviours.[17] In the deepest layer of computing systems we find the 'logic gates' that are baked into the hardware (eg vacuum tubes or transistors, operating as switching circuits), based on the either/or (physically 'on' or 'off') state of their components. The development of two-value Boolean algebra in the nineteenth century, based on a digital instead of a decimal notation system, enabled the digital computer, which is based on the digital expression of complex manipulations of numbers in the physical hardware of the computer's 'motherboard'. Any operation or behaviour of any digital computing system is enabled – and thus constrained – by the Boolean logic that is hardwired into the logic gates. The logic gates require that any input into the system is

[14] J Waldron, *Nonsense upon Stilts: Bentham, Burke and Marx on the Rights of Man*, Routledge Revivals (Abingdon, Routledge, 2015).

[15] M Hildebrandt, 'A Philosophy of Technology for Computational "Law"' in D Mangan, A Daly, and G van Dijck (eds), *Philosophical Foundations of IT Law* (Oxford, Oxford University Press) (forthcoming

[16] I will use the term computer, computing system and computational system as synonyms, though their emphasis is different. The computer highlights the machine-dimension (noting that originally computers were human beings brought together in a room to conduct and integrate a large number of computations), computing system highlights the network-dimension and computational system highlights the mathematical dimension that is key. One could also say that 'computer' is often used to refer to the concrete, physical hardware, whereas the 'systems' approach is often used to refer to the abstract models and computer code. The point is of course that the distinction is not always helpful and both depend on each other.

[17] The distinction goes back to Kant and has been elegantly developed by J Rawls, 'Two Concepts of Rules' in Philippa Foot (ed), *Theories of Ethics* (London, Oxford University Press, 1967). See also M Hildebrandt, 'Legal and Technological Normativity: More (and Less) than Twin Sisters' (2008) 12 *Techné: Journal of the Society for Philosophy and Technology* 169.

provided in a way that can be 'handled' by one of the following logical rules: AND, OR, NAND, NOR, XOR, XNOR. These rules exemplify a discrete logic, with logical operators such as conjunction (and), disjunction (or) and negation (not). This is the reason why computing systems require unambiguous input, even in the case of machine learning (based on detecting stochastical patterns in training data).[18] Boolean algebra and its hardwired descendants (digital computing systems) have enabled extremely efficient and fast ways of performing highly complex calculations; computations that would have taken a room full of human computers light years can now be computed in nano-seconds. We must remember, however, that reality is not digital and that, for computers to engage with reality, 'the' reality must first be framed in a way that can be processed by the logic gates. Thus, there is a specific type of translation that precedes the input of a computing system which, in turn, defines what output is possible. As a consequence of the fact that computing systems depend on – and are limited to – what can be processed by the logic gates, I have articulated the three constitutive rules that define both the affordances and the limitations of computational systems: (1) reality is not computable, (2) it can, however, be *made* computable, (3) this can be done in *different ways* (though not in any way) and the difference matters. Next, I will discuss each of these constitutive rules for computational systems that engage reality.

2.1.2 Reality Is Not Computable

When I say that reality is not computable, I mean that reality is – ultimately – incomputable, because a computation requires discrete mapping and/or representing of whatever is computed, thereby *making* the difference between that which is mapped or represented and its mapping or representation. Though there is a neo-Platonic belief that the unreasonable effectiveness of mathematics in physics implies that the ontological status of reality is mathematical, this does not at all follow from the fact that mathematics makes great maps of the world we navigate.[19] Believing that reality is 'really' mathematical is confusing the proxy with what it stands for.

The key issue here is the fact that physical, chemical, biological and human reality are themselves already different mappings of an undivided reality that can be trapped for a moment but remains in flux, meaning that every representation and anticipation is always based on inferences from past 'data', while the inferences we make, in turn, impact the reality we navigate, insofar as they enable and constrain

[18] On the limits of computational systems, see J Weizenbaum, *Computer Power and Human Reason: From Judgment to Calculation* (San Francisco, W.H. Freeman and Co, 1976); HL Dreyfus, *What Computers Can't Do: The Limits of Artificial Intelligence* (New York, Harper & Row, 1979); HL Dreyfus, *What Computers Still Can't Do: A Critique of Artificial Reason*, vol Rev (Cambridge MA, The MIT Press, 1992); BC Smith, *The Promise of Artificial Intelligence: Reckoning and Judgment* (Cambridge MA, The MIT Press, 2019).

[19] EP Wigner, 'The Unreasonable Effectiveness of Mathematics in the Natural Sciences: Richard Courant Lecture in Mathematical Sciences Delivered at New York University, 11 May 1959' (1960) 13 *Communications on Pure and Applied Mathematics* 1; D McQuillan, 'Data Science as Machinic Neoplatonism' (2018) 31 *Philosophy & Technology* 253.

how we act on the world.[20] The latter effect, also called 'the Goodhart effect' is related to the fact that we are capable of imagining alternative *present futures* that, in turn, define our actions and thereby shape the only *future present* we 'have'.[21] To sum up, reality is ephemeral and should not be confused with the computational models we make to navigate and reconfigure it.[22]

2.1.3 *It Can Be Made Computable*

Reality may thus be incomputable, but we can and do *make* it computable. Just like a map of a territory is not that territory, we can and do nevertheless make maps to help us navigate the space. And, like in the case of maps, computational models of reality can be good or bad, depending on the purpose (for maps: tourism, commuting, political, mining) and depending on the agent (for maps: who may drive a car, walk, take public transport or may be blind or in need of water or who may have to defend themselves against dangers unknown to whoever developed the map). Computational surveillance technologies, such as remote biometrics, hotspot mappings or tools to predict recidivism, may be good for crime fighters and bad for vulnerable persons, good for the short term and bad in the long run, they may invite new types of criminal behaviour by those who manage to work around the output models or by those who know that attention is going elsewhere.[23] All this depends on how the model was generated, eg based on what training data, and on how it is deployed, in what environment and with what purpose.

2.1.4 *In Different Ways (Though Not in Any Way), and the Difference Matters*

Gregory Bateson, one of the founding fathers of cybernetics, wrote, in his *Steps to an Ecology of Mind*, that for the 'map' or 'form' that frames a 'territory' or 'substance', the key notion is 'difference'.[24] His point was that a good map/form/model marks out *the difference that makes a difference*. The territory or substance (let's say reality) that is mapped or modelled consists of myriad differences and for

[20] See also the fact that 'things' do not remain the same without hard work, as everything is forever 'becoming', see especially AN Whitehead, *Process and Reality* (New York, Macmillan, 1929). And, in relation to AI, Smith (n 18); this relates to what Parsons and Luhmann have called the 'double contingency' that is core to human interaction, see, eg R Vanderstraeten, 'Parsons, Luhmann and the Theorem of Double Contingency' (2007) 2 *Journal of Classical Sociology* 77; M Hildebrandt, 'Profile Transparency by Design: Re-Enabling Double Contingency' in M Hildebrandt and K de Vries (eds), *Privacy, Due Process and the Computational Turn: The Philosophy of Law Meets the Philosophy of Technology* (Abingdon, Routledge, 2013).

[21] In econometrics so-called 'Goodhart effect' tells us that 'when you use a measure as a target, it ceases to be a good method', see especially; E Esposito, *The Future of Futures: The Time of Money in Financing and Society* (Cheltenham, Edward Elgar Publishing, 2011).

[22] See A Frank, M Gleiser and E Thompson, *The Blind Spot: Why Science Cannot Ignore Human Experience* (Cambridge MA, The MIT Press, 2024); B Cantwell Smith, *Computational Reflections* (Cambridge MA, The MIT Press, 2026).

[23] BE Harcourt, *Against Prediction: Profiling, Policing, and Punishing in an Actuarial Age* (Chicago, University of Chicago Press, 2006).

[24] G Bateson, *Steps to an Ecology of Mind* (New York, Ballantine Books, 1972).

a map or model to be a good map or model, those who do the mapping/modelling must elicit the differences that make a difference in terms of the purpose of the mapping/modelling. In point of fact, this is how Bateson defined 'information': 'the difference that makes a difference'.[25] This implies that the question of whether something qualifies as information depends on the purpose and – obviously but importantly – on the agents who share or receive the information: what is information to me may not be information to you and what was information to me yesterday may not be information to me today. In other words, Bateson highlighted the issue of relevance: for something to be 'information' for an agent, it must be relevant to that agent, in view of their objectives.

The mere fact that the same substance/reality/territory can be made computable in different ways confirms its incomputable nature, in the sense that no computational representation can claim absolute equivalence with what it represents. One way of modelling may result in other output compared to another way of modelling, thus affecting both those deploying the model and those being targeted by it. In other words, there is no free lunch; a model that is good for achieving one purpose or aligning with the objectives of one agent may be bad for achieving another purpose or aligning with the objectives of another agent.[26] In terms of machine learning, for instance, *the decision on the objective function* defines how reality is made computable, stipulating in view of what objective the model is – mathematically – optimised.[27] And this optimisation, in turn, defines the output model. The same goes for the choice and curation of the training data that define what models can be inferred, thus not only enabling the machine to learn but also restricting the learning process to the distribution of the input data. The fact that alternative objective functions or training data are possible does not imply that any training data or model would make sense; whether it does will depend on the agent and on the purpose. An output model, therefore, will present patterns that are deemed relevant by the developers of the model, at the cost of other models that could have been chosen – there is no master algorithm.[28]

[25] ibid 135. Digging deeper into the computational concept of 'information', which is of key interest for the use of 'legal technologies', see M Hildebrandt, 'Law *as* Information in the Era of Data-Driven Agency' (2016) 79 *MLR* 1; Bateson (n 23).

[26] Even from a computational perspective, this has been 'proven': DH Wolpert and WG Macready, 'No Free Lunch Theorems for Optimization' (1997) 1 *IEEE Transactions on Evolutionary Computation* 67; DH Wolpert, 'Ubiquity Symposium: Evolutionary Computation and the Processes of Life: What the No Free Lunch Theorems Really Mean: How to Improve Search Algorithms' (2013) 2013 *Ubiquity* 1.

[27] On the way the objective function could be deployed to actually protect natural persons: S Gürses, R Overdorf and E Balsa, 'Stirring the POTs: Protective Optimization Technologies' in E Bayamlıoğlu et al (eds), *BEING PROFILED: COGITAS ERGO SUM: 10 years of Profiling the European Citizen* (Amsterdam, Amsterdam University Press, 2018).

[28] P Domingos, *The Master Algorithm: How the Quest for the Ultimate Learning Machine Will Remake Our World*, 1st edn (New York, Basic Books, 2015), see especially 62–65, where he discusses Wolpert. Domingos seems to miss out on the difference between the average outcome if the same model is applied across the board (where any specific output is undone by another specific output) and the fact that the application of a specific outcome to a specific case can be very helpful (even though we may not be sure and noting that adding prior knowledge will contribute to getting things right).

2.2 The Logic Gates and the Issue of Proxies

2.2.1 Qualification Precedes Quantification

For digital monitoring that deploys computational systems it is key to understand the assumptions on which AI systems are based, notably with regard to the nexus of counting and calculation on the one hand and what is being counted in terms of what units on the other hand.

Two plus three is five. Or is it? In fact, it depends. In mathematics, the assumption is that the *units* of two and five are the same; in real life, that is the question. Two apples plus three strawberries is five pieces of fruit, but not five apples or five strawberries. Two desks and three chairs are five pieces of furniture, but not five desks or five chairs. Two cats and three spoons are neither five cats not five spoons and it will take some creative intervention to find a level of abstraction where both types can be added up. Obviously, we could say that two things plus three things are five things, but some may object to qualifying a cat as a thing, even though others will argue that, depending on the purpose, that is not necessarily problematic. Is two convictions for theft sufficiently similar to three convictions for speeding to speak of five convictions? On what does this depend? For instance, on whether violence was used when stealing and/or on whether the speeding was a minor or a major violation of the maximum speed limit? Does it make a difference whether the 'counting' is done in the context of criminological research or in the context of a court's sentencing decision?

Here, the point is that quantification is necessarily preceded by a qualification that allows the quantification.[29] This is not only the case in traditional quantitative research, but also in the case of machine learning. Supervised learning requires prior 'labelling' of the data, for instance deciding whether apples and pears should be 'counted' under the joint heading of fruits or counted separately as either apples or pears. Or, whether a conviction for stealing and one for speeding should be labelled under the joint heading of 'criminal convictions' or under the joint heading of 'violent behaviours', depending on whether either or both qualify as such. This is also relevant when artificial intelligence (AI) systems are capable of self-supervision, where the 'labelling' is decided by the system, based on the stochastical patterns it detects in the training data. These kinds of systems, using deep learning methods, are based on highly complex mathematical functions that do not offer insights into what labels are chosen and how they have been attributed to what data, even though the decisions on what pattern is relevant will have a major impact on the output. In this case it is not a label but the so-called 'objective function' that defines the output, as we saw above. Although the choice of the objective function may be seen as a technical decision by the developers of the system, it is based on qualifying a specific output configuration as a proxy for whatever the

[29] M Callon and J Law, 'On Qualculation, Agency, and Otherness' (2005) 23 *Environment and Planning D: Society and Space* 717.

system should achieve (its objective), followed by qualifying specific outputs as relevant approximations of the targeted output. Until recently, the objective would be finding and ranking specific information (search) or identifying the 'right' decision from a distributed decision space (prediction). The recent prominence of large language models (LLMs) has another type of objective, that is language *generation* rather than language *'understanding'*.[30] In the case of LLMs, the output configuration is based on 'stochastically correct next word-token guessing', where 'stochastically correct' means that the guess makes sense from the perspective of native language users.[31] The output of a machine learning system is usually a model that may be applied to make certain decisions, from detention or parole decisions (COMPAS) to decisions on what information to select as search results and how to rank them (Westlaw, Lexis Nexus) and to decisions on social security or tax applications. Some qualification is going on here, even if it not explicit and even if impossible to trace.

2.2.2 The Act of Translation Is a Performative Act

Building a computing system thus implies the choice and construction of proxies, whether in the form of using a specific programming language, dedicated training data or learning algorithm. The act of translation that is involved in selecting, curating and developing the proxy, *does what it says*; it qualifies a programming language, set of data or objective function as a stand-in for what is sometimes called the 'ground truth'.[32] In machine learning, 'ground truth' is what must be made computable to allow the machine to learn. By defining specific code, data or mathematical functions as, for instance, the risk of reoffending, defaulting on a loan or tax fraud or as eligibility for social security, medical insurance or access to higher education, the relevant real-world risks or rights must first be translated into what a computing system can handle. By trusting the output of the system, this act of translation gains performative effect; the alleged ground truth is affirmed in computational terms, defining the choice architecture of those who 'ground' their decisions in the output models. In that sense, the many seemingly technical micro-decisions made by upstream model-developers have downstream performative effect: they reconfigure the real world in line with the assumptions made when building the model. Translating real-work phenomena, including risks and rights, into computational terms, thus involves proxies that have performative

[30] LLMs do not actually understand anything, they merely simulate, parasitising on the statistical regularities of our language behaviours, see, eg EM Bender and A Koller, 'Climbing towards NLU: On Meaning, Form, and Understanding in the Age of Data' in D Jurafsky et al (ed), *Proceedings of the 58th Annual Meeting of the Association for Computational Linguistics* (Stroudsburg, The Association for Computational Linguistics, 2020).

[31] A Sobieszek and T Price, 'Playing Games with Ais: The Limits of GPT-3 and Similar Large Language Models' (2022) 32 *Minds and Machines* 341.

[32] JL Austin, *How to Do Things with Words*, 2nd edn (Cambridge MA, Harvard University Press, 1975). The act of translation/qualification is a performative speech act: once the proxy is chosen the proxy 'counts as' what it stands for.

effects in the real world: 'If machines define a situation as real, it is real in its consequences.'[33]

2.2.3 *Reducing the Interpretation-Space of Legal Norms*

When surveillance technologies are deployed to attribute risks or rights to natural or legal persons, this may limit the interpretation-space for public administration and the courts. This is due to the fact that the proxies used to develop these technologies (upstream) entail an unambiguous interpretation of the relevant legal norm and the relevant facts at stake. That interpretation will be leading when acting upon the output models that are contingent upon the chosen interpretation (downstream), even if that interpretation is hidden under the cloak of a technical design decision.[34] In a sense, those targeted by the output model that is deployed, may become invisible. Those who decide about, for instance, providing social security, allowing parole or charging someone with a criminal offence may not see a person but first and foremost an applicable computational profile or score.

3 Computational and Human Agency

3.1 Agency of Computational Systems: Adaptive Behaviours

To understand the nature and the impact of digital monitoring it is not enough to critique its potential for unjustifiable discrimination, automated exclusion or its nefariously technocratic outsourcing of decision making. In this section, I will argue that AI systems have a specific type of agency that is at the heart of the problems generated by digital monitoring, such as exclusion, discrimination and erosion of the human agency of those administering the decisions that make a difference. It is important to acknowledge that the AI systems deployed for digital monitoring display a specific type of agency, to better grasp the difference with plant/animal/human agency and to better protect our own kind of agency from reduction to machinic agency.[35] From the preceding sections, we can conclude that surveillance systems that make or prepare decisions based on logical or stochastical predictions do not, as Hannah Arendt would say, 'have a world'; they do not have, first-hand, experience of the real world.[36] Instead, they develop models of

[33] A modulation of RK Merton, 'The Self-Fulfilling Prophecy' (1948) 8 *The Antioch Review* 193. 'if men define a situation as real, it is real in its consequences' in M Hildebrandt, 'Who Needs Stories If You Can Get the Data? ISPs in the Era of Big Number Crunching' (2011) 24 *Philosophy & Technology* 371, 379.

[34] PN Meessen, 'On Normative Arrows and Comparing Tax Automation Systems' in *Nineteenth International Conference on Artificial Intelligence and Law: Proceedings of the Conference* (New York, Association for Computing Machinery, 2023).

[35] Hildebrandt, *Smart Technologies and the End(s) of Law* (2015), ch 2.

[36] In detail, on the concept of 'world', see the next subsection and ibid, ch 3.

various aspects of the world. Depending on the reliability of these models, they may expand or reduce the agency of those who develop and deploy them.

The key point is that they model human behaviours to make certain predictions, upon which they or those who deploy them subsequently act. Note the use of the term 'behaviours' instead of 'behaviour', which highlights the fact that computational modelling of human behaviour implies discretising human behaviour in chunks that can serve as input data, eg speech, mobility, location, eating, reading or simply click behaviours. Such behavioural data function as a proxy for what we might otherwise call behaviour or action. The reason for attributing 'agency' to computational systems is the fact that they foresee our future behaviours, whether correct or incorrect, and thus transform our environment based on what they infer from our behavioural data. In cognitive and computer science, agency is often defined as the capacity to act on an environment based on inferred expectations about the environment, in view of specific goals.[37] Things like stones, tables, volcanoes and chairs, do not anticipate the behaviour of their environment; in that sense, they lack agency. Living organisms, instead, anticipate and act – whether plant, animal or human. We have not recognised agency in machines, because we assumed that agency is an attribute of living organisms; with AI systems acting on their environment based on what they infer from our behaviours, it becomes important to acknowledge their particular type of agency – without, however, mistaking it for human agency.

AI systems, including surveillance systems, ground their behaviours in data- or code-driven predictions of their environment – including the humans. If we fail to understand the impact of this agency, we may diminish our own agency. In the next subsections, we will dig into what makes a difference between human and computational agency.

3.2 Agency of Human Beings: The Self as Another

Human agency differs from plant and animal agency due to our ability to look at ourselves from the perspective of another. This ability is linked with our use of language. When I speak to my one-and-a-half-year-old daughter and tell her that 'you are Maria (pointing to her)' and that 'I am Mireille (pointing to myself)', she will agree by saying 'you are Maria (pointing to herself)' and 'I am Mireille (pointing to me)'. This is an entirely reasonable way of responding, but I will nevertheless tell her that 'no, you are Maria, I am Mireille'. It will take her some time (weeks) to switch perspective, understanding that she is 'you' to me and 'I' to herself. This ability to take the perspective of her close others, later followed by taking the more complex perspective of what Mead called 'the generalised other', is what makes us human(s). It allows us to speak *about ourselves* due to a new ability to *de-centre* and

[37] ibid (n 34).

it is key to realise that this ability is born from *being addressed* and not from developing mental models of others. The latter is predicated on (preceded by) being addressed as another by another. Both the American pragmatist social psychologist George Herbert Mead and the French philosopher Paul Ricoeur developed this point in their work.

Ricoeur developed an incisive analysis of the birth of the self as another and the implications of this insight for the continuity and discontinuities of the self, tracing the difference and interrelationship between what he called *idem*-identity and *ipse*-identity.[38] *Idem* refers to sameness or similarity (assuming a third-person perspective), while *ipse* refers to the irretrievable subjective perspective that necessarily precedes the third-person perspective. We should note that any reflection on the subjective (*ipse*) perspective inevitably results in a third person (*idem*) perspective.

Mead discussed self-identity in a similar, though not identical, way. He distinguished between the 'I' as the irretrievable subject and the 'I's understanding of itself under the heading of 'me'. Mead explained how my sense of self develops when 'I' anticipate how others anticipate 'me', noting that we can never be sure how my actions, including my speech acts, will be understood.[39] In the pragmatist tradition, 'understanding' is a matter of anticipation, it concerns the consequences of my language usage; developing a self is learning to anticipate how others interpret my words and actions.[40] Developing a self is therefore about a double anticipation: about how 'I' anticipate others to anticipate 'me'. Mead's followers, notably Parsons and Luhmann, spoke of 'double contingency' when referring to this double anticipation.[41] They highlighted the fundamental uncertainty (contingency) this generates, as I can never be sure how another 'I' anticipates me, which means that I can never be sure of how my words and actions will be interpreted and thus what consequences they will have – while being aware that others face the same uncertainty that affects me. For Parsons and Luhmann, this uncertainty was a fundamental problem that affects the constitution of society. Parsons highlighted the role of culture in achieving sufficient consensus on the meaning of our actions, while Luhmann highlighted the productive nature of this uncertainty. The latter reminds one of De Beauvoir's work on ambiguity, Butler's work on the construction of human identity, Arendt's concept of 'natality' and the importance of speech act theory for a proper understanding of the 'world' we find ourselves 'thrown into'.[42] The productive nature

[38] P Ricoeur, *Oneself as Another* (Chicago, The University of Chicago Press, 1992).

[39] GH Mead, *Mind, Self, and Society from the Standpoint of a Social Behaviorist*, CW Morris ed (Chicago, The University of Chicago Press, 1962).

[40] See the pragmatist maxim on the meaning of meaning, of CS Peirce and PA Turrisi, *Pragmatism as a Principle and Method of Right Thinking: The 1903 Harvard Lectures on Pragmatism* (Albany, State University of New York Press, 1997) 111.

[41] Vanderstraeten (n 20).

[42] S Kruks, *Simone de Beauvoir and the Politics of Ambiguity* (Oxford, Oxford University Press, 2012); J Butler, *Giving an Account of Oneself*, 1st edn (New York, Fordham University Press, 2005); H Arendt,

of the challenges of double anticipation requires us to walk the fine line between, on the one hand, an anomia that would make action impossible and, on the other hand, attempts to petrify the concrete order.[43] This links to Austin's speech act theory, which highlights the institution and sustainability of meaning as part of a practice and it is interesting to note that speech act theory was 'born' in the context of Wittgenstein's concept of 'rule following', which influenced Hart's concept of law, via the brilliant work of Anscombe, writing on the difference between 'brute' and 'institutional' facts.[44]

My point here is that law and legal certainty provide one way of consolidating and stabilising the ambiguity that is key to the human condition, noting that law does not aim to 'solve' the problems of ambiguity and uncertainty but instead aims to offer effective and fair ways of addressing them. Acknowledging that the nature of the self is being triggered and co-constituted by relevant others, is not 'just' a matter of justice or morality, but part of the human condition.

4 Legal Subjectivity: The Mask That Enables and Shields

4.1 The Persona: Freedom to and Freedom From

Having legal subjectivity involves the ability to invoke both the positive *freedom to* act, for instance to rent a house, to buy a car, to vote or to voice one's opinion and the negative *freedom from* interference that requires others to refrain from unjustified intruding or trespassing. Here, the Latin term 'persona', which stood for a theatre mask, helps to understand the role of legal subjectivity when protecting the rights of natural persons. Legal subjectivity is like a mask that enables the person who wears the mask to 'act in law', taking a specific role, while simultaneously shielding that person from the gaze of others. In other words, the living person should not be confused with the role they play as a legal subject; the living person is both more and less. Even though a person may be a suspect, a defendant or a convicted offender in terms of the law, this does not define the whole of that person. In the context of criminal law this means that the law condemns an act, not a person, even though the legal effect of such condemnation may be that the person is punished (not because they are bad but because they did something they should have known to be a criminal offence).

In law, only 'legal subjects' can act and be held to account. Only they can generate legal effect, whether deliberately (when performing a juridical act such as

The Human Condition (Chicago, The University of Chicago Press, 1958); Austin (n 31).

[43] Hildebrandt (n 1).

[44] Austin (n 31); GEM Anscombe, 'On Brute Facts' (1958) 18 *Analysis* 69.

concluding a contract or issuing a will) or not (when committing a tortuous act or a criminal offence). Though, in the latter case, the action may be deliberate (defaulting on a payment or causing physical harm), the intent is not on creating the legal effect (having to pay compensation or being liable to punishment). Positive law attributes legal subjectivity to two types of legal subjects: natural persons (individual human beings) and legal persons (corporations, public administrative bodies etc). In principle, positive law could attribute legal subjectivity to animals, trees or to AI systems. The fact that it does not generally do so is not because it is not possible, but because legislatures do not see the advantage. Legal persons must, necessarily, be represented by natural persons. This is a complication that requires keen attention before attributing legal subjectivity to animals or machines; who will represent them, based on what justification? Under what conditions can those who represent a legal person be held accountable for the harm caused by the legal person?

In this chapter, I focus on natural persons, to unravel what kind of legal protection is offered by legal subjectivity. Hannah Arendt famously wrote that the most important right is the right to have rights, thereby pinpointing the fundamental nature of legal subjectivity, as this is what gives natural persons the right to have and invoke rights.[45] Arendt's seminal argument also addresses the fact that this 'right to have rights' cannot be an abstract, moral principle. For this right to offer real-world protection, it must be tied to the status of citizenship in a polity (state) capable of guaranteeing that right.

The right to have rights concerns both the positive freedom to act in law and the negative freedom from unreasonable constraints or unjustified intrusions. As indicated above, legal subjectivity is like a mask that should not be equated with the person attributed with such subjectivity. Instead, legal subjectivity should protect natural persons from overdetermination by the state or other big players. To understand the importance of this point, we can turn to Mead's distinction between the 'I' and the 'me', noting that the 'me' is always lagging behind, as it tries to capture the 'I'. The 'me' refers to how others frame a subject (adscription) and to how that subject frames themselves (inscription), where the constitution of *the self happens* on the cusp of the 'I', who 'does' the framing and the 'me' that is framed. The self is the resulting self-understanding, born from the continuous interaction between ad- and inscription. Neither is immutable, both are in the process of becoming and sensitive to how others and institutional contexts frame them. But there is no 'me' without an 'I' and the 'I' is what cannot be determined, as this determination would be the 'me', not the 'I'. To nourish and protect the 'I' we must ensure that the 'me' is not overdetermined, meaning that the 'I' has sufficient freedom to reconfigure the 'me' while navigating their real life and real world environment. The 'me' necessarily entails some level of determination, as it is contingent upon the ex-centric

[45] H Arendt, *The Origins of Totalitarianism* (San Diego, Harvest, 1979); DeGooyer et al (n 9).

positionality of a human agent, so the point is not to claim that the self is indeterminate. The best way to describe the moving target of the 'I' and 'me' would be to say that the self is '*under*determined'. This is directly related to the capability to contest the way others frame a person, especially when the framing is imposed in a way that overdetermines them (eg in the case of digital monitoring). This is where a proper understanding of self, mind and society contributes to a proper understanding of what legal protection means. Instead of falling into the traps of naïve behaviourism, including behavioural economics and cognitive computationalism, Mead's sophisticated behaviourism marks out both the observer's position (that affords a 'me') and the subject who takes that position (the 'I' that is a precondition for a 'me').

4.2 Legal Protection as the Protection of the Incomputable Self

4.2.1 A Practical and Effective Right to Have Rights

Legal protection against overdetermination or petrification of the dynamic and artificial nature of the self requires keen attention to the antinomian goals of the law, notably to the interaction between legal certainty, justice and instrumentality. Understanding the self as a continuous dynamic between an ever changing 'I' and 'me' does not ignore the need for a self to identify as themselves. This process of identification implies the construction of a self that achieves continuity while developing discontinuity, making sure the line is not broken while taking the freedom to grow and reinvent oneself. This curious interplay between continuity and discontinuity (both in time and space) is also key to legal certainty and justice. If the subject were forever in flux, it would not be possible to hold a person to account, as they could claim to be another person, not liable for whatever their previous self did. If the self were identical with itself it would not be alive, because being alive implies adaptiveness and in the case of a human being it implies a continuous process of reimagining the self from the ex-centric position.

Legal protection can be seen, in that light, as safeguarding the underdetermined nature of the self that, in turn, implies its incomputability. As indicated above, this does not ignore that fact that the self can be *made computable*. Instead, it vouches for the fact that this can always be done in different ways, while such difference can make the difference between having or not having access to, for instance, employment, healthcare, education or insurance.

Legal protection of the incomputable self would mean that a natural person can act in law and contest the way they have been made computable, thus resisting overdetermination. In the context of the rule of law, legal protection also means that the burden of resisting overdetermination should not be shifted to individuals, who may otherwise have to take big players with deep pockets to court that have access to big law, which allows them to instrumentalise the law to intimidate those less fortunate by means of procedural delays and irrelevant formalities.[46] To prevent such instrumentalisation, legislatures must create appropriate information duties on the side of those with dominant economic or political power and place the burden of proof on those who take risks with the assets, capabilities or even lives of others. Whether legislatures have such power may, however, depend on geopolitical and geo-economic checks and balances, see section 5 below.

Legal subjectivity, entailing the right to have rights, while also shielding the human subject from overdetermination, provides for standing in a court of law. In terms of the European Court of Human Rights, such standing should provide individuals with 'practical and effective protection' of their human rights.[47] This is often a matter of calling a contracting state to account for failing to actively enable a person to enjoy the substance of their right, which not only concerns respecting a right by refraining from an interference but may imply positive obligations to make the substance of the right available or to prevent other big players from violating the right. Protecting legal subjects, notably natural persons, against a type of computability that has potentially adverse effects and may be hard to contest, is thus key to legal protection.

4.2.2 *Protecting EU Charter Rights, the GDPR and the AI Act*

Both the GDPR and the AI Act aim to explicitly protect the fundamental rights of natural persons.[48] Though the GDPR often protects a subset of natural persons, namely data subjects (those whose personal data is being processed), Articles 1, 24, 25, 32 and 35 explicitly require that data controllers assess and mitigate the risk to fundamental rights and freedoms of *natural* persons. This refers to the protection of all the rights and freedoms articulated in the CFREU, not merely the rights to privacy and data protection. By extending the protection to natural persons, the GDPR acknowledges that in a surveillance society, aggregates of personal data may be used to infer information about individuals whose data was not part of this aggregate. Data controllers must thus foresee how the models they deploy,

[46] See eg, the way META threatened various NGOs who tried to infer how META profiles consumers: N Kayser-Bril, 'AlgorithmWatch Forced to Shut down Instagram Monitoring Project after Threats from Facebook' (*AlgorithmWatch*, 13 August 2021). Available at: https://algorithmwatch.org/en/instagram-research-shut-down-by-facebook/. For a more in-depth analysis of how private law has been instrumentalised to protect the wealthy, see K Pistor, *The Code of Capital: How the Law Creates Wealth and Inequality* (Princeton NJ, Princeton University Press, 2019) and section 5 below.

[47] The European Court of Human Rights has asserted time and again in its case law that Convention rights must be 'practical and effective, not theoretical and illusionary'. See in detail J McBride, 'The Doctrines and Methodology of Interpretation of the European Convention of on Human Rights by the European Court of Human Rights' (*Council of Europe*, 2021). Available at: https://rm.coe.int/echr-eng-the-doctrines-and-methodology-of-interpretation-of-the-europe/1680a20aee.

[48] In other work I have argued, based on philosophical anthropologists H Plessner, that and how EU law builds on the artificial intelligence of a human legislature, court and administration, see: M Hildebrandt, 'The Artificial Intelligence of European Union Law' (2020) 21 *German Law Journal* 74.

built on massive amounts of personal data, may affect the rights and freedoms of natural persons, even when the models themselves do not qualify as personal data. For instance, modelling potential suspects involves the risk of infringing the presumption of innocence or even the right to a fair trial, to the extent that individuals are not aware of being monitored, based on their matching such models. If social networks were to share these models with the police or justice authorities, or if the output of software systems that calculate the risk that a person will commit fraud is taken for granted, the burden of proof may de facto be reversed against citizens who are asked to prove their innocence while the key to such proof is in the hands of private companies that hide behind intellectual property (IP) rights or trade secrets.

The AI Act similarly requires that providers of high-risk AI systems assess the risks of infringing natural persons' fundamental rights, due to the design of the system, requiring that they mitigate the risk of infringement due to the deployment of the system, including reasonably foreseeable deployment for other purposes than those intended by the provider. The Act also requires deployers of some high-risk systems to conduct and document a fundamental rights impact assessment (FRIA). These are far reaching legal obligations, meant to offer legal protection against adverse effects of making a person computable, asserting that persons can be made computable in different ways and obliging providers to make sure that it is done in a way that has the least impact on fundamental rights.

The risk approach to fundamental rights, therefore, should not be seen as a way to manage risks to the assets of the data controller (in the case of the GDPR) or the provider of deployer (in the case of the AI Act) but as a precautionary approach that requires data controllers and providers to foresee and avoid or to mitigate risks to fundamental rights of natural persons.

5 Economic Power, Democracy and the Rule of Law

The key question as to legal protection against types of digital monitoring that diminish, overrule or eradicate human agency is to what extent such protection is practical and effective. This is not a matter of formal legal positivism or social science legal positivism. The elephant in the room is the extent to which powerful actors can instrumentalise the law to their own advantage. This depends on the relationship between law and economics in the market economies of constitutional democracies. In this section I will explore the connection between AI systems that erode human agency and a specific type of neoliberal capitalism, in turn rooted in utilitarian ideology, to situate digital monitoring as liable to denying and potentially destroying the incomputable self.

The incomputable self goes against the grain of raw, predatory capitalism, where anything must be made available for surplus extraction. This type of capitalism is based on the assumption that anything can be made calculable to enable exchange, with the idea of the price as the universal *tertium comparationes*.[49] Such capitalism is not a given but the result of a specific set of legal institutions. This also goes for the type of economic markets touted by those who believe that unrestricted capitalism will benefit, in the end, even the poor, due to the so-called trickle-down effect.[50] There is no scientific evidence for such effect and much of the wealth of the very rich is due to a trickle-up effect, usually called surplus extraction.[51] By asserting that economic markets are instituted and shaped by positive law I reject economic determinism, whether based on mainstream econometric modelling or on neo-Marxist belief systems.[52]

Economic markets don't grow like grass; they are created by the intricate set of private and public law constraints that define who and what can act in law (that is, act as a legal subject), the validity of contracts, liability for damage caused, the burden of proof in case of enforcement, competition law, property rights and corporate law, and, insofar as relevant, economic markets are subject to, and thus made to fit with, the requirements of environmental law, labour law, consumer law and many other dedicated types of administrative law. If markets are not given but made, the extent to which big economic players can overrule other players, notably those who depend on them or compete with them, depends on *how* markets are made. This includes the extent to which the responsibility for public goods and general interests can be outsourced to private players.

Pistor, Cohen, Pasquale and many others have argued that the law has been and is instrumentalised by big economic players.[53] Big Tech can afford to hire Big Law to defend their private interests and by throwing sand in the machinery of legal procedure, or they can invest in bending legislation to match their interest by way of lobbying. Both politics and public administration in the Global North are largely based on a tacit belief in the kind of neoliberal economics that has also infiltrated

[49] R Bronk, 'Hayek on the Wisdom of Prices: A Reassessment' (2013) 6(1) *Erasmus Journal for Philosophy and Economics* 82.

[50] JA Hübner, 'Neoliberal Justifications of Economic Inequality' in R Baikady et al (eds), *The Palgrave Handbook of Global Social Problems* (Palgrave Macmillan Cham, 2024). Available at: https://link.springer.com/rwe/10.1007/978-3-030-68127-2_434-1.Cham 2024

[51] M Mattern, *The Trickle-Up Economy: How We Take from the Poor and Middle Class and Give to the Rich* (Boulder CO, Lynne Rienner Publishers Inc, 2021).

[52] C Thomasberger, 'The Belief in Economic Determinism, Neoliberalism, and the Significance of Polanyi's Contribution in the Twenty-First Century' (2012) 41(4) *International Journal of Political Economy* 16; PG Stillman, 'The Myth of Marx's Economic Determinism' in Peter G Stillman (ed), *Marx Myths and Legends* (2005). Available at: www.marxists.org/subject/marxmyths/peter-stillman/article.htm.

[53] Pistor (n 45); JE Cohen, *Between Truth and Power: The Legal Constructions of Informational Capitalism* (New York, Oxford University Press, 2019); McQuillan (n 19) MT McCluskey, FA Pasquale and J Taub, 'Law and Economics: Contemporary Approaches' (2016) 35 *Yale Law & Policy Review* 297. See also the 2018 special issue of the *Georgetown Law Technology Review* (vol 2) on *Information Platforms and the Law* and the special issue of Critical Analysis of Law, notably the introduction: FA Pasquale, 'New Economic Analysis of Law: Beyond Technocracy and Market Design' (2018) 5 *Critical Analysis of Law* 1."plainCitation":"Frank Pasquale, 'New Economic Analysis of Law: Beyond Technocracy and Market Design' (2018) 5 *Critical Analysis of Law* 1.

legal education in the form of courses on 'law and economics'.[54] The vocabulary of transaction costs, the Coase theorem, Pareto optimal outcomes and other core methodological beliefs based on rational choice theory are steeped in the ideology of utilitarianism, while sold as if part of a neutral scientific theory. Though most lawyers would not be able to reproduce the meaning of the Coase theorem or the implications of being guided by a belief in Pareto optimal outcomes, both permeate policy making on the left and the right, perhaps because most policy makers don't understand the technicalities but accept the expertise of those who supposedly do. The quasi-neutral scientific claims made on behalf of 'law and economics' generate a specific kind of economic determinism that hides the legislative choices that shape economic forces.

Digital monitoring fits the economic incentives that prevail in neoliberal economics, because both have to assume that what matters can be measured and predicted based on dedicated metrics.[55] Both surveillance and economics require calculations that are, however, necessarily preceded by qualifications (see section 2(b)(i) above); to calculate assumes that the unit of calculation is clear, such that real world phenomena can be qualified as fitting the relevant unit.[56] The act of qualification will often have normative implications and the same phenomenon can almost always be qualified in more than one way, depending on the purpose of quantification. In neoliberal econometrics, such choices are hidden behind quasi technical jargon; the same goes for the labour of data labelling and prompt engineering that informs the building of AI models, especially in relation to surveillance.[57]

A participatory democracy, built on the countervailing powers of the Rule of Law, should make sure that both its economic system and the digital monitoring it deploys are informed by normative, qualitative choices that align with the outcome of public engagement.[58] Agreeing on such choices in a *constitutional* democracy will

[54] P Mirowski and D Plehwe (eds), *The Road from Mont Pelerin: The Making of the Neoliberal Thought Collective*, 1st edn (Cambridge MA, Harvard University Press, 2009); M Baradaran, *The Quiet Coup: Neoliberalism and the Looting of America* (New York, WW Norton & Company, 2024).

[55] LP Syll, *The Poverty of Fictional Storytelling in Mainstream Economics* (Bristol, World Economics Association Books, 2023).

[56] Callon and Law (n 28).

[57] P Terzis, 'Law and the Political Economy of AI Production' (2023) 31 *International Journal of Law and Information Technology* 302. Note that outsourcing of AI labour is no longer restricted to data labelling (for supervised AI and content moderation) but now also concerns prompt engineering, see, eg SuperStaff Editorial Board, 'Unlock Your AI Potential By Nearshoring Prompt Engineering Projects' (*SuperStaff*, 24 November 2023). Available at: www.superstaff.com/blog/nearshoring-prompt-engineering-projects/.

[58] J Dewey, *The Public & Its Problems* (New York, Henry Holt and Company, 1927); C Mouffe, *The Democractic Paradox* (London, Verso, 2000). Note that I am not referring to a 'liberal democracy' that seems to inform Anglo-American common sense when it comes to political theory. Constitutional democracy is not equivalent with liberal democracy, if only because the notion of liberty has myriad meanings, often reduced to honouring arbitrary, individual preferences (which fits neoliberal economic and utilitarian political theories). See also M Hildebrandt and S Gutwirth, '(Re)Presentation, pTA Citizens' Juries and the Jury Trial' (2007) 3(1) *Utrecht Law Review* 24: KM Schönfeld, 'Rex, Lex et Judex: Montesquieu and La Bouche de La Loi Revisted' (2008) 4 *European Constitutional Law Review* 274.

require real-world investigations, adversarial discussion and compromise, as well as respecting the negative and the positive obligations implied in fundamental rights. This will ensure that the polity respects the incomputable self of its citizens, and the incomputable nature of the public goods and shared values that allow folk to identify as a polity – even if these values will often be contested and rearticulated. But real-world democracies are under threat as authoritarianism is on the rise, while private corporations achieve levels of economic power that are incompatible with both democracy and the practical and effective protection of fundamental rights. A global oligarchy of outrageously rich Big Tech investors has reached disproportional economic powers, capable of overruling sovereign self-determination and steering geopolitical relations based on private geo-economic priorities. The current race for AGI involves a global battle to mine and hoard rare earth minerals to 'fuel' the batteries of AGI applications, while competing to build data centres and to source the energy and water to feed and cool them. Combined with a leap in governmental spending on defence (betting on integrating AI) it should be clear that this oligarchy has a nefarious impact on the ability of states to uphold the practical and effective legal protection of the incomputable self.

In 2023, Gebru and Torres published an article on TESCREAL, an acronym that stands for transhumanism, extropianism, singularitarianism, cosmism, rationalism, effective altruism and long-terminism.[59] They demonstrate the ideological background of the billionaires and trillionaires who invest in AGI, which they qualify as a highly problematic quest to achieve super- and supra-human 'intelligence', mixed with dreams of immortality, various types of supremism and the wish to invest in the colonisation of outer space. Their article asserts that the race to achieve AGI is built on ideology rather than science or engineering. They refer to fundamental engineering principles, pointing out that in order to develop reliable AI systems or models, these must be 'well-scoped and well-defined' (often referred to as 'narrow AI'), because otherwise they cannot be tested and validated. The whole point of AGI, however, is to develop models and systems capable of performing any task or function for any goal under any circumstances. As indicated above, in section 2(a)(iv), this flies in the face of Wolpert's *no free lunch theorems* that prove mathematically that no algorithm can optimise for all problem domains. AGI is part of an ideological pursuit, based on the exploitation of labour in the Global South, while the real-world effects speed up climate change.[60]

[59] T Gebru and ÉP Torres, 'The TESCREAL Bundle: Eugenics and the Promise of Utopia through Artificial General Intelligence' (2024) 29 *First Monday*. Available at: https://firstmonday.org/ojs/index.php/fm/article/view/13636. Note that Gebru was co-author of the seminal article on LLMs for which she 'was resigned', published before the release of ChatGPT, see EM Bender et al, 'On the Dangers of Stochastic Parrots: Can Language Models Be Too Big? 🦜' in *FAccT '21: Proceedings of the 2021 ACM Conference on Fairness, Accountability, and Transparency* (New York, Association for Computing Machinery, 2021).

[60] SS Regilme, 'Tech Imperialism Reloaded: AI, Colonial Legacies, and the Global South' (*E-International Relations*, 17 February 2025). Available at: www.e-ir.info/2025/02/17/tech-imperialism-reloaded-ai-colonial-legacies-and-the-global-south/.

The argument for legal protection as the protection of the incomputable self, presented in this chapter, should be read in conjunction with a critique of a global capitalism that is built on dangerous assumptions about the computability of human interaction. Though this subsection offers only a brief introduction to that critique, it is key to note that and how the quest to make us computable is aligned with an economic ideology that has justified grotesque inequality and invited populism which oftentimes – though not necessarily – results in authoritarianism.[61]

6 Conclusions

In previous work I have argued that privacy should be understood as including the protection of the incomputable self. In this chapter, I have extended the argument by framing the concept of legal subjectivity for natural persons as key to an effective and practical protection of the incomputable self. This is a more powerful argument that informs the protection of privacy, because without legal subjectivity privacy may be a value or an interest but not a right, thus making its protection dependent on economic and political power relationships. By extending the argument to the level of Arendt's right to have rights, it becomes possible to involve all human rights as key to the protection of the incomputable self.

The argument builds on a specific understanding of the difference between machinic and human agency, more specifically between the limitations inherent in computational agency on the one hand and the productive ex-centrix agency that defines the human condition. Before doing so, I have introduced the three laws of computational agency, discussed in my work on privacy as the protection of the incomputable self: (1) reality is not computable, (2) it can be made computable and (3) this can be done in different ways and the difference makes a difference. I have detailed these laws as based on the constraints imposed on computing systems by the logic gates that define their affordances. This allowed me to highlight the issue of proxies that is inevitable when using computational models to frame aspects of the real world, requiring developers to take several technical design decisions whose downstream impact will make a difference to those targeted by the output models.

A surveillance society that makes an entire network of fine-grained decisions dependent on AI design and deployment can only survive as a constitutional democracy if the *under*determinacy and incomputability of its human agents is respected and protected. This requires key attention to the normative implications of upstream design decisions. For lawyers this means keen attention to the limitations of the computational systems that 'softwire' the administrative decision engines of the welfare state and the rule of law. The digital transformation that is

[61] G Halmai, 'Populism, Authoritarianism and Constitutionalism' (2019) 20 *German Law Journal* 296; D Győrffy, 'Populism and Authoritarianism in the EU: What Is the Role of the Euro?' (2024) 25 *European Politics and Society* 643.

upon us should not be seen as an inevitable and neutral update of both the state and economic markets, but as a challenge that raises question zero (should specific processes, events and decisions be transformed at all?) and requires both curiosity and a more in-depth understanding of what computing systems can and cannot achieve.

In that light, this chapter has also offered a brief critique of the legal frameworks that create and sustain economic markets. Though both the GDPR and the AI Act offer key protection of the incomputable self by addressing risks to fundamental rights, we must prevent the law and the Rule of Law from being instrumentalised by big economic players. Untamed, rogue capitalism aligns well with the idea that human action can be reduced to computable behaviours and made available for profitable manipulations. This, in turn, requires and rewards digital monitoring and profiling as part of Big Tech's business model, which can be used by states to control human interaction as a computable commodity. The ideology of neoliberal economics, which pervades much of legal education, must be countered by keen attention to the nefarious consequences of disproportionately rich players who have an interest in the computability of the human self, which to them is but an instrument to feed their data engines.

INDEX

www.ingramcontent.com/pod-product-compliance
Ingram Content Group UK Ltd.
Pitfield, Milton Keynes, MK11 3LW, UK
UKHW021824230926
475688UK00003BC/95

9 781509 991891